Olexander Hryb

Understanding Contemporary Ukrainian and Russian Nationalism

The Post-Soviet Cossack Revival and Ukraine's National Security
With a foreword by Vitali Vitaliev

UKRAINIAN VOICES

Collected by Andreas Umland

The book series "Ukrainian Voices" publishes English- and German-language monographs, edited volumes, document collections, and anthologies of articles authored and composed by Ukrainian politicians, intellectuals, activists, officials, researchers, entrepreneurs, artists, and diplomats. The series' aim is to introduce Western and other audiences to Ukrainian explorations and interpretations of historic and current domestic as well as international affairs. The purpose of these books is to make non-Ukrainian readers familiar with how some prominent Ukrainians approach, research, and assess their country's development and position in the world. The series was founded in 2019, and the volumes are collected by *Andreas Umland*, Dr. phil. (FU Berlin), Ph. D. (Cambridge), Senior Research Fellow at the Institute for Euro-Atlantic Cooperation in Kyiv.

Olexander Hryb

UNDERSTANDING CONTEMPORARY UKRAINIAN AND RUSSIAN NATIONALISM

The Post-Soviet Cossack Revival and Ukraine's National Security

With a foreword by Vitali Vitaliev

ibidem Verlag

Bibliografische Information der Deutschen Nationalbibliothek
Die Deutsche Nationalbibliothek verzeichnet diese Publikation in der Deutschen
Nationalbibliografie; detaillierte bibliografische Daten sind im Internet über
http://dnb.d-nb.de abrufbar.

Bibliographic information published by the Deutsche Nationalbibliothek
Die Deutsche Nationalbibliothek lists this publication in the Deutsche Nationalbibliografie; detailed
bibliographic data are available in the Internet at http://dnb.d-nb.de.

ISBN 978-3-8382-1377-4
© *ibidem*-Verlag, Stuttgart 2020
Alle Rechte vorbehalten

Printed in the EU

How to read this book

Nationalism, national identity and ethnicity are such complex social phenomena that academic researchers worldwide are divided in even defining these terms. Therefore the first two chapters are dedicated to definitions, so that readers will have a clear understanding of the relevant theoretical framework before Ukrainian and Russian nationalisms are discussed. Considering that a lot of the content in such discussions is of mostly academic value, readers interested in the actual nationalist narratives can go straight to chapter 4 and 5 and the case studies on Russia and Ukraine. Professionals who are interested in the security implications of paramilitary movements with a nationalist ideology (i.e., Cossacks) as well as potential conflict resolution can skip straight to Chapter 5. Social scientists interested in the actual fieldwork methodology, data collection and findings might want to start reading from the Appendixes 1 & 2.

PREFACE

The sources from which information for this monograph has been taken are published works, official documents, lectures and interviews. The conceptual idea of research evolved as a result of my studies beginning at the Graduate School for Social Research (Institute of Philosophy and Sociology, Polish Academy of Science) in 1994-1996 where I greatly benefited from the supervision of professors Janusz Reykowski and Henric Domanski as well as from the seminars of Joanna Kurczewska and Erica Benner. I also participated in the seminars at the University of Warsaw given by Professor Ernest Gellner and gratefully remember his comments on the initial research outline of my PhD thesis. I have also to thank Claire Wallace (Central European University, Prague) and Birgit Muller (Marc Bloch Centre for Social-Anthropological Research, Berlin) for their help in starting up my field–work research among the Cossack Communities in Southern Ukraine in 1995.

During the summer of 1995 the first fieldwork findings were researched together with Austrian sociologist Sabine Haas to whom I am especially indebted for her thoughtful insights, which are reflected in my fieldwork analysis. The fieldwork proceedings at a later stage in 1996-1997 would have been impossible without a grant from the GSSR, so my gratitude is addressed to the Head of the School, Professor Stefan Amsterdamski. I would like also to thank Ukrainian scholars: Professor Natalia Chernysh (University of Lviv), Dr. Olena Bachynska and Dr. Anatoliy Mysechko (University of Odesa), Dr. Olga Philipova (University of Kharkiv) and Dr. Taras Chuhlib (Center for Research of Cossack History, Institute of History, Ukrainian National Academy of Science). Finally, my work could not have been completed without the assistance of many others, whom I also thank wholeheartedly.

Understanding Contemporary Ukrainian and Russian Nationalism
The Post-Soviet Cossack Revival and Ukraine's National Security

SUMMARY

This monograph explores the causes and conditions of nationalist revivals as such and in post-Soviet Ukraine and Russia specifically. It does so by, first, developing a framework based on a synthesis of Eastern and Western European perspectives on nationalism; and, then, applying this framework to the case of the Cossack nationalist revivals in Russia and Ukraine.

In order to develop a framework for analyzing nationalist revivals, the monograph explores Eastern (Russian and Ukrainian), as well as Western, theoretical perspectives relating to national identity, national and ethnic communities, and nationalist movements. Soviet ethnography and Soviet ethnic engineering continue to influence both academic discourse and state policies in the Russian Federation and Ukraine with respect to post-communist nation building. Understanding Soviet and post-Soviet theoretical perspectives on nationalism can contribute much to the study of nationalist phenomena, in the West as well as in the East. Thus, the monograph not only introduces into the English-language literature often overlooked Russian and Ukrainian (Soviet and post-Soviet) theories, but also suggests how these theories might be synthesized with Western traditions to produce a better framework for understanding nationalism. To this end, this monograph proposes a synthetic framework based on an analysis of commonalities and divergences in the Western and Eastern traditions.

Central to this framework is the concept of societal or identity security. The monograph endeavors to show the importance of societal security to an understanding of when and why nationalist movements turn violent by applying it to the case of the Cossack nationalist revival in Russia and Ukraine. Research on Cossack nationalism not only demonstrates the utility of the proposed framework and its central concept (societal security); it also clarifies the distinction commonly drawn between "ethnic" and "civic" nations. In doing this, it provides insight, not only into nation building in the former Soviet Union, but also into the origins and evolution of "Eastern" vs. "Western" nations.

Contents

ABBREVIATIONS

ASSR	Autonomous Soviet Socialist Republic
BBC	British Broadcasting Corporation
CIS	Commonwealth of Independent States
CPSU	Communist Party of the Soviet Union
ESO	Ethno-Social Organism
EU	European Union
EAEU	Eurasian Economic Union
FSU	Former Soviet Union
GMT	Greenwich Mean Time
IMF	International Monetary Fund
IR	International Relations
ITAR	TASS—Russian Information Agency
KGB	Soviet Security Service
KLA	Kosovo Liberation Army
MOD	Ministry of Defense
MP	Member of Parliament
MVD	Ministry of Interior in the USSR or the Russian Federation
NATO	North Atlantic Treaty Organization
NCA	National Cultural Autonomy
NEO	New European Order
NIS	Newly Independent States
NTV	Russian National Television
NUAS	National Ukrainian Academy of Science
OSCE	Organization of Security and Cooperation in Europe
RSK	Republic of Serbian Krajina
RSFSR	Russian Soviet Federative Socialist Republic
SBU	Ukrainian Security Service
SWB	Short Wave Broadcast reports by the BBC Monitoring
UAF	Ukrainian Armed Forces
UK	Ukrainian Cossack Organization
UK	United Kingdom

UNIAR	Ukrainian Independent News Agency *Respublika*
UPA	Ukrainian Resurgence Army
USA	United States of America
USSR	Union of Soviet Socialist Republics
VDV	Soviet and then Russian or Ukrainian paratroopers' military formations
WW2	Second World War

Foreword

Strangers to Themselves

By Vitali Vitaliev

Olexander Hryb has written an extremely topical book, the main subject of which is national identity.

Let's face it: nationalism — in all its different guises and manifestations — remains one of the main divisive factors on the global, read federal, scale and, at the same time, one of the main uniting ideologies on the local, read provincial, level. There's no need to give examples — suffice it is to open a daily newspaper, turn on radio or TV, or do a quick browse of the Internet — and you will be showered with them.

But what exactly is nationalism, often wrongly confused with hooray patriotism of the type which Dr. Samuel Johnson famously (and rather categorically) branded "the last refuge of a scoundrel"? My online dictionary defines it (nationalism) as identification with one's own nation and support for its interests, especially to the exclusion or detriment of the interests of other nations. If so, then nationalism and national (or cultural) identity are very close relations, and one cannot exist without the other. In the words of the former US President Bill Clinton, "If you don't remember anything else I say, remember this: every single fundamental problem of the independent world is rooted in an imperfect sense of identity." And in a stubborn and often violent search for it, I would add.

"Cultural identities . . . were never monolithic and are becoming much less so," — in the words of Professor Paul Gifford, Director of the Institute of European Cultural Identity Studies at St. Andrews University. It important to remember that nationalism often appears first as a result of a repressed, or otherwise weak (non-monolithic) cultural identity. To me, that explains why Julia Kristeva, a Bulgarian-born and Sorbonne-educated French writer and scholar, once referred to herself and her fellow Europeans as "strangers to ourselves".

Olexander Hryb—a British Ukrainian scholar, who also speaks fluent Russian, Polish and English, is the right person to compare Russian and Ukrainian forms of nationalism, with all their striking similarities and differences. The main difference between the two has always been the fact that Ukrainian nationalism, in most instances, was directed again the oppressor (read Russia, or the USSR), whereas Russian nationalism was mostly of the imperialist nature and was aimed at dissolving national identities of the oppressed.

Hryb is the native of Lviv, where Ukrainian nationalism was kept alive (if not particularly well) all through the darkest Soviet times. It was the only major city in the whole of Ukraine where Ukrainian was routinely spoken in the streets. As for my own native city of Kharkiv, it was russified to the extreme: out of 200 secondary schools in city, only 1 (one) was Ukrainian, and even that one was not a complete school but a curtailed *'vos'miletka'* (with 8-year course of studies as opposed to a normal secondary school course of ten). In the belief system of the Kharkiv Communist Party rulers, anything Ukrainian was nationalism. At my University, founded by the great Ukrainian philosopher Hryhorii Skovoroda and then (in the 1970s) bearing the name the Russian proletarian writer Maxim Gorky (!), all disciplines were taught in Russian, and speaking Ukrainian during classes and the intervals was actively discouraged. The point came when (in the mid-1970s) two of my fellow students at the foreign languages faculty were expelled from the University for" stubbornly and despite several warnings" carrying on speaking Ukrainian to the lecturers and to each other. They were accused of (wait for it) "Ukrainian bourgeois nationalism" and expelled! What was so nationalistic, let alone "bourgeois", about speaking their own language in their own country, only God (and perhaps Brezhnev too) knew... That was my first direct encounter not with nationalism per se, but with a normal human behaviour branded as such—the attitude that kept transforming 'nationalism' into a kind of a swear word (often preceded with the meaningless adjective 'bourgeois') for all the seventy odd years of the Soviet regime. No wonder that in the perception of many of those who had lived in the USSR, that word still carries a kind of negative connotation...

Hryb's choice of Cossacks, both Russian and Ukrainian — a peculiar paramilitary movement which, at different times of their history, served both the oppressors and the oppressed — as the main object of the study is very well justified.

What most Russian and Ukrainian people would know about early Cossacks is that they were effectively bands of young men fleeing from serfdom: criminals, deserters and Old Believers who rejected the reformed Orthodox church. This mixed bunch of misfits established a kind of wandering, militarised democracy of self-rule under their chieftain, the Ataman. They lived by hunting, fishing, fighting and plundering — whatever served their needs. Sometimes they supported the Tsars, sometimes not... Driven out of central Russia to the remote provinces, they ended up both in the North and South of the Russian Empire. As for the Cossack state of the Zaporozhian Sich on the territory of modern Central Ukraine, it was formed in the 15th century from serfs fleeing the Polish-Lithuanian Commonwealth. With time, the Sich became a fiercely independent political and military force in its own right...

In his research, Hryb goes far and wide. He starts with pointing out the growing "insecurities" of identities (national, cultural and ethnic) and their role in the nationalist revival. He then closely examines the concepts of ethnic and national consciousness before delving into the history of nationalism, Soviet attitudes to the eternal 'natsionalniy vopros' (issues of nationalities), Putin's ethnogeopolitics and the ongoing Cossack revival in both Russia and Ukraine. The final chapter is devoted to defining nationalism as a fast-growing belief system of modern times and its role in the post-Communist world.

The book completes with the impressive case study of the Black Sea Cossack revival which involved extensive and thorough fieldwork by the author who comes to the conclusion that by continuing to ignore the threatened people's identities at the lowest level, modern powers that be (including present-day Ukrainian and Russian authorities) keep undermining their societies' security. The case study was completed long before the Maidan and the recent political changes in Ukraine, so I would like to hope that, with the new and extremely popular Ukrainian President in power, the situation will soon change for the better and the citizens of both Russia and Ukraine will stop being "Strangers to themselves".

1 Insecure Identities and the Nationalist Revival

Fundamental changes in Europe since the 1990s, with the further integration of the European Union (EU) and a restructuring of the political space in Eastern Europe, have highlighted the limits of our understanding of European nation building, national revival and nationalist movements. In Western Europe, the nation-state is being challenged by EU processes of legal and socio-economic integration that some fear may lead to the creation of a super-state and at least partly helps explain the Brexit logic. In Eastern Europe, the Euro-Atlantic integration of former Warsaw Pact countries led to the Russian neo-imperialist attempt to create an EU alternative, the Eurasian Economic Union. The re-emergence of ethnic violence and of militant forms of nationalism in Eastern and Central Europe were as unexpected as the fall of the Soviet Union. Russian-Ukrainian armed conflict over Crimea and Donbas could be viewed as a delayed Ukrainian war of independence that was not foreseen by the mainstream academia. Scholars continue to debate about the nature of nationalism and of nations; about definitions, typologies, the role of ethnicity and ethnic heritage, and the conditions and mechanisms of national revival. There is no general consensus about these, nor is there a unified theory of nationalism or a clear understanding of its causes or prospects. And yet the future of the European community depends on the evolution of the EU member nation-states, hence understanding nationalism would help to secure peace in its own expanding home.

This monograph explores the causes and conditions of national(ist) revivals. It does so by, first, developing a framework based on a synthesis of Eastern and Western European perspectives on nationalism; and, then, applying this framework to the case of the Cossack nationalist revivals in Russia and Ukraine.

In order to develop a framework for analyzing nationalist revivals, the monograph explores Eastern (Russian and Ukrainian), as well as Western, theoretical perspectives relating to national identity, national and ethnic communities, and nationalist movements. Soviet ethnography and Soviet ethnic engineering continue to influence both academic discourse and state policies in the Russian Federation and Ukraine with respect to post-communist nation building. Moreover, elements of Soviet and post-Soviet theoretical perspectives on nationalism can contribute much to the study of nationalist phenomena, in the West as well as in the East. Thus, the monograph not only introduces largely unknown Russian and Ukrainian (Soviet and post-Soviet) theories into the English-language literature, but it also suggests how these theories might be synthesized with Western traditions to produce a better framework for understanding nationalism. To this end, this monograph proposes a synthetic framework based on an analysis of commonalities and divergences in the Western and Eastern traditions.

Central to this framework is the concept of societal or identity security. The monograph endeavors to show the importance of societal security to an understanding of when and why nationalist movements turn violent by applying it to the case of the Cossack nationalist revival in Russia and Ukraine. The term "security," therefore, is used in this research in reference to the individual (e.g., Cossack individuals), the group (Cossacks/nationalist organizations), the state (e.g., the Ukrainian nation-state, the Russian Federation), the international system (the European Union/NATO security community vs. the Eurasian Economic Union) and is looked at on the different levels of analysis discussed in Chapter 3. For other conceptual uses of the term security, see the discussion by David Baldwin, "The Concepts of Security" (Baldwin 1997).

Research on Cossack nationalism not only demonstrates the utility of the proposed framework and its central concept (societal security); it also clarifies the distinction commonly drawn between "ethnic" and "civic" nations. In doing this, it provides insight, not only into nation building in the former Soviet Union; it also clarifies the similarities and differences in origin and evolution of "Eastern" and "Western" nations.

1.1. Why is There not "a" Theory of Nationalism?

The major approaches to the study of nations and national identity are represented by "modernist" and "primordial" traditions in the West, and by "socio-spherical" and "bio-spherical" traditions in the Soviet Union, Russia and Ukraine. However, there are similar trends in the study of nationalism generally.

In the West following the Second World War, Hugh Seton-Watson (1977) drew a distinction between "old" and "new" nations, replacing the nineteenth-century distinction between "historic" and "non-historic" nations of mostly Western and Eastern European origin respectively. In the 1960s, Miroslav Hroch (1985) defined three major periods of national revival in Europe concerning, largely, the category of "new" nations. Two major trends in the studies of nationalism developed, since then, in order to explain the origin of nations—primordialism and modernism. Clifford Geertz (1962) and later Anthony Smith (1983) argued that there were primordial or perennial elements in the history of nations that link them with their particular ethnic and religious past, while modernists like Ernest Gellner (1983), Eric Hobsbawm (1990) and Benedict Anderson (1991) insisted that nations are a purely modern phenomenon, "imagined" to a large extent with the spread of mass communication and literacy. Both trends continue their existence in the present and more or less dominate the study of nations and nationality in Europe.

In the Soviet Union, a separate school of thought developed that combined elements of both modernist and primordialist perspectives. A "Marxist-Leninist" dogma on nations and nationalism was postulated by Joseph Stalin (1947), and developed subsequently by several generations of Soviet ethnographers. Whatever the merits of this perspective, the Soviet state was committed to implementing a nationality policy that was consistent with it, and in so doing, it created a national hierarchy which continued to affect social processes, after the disintegration of the Soviet Union and to this day.

Although the large amount of literature produced on nations and nationalism is said to have resulted in an "overproduction of theories," in fact neither of the two dominant currents of thought on the subject has succeeded in producing a definitive breakthrough. Rogers Brubaker has concluded that perhaps there is no possibility of creating a valid comprehensive theory:

> The search for "a" or "the" theory of nationalism—like the search for "a" or "the" solution to nationalist conflicts—is in my view misguided: for the theoretical problems associated with nationhood and nationalism, like the practical political problems, are multiform and varied, and not susceptible of resolution through a single theoretical (or practical) approach. (Brubaker 1998, 301)

Ironically, Brubaker arrived at this conclusion at the end of a collection of articles reflecting on Ernest Gellner's philosophical heritage, and Gellner is generally credited with producing a theory of nationalism that is, as yet, unmatched. Gellner's theory (Gellner 1983), which defines the causes of nationalism within the framework of a modernization paradigm, has been criticized for its functionalism and reductionism. Gellner believed that nations and nationalism are related to the transition from agrarian to scientific-industrial society, the latter requiring a homogeneous society based on one high culture. Single high cultures within single states that are reproduced by a centralized education system require a common language. The necessity, for a modern industrial economy, of a common language, education and high culture within the boundaries of a single political unit, was the basis for the creation of the "nation."

For Gellner, the principle of one culture, one state is the essence of nationalism. However, he distinguished four basic forms of nationalism (1983, 1997):

1.   Early Industrialism Nationalism without an ethnic catalyst within strong Dynastic states such as those based in Lisbon, Madrid, Paris and London. Power-holders in these states on the Atlantic coast of Europe shared the same culture as their subjects long before the age of nationalism arrived, so when it did arrive the State and culture already constituted one unit.

2. Classical Unification (Western) Nationalism, which was the model of national unification in nineteenth-century Germany and Italy, when already existing high cultures needed to acquire a political roof that would correspond to those culture states.

3. Classical Habsburg-East-and-South Nationalism, which arose when power-holders who shared a single high culture with their subjects sank into local folk and ethnically marked cultures, which might be turned into high cultures by the nationalist agitation of small groups of intelligentsia belonging to the same ethnic groups. If the efforts of intellectuals-awakeners succeeded, then such a group would create a state of its own that would reproduce a newly established or re-established high culture.

4. Diaspora Nationalism, or the nationalism of predominantly ethnically marked groups who served during the transition from *Agraria* to *Industria* as a "middle-man" between power-holders and the ruled. Being ethnically distinct from both the rulers and the ruled such historically dispersed groups as Jews, Greeks, Armenians and Parsis are good examples of Diaspora nationalism.

Gellner's delineation of historical forms of nationalism sought also to reject at least four false theories of nationalism shared, at times, by nationalists, and at other times by scholars of nationalism, and sometimes by both. These are that nationalism is

1. Natural, self-evident and self-generating unless forcefully repressed;

2. A consequence of ideas that emerged as a result of a regrettable accident;

3. An awakening message that was intended for *classes* but that, by some error, was delivered to *nations* ("the Wrong Address theory" favored by Marxism);

4. The re-emergence of atavistic notions of blood or territory (the "Dark Gods theory").

Although most contemporary scholars agree that nationalism is a modern phenomenon, there is no consensus as to its causes or how it is related to processes of socio-economic modernization. Typologies of different forms of nationalism and their historical phases also vary widely. Scholars distinguish between Eastern and Western cultural and political, ethnic and civic, totalitarian and democratic, illiberal and liberal; aristocratic, bureaucratic, revolutionary, "actually existing" and even banal versions of nationalism. All of these and many other definitions use different criteria and approaches. The most important distinctions are discussed below.

Among the most "popular" distinctions of nationalism is that between Eastern and Western nationalism. After the Second World War, Hans Kohn (1944), and later John Plamenatz (1973), developed a set of criteria that defined Eastern nationalism as ethnocentric and irrational and Western nationalism as rational and liberal. Hans Kohn argued that the Renaissance and the Reformation in the West had produced a conception of nationality that related it to individual liberty and even rational cosmopolitanism. Nationalism in Germany, Central and Eastern Europe, and Asia, on the other hand, emerged without the "enlightenment" of a Renaissance and Reformation and on the basis of ethnographic demands. These later nationalisms "lacked self-assurance" and their "inferiority complex was often compensated by over-emphasis and overconfidence" (Kohn 1944, 330). In a similar vein, Plamenatz characterized Western nationalism as civilized and liberal, and the Eastern nationalism adopted by more primitive nations to the "East of Trieste," as "nasty." This distinction, however, included German and Italian nationalism in the Western model (Plamenatz 1973).

Anthony Smith defined a distinction between the civic and political nationalism of the West and an ethnic and genealogical Eastern variant. Smith, however, argued in his later works that these historical distinctions did not imply that one was necessarily better than the other. According to Smith, civic nations, which are more typical in the West

> may demand eradication of minority cultures on the common assumption, shared by Marxists and liberals, not just of equality through uniformity, but also of the belief that the "high cultures" and "great nations" are necessarily of greater value than "low" cultures and small nations or *ethnies.*

In support of his arguments concerning the ethnic origin of nations, Smith further maintained that the "pedagogical narrative of Western democracies turns out to be every bit as demanding and rigorous – and in practice ethnically one-sided – as are those of non-Western authoritarian state-nations, since it assumes the assimilation of ethnic minorities within the borders of the national state through acculturation to a hegemonic majority ethnic culture" (Smith 1995: 101). In other words, Western civic nationalism is not necessarily as tolerant and ethnically unbiased as its self-image suggests.   The distinctions defined between Eastern and Western, ethnic and civic nationalism, however, are widespread and difficult to avoid, as all scholars agree that there are differences in how nationalism evolved in various parts of Europe and in the world in general. The notion of "good" civic Western nationalism in relation to "bad" ethnic Eastern nationalism is especially widespread in the media, and in political rhetoric (and therefore in public discourse). However, this distinction is rather more deceiving than revealing.

So, is there a theoretical justification for distinguishing between Eastern and Western, Ethnic and Civic nationalism? Do these distinctions point to important and inherent characteristics of nationalism?

In fact, the cultural and political dimensions of nationalism have not been clearly and persuasively elaborated. An attempt by Michael Ignatieff (1993) to equate "ethnic" and "cultural" nationalisms in order to explain why such nationalisms tend to be exclusive, as opposed to civic inclusive nationalism, has been criticized as short-sighted. Will Kymlicka has argued that Ignatieff and others have defined a false distinction, since both ethnic and civic nationalisms have a cultural component. As he points out:

> Membership in the American nation, just as in the Quebecois nation, involves participation in a common culture. It is a legal requirement for children to learn the English language and American history in schools, and all levels of American government had insisted that there is a legitimate governmental interest in promoting a common culture (Kymlicka 1999, 133).

Rogers Brubaker (1998) argued that the distinction between civic and ethnic nationhood and nationalism is both normatively and analytically problematic. His view is similar to Kymlicka's: he argues that, if we consider *what is cultural in ethnic nationalism*, virtually all nationalisms would be coded as ethnic or ethnocultural. In this sense, even the "paradigmatic cases of civic nationalism — France and America — cease to be counted as civic nationalism, since they have a crucial cultural or ethnocultural component" (Brubaker 1998, 299).

An enquiry into the history of the American nation and nationalism brings yet another dimension to the discussion. Not all authors agree that the American nation is similar in nature to European ones such as, for instance, the German or French nations. It is argued that this nation of immigrants from Europe is inclusive, democratic and liberal in its nature and therefore is not a nation with an ethnic, "bad" nationalism (See Yack 1999). On the other hand, as Kymlicka argues, America's civic nationalism has historically justified the conquering and colonizing of national minorities and the coercive imposition of English-language courts and schools. The experience of the United States, and of other American nations, namely those in Latin America, illustrates that civic nations can be military dictatorships as easily as liberal democracies (e.g., Peru and Brazil, which are multiethnic societies, granting equal citizenship to whites, blacks, Indians and Asians). According to Kymlicka, North Americans often overlook this fact, because they fail to distinguish immigrants from national minorities. In fact, nationalist policies of the U.S. government led to the forced incorporation of Indian tribes, native Hawaiians, and Puerto Ricans into the American state and their coerced assimilation into American culture. This is, according to Kymlicka, only one example of the link between aggressive expansionism and civic American nationalism.

However, other scholars have pointed out that there is a cultural aspect of American nationalism that has been evident in attempts to define an ideological norm for the American nation as a whole. As Anthony Richmond pointed out, the McCarthy era in the United States was an attempt to impose a single nationalistic ideology and to regard any non-conformity as "un-American" (Richmond 1984, 11). The British social psychologist Michel Billig, however, pointed out that such "philosophical" American nationalism is just as easily adaptable to the post-communist world. Since 1991, the old Soviet demons were quickly replaced in the nationalism of *Pax Americana* with new enemies: the religious fundamentalists and misguided extremists. He describes this as follows:

> This philosophical nationalism, unlike some other forms, does not speak with narrow ferocity. Instead, it draws its moral force to lead the nations from its own proclaimed reasonableness. The global ambitions are to be presented as the voice of tolerance ('our' tolerance), even doubt ('our' doubt, 'our' modesty). All the while, 'we' are to keep a sense of 'ourselves'. And a sense of 'others': the mad and the bad, who cling to dangerous absolutes, opposing 'our' pragmatic, non-ideological politics (Billig 1995, 172).

Billig calls this sort of nationalism "banal nationalism," because it denies its own nationalism while arguing at the same time for loyalty to the nation-state, to "our" nation. Such banal nationalism is, in his opinion, typical for all Western democracies that deny that "their" nationalism is nationalist, because "it is a part of common-sense imaging of 'us', the democratic, tolerant and reasonable nation, rightfully inhabiting 'our' homeland" (Billig 1995, 161).

If, in fact, Western democracies are not less nationalist when it comes to "their" homeland, even though they repress and deny this fact, can nationalism be democratic and liberal? As Erica Benner (1995) discovered (in the writings of Marx and Engels), in the mid-nineteenth century nationalist movements in Europe were in fact either politically conservative or indeed democratic. In fact, this was, according to Benner, the main contribution of Marxism — to distinguish democratic and non-democratic nationalism and, thereby, to bring politics back into the study of nationalism. The founders of Marxism believed that both within oppressed nations and within their oppressor states, there were despotic as well as democratic nationalists, chauvinists and internationalists. Benner reflects on how Marx viewed the political nature of different nationalisms:

> To be eligible for support, he argued a nationalist movement should demonstrate that it is authentically 'national' in his democratic sense: it should, that is, positively address the concerns of a broad section of a nation's people by improving social conditions and expanding the bases of political participation. He cited the Krakow insurrection of 1846 as an example of such a movement,

applauding not only the political reforms advanced by the nationalist rebels but also their social and economic programme which represented, as Marx declared, Poland's attempt to 'break the chains of feudalism' (Benner 1995, 155).

If it was possible to distinguish democratic forms of nationalism among the nineteenth century nationalist movements struggling for the right of self-determination, is it possible to apply the same principles to contemporary Europe with mostly established frontiers? Is it possible to do so outside a Marxist paradigm that, in fact, proved ineffective in handling nationalism?

There is a growing school of thought suggesting that liberal nationalism is not only possible, but also the only acceptable future for nationalism, if it is to have any future at all. The Israeli scholar Yael Tamir (1993) proposed combining the liberal admiration of personal freedom and individual rights with the nationalist emphasis on belonging, loyalty and solidarity. Tamir believes that people have the right to their own culture, and that it is possible to provide them with this right within the framework of a liberal society, if equal opportunities are provided for all members of that society. A similar approach was suggested by Will Kymlicka. Kymlicka's liberal theory of minority rights argues for "freedom within minority groups and equality between minority and majority groups" (Kymlicka 1995, 152). However, as Judith Lichtenberg argued, this poses the difficult question of whether the state may or must privilege certain cultural practices, and disadvantage others, in the interests of social unity. Indeed, how *liberal* can nationalism be within or beyond state borders? And if it can provide cultural equality within a state and internationally, which is a moral prerequisite of liberal nationalism, then how different would such nationalism be from a cosmopolitan perspective? If the answer to the latter question proves difficult, Lichtenberg believes that liberal nationalism might be hard to distinguish from cosmopolitan-*ism* (Lichtenberg 19991, 167-88). In fact, it is difficult to disagree with such an argument precisely because nationalism is understood as relating to a single culture in a single state. So, is there any "good" nationalism that is possible or necessary? In order to address this question, it is useful to consider the relationship between democracy and nationalism on the one hand, and patriotism and nationalism on the other hand.

It is easy to observe that both contemporary democracy and nationalism became potent movements at approximately the same time, after the French Revolution, when a new concept of nation was born, within which it was people who possessed the right of sovereignty, and not the rulers as before. So, despite the popular, but mistaken, belief that democracy has nothing in common with nationalism or at least with "bad" nationalism – scholars cannot ignore the fact that, in one way or another, there must be an important correlation between the two.

Jürgen Habermas has argued that the modern state solved two important problems by its unique fusion of state institutions and the homogenizing idea of the nation. The national state established a democratic mode of *legitimation,* and it provided a new and more abstract form of *social integration.* This, however, caused an uneasy tension between a nationalist and a republican self-understanding of national society. According to Habermas, the fate of democracy depends on which of these self-understandings dominates (1996, 281-294). The normative conclusion drawn from the European history of nation-states should therefore be simple: to get rid of that ambivalent potential of nationalism, which was originally the vehicle for its success, and to replace it with constitutional patriotism. Habermas admits, however, that in comparison with nationalism, constitutional patriotism appears too thin to hold societies together. He uses, as an example, the United States which, in his view, is the prototype of a country which is united by a civic patriotism that is ultimately self-defeating: for, as he argues, "surging fundamentalism and terrorism (such as in Oklahoma [the 1995 bombing]) are alarming signs that the safety curtain of a civil religion, interpreting a constitutional history of two hundred years, may be about to break" (Habermas 1996, 290).

Jack Snyder proposed an "elite-persuasion" theory of nationalism to explain the relationship between democratization and nationalist conflict. Snyder argues that democratization produces nationalism in the early stages of democracy building, when national elites use nationalism for their own self-interests in order to organize masses behind them for the tasks of war and economic development. Snyder explains the use of nationalism by national elites, historically first in Western Europe and later in Eastern Europe, as related, not to the logic of industrialization as Gellner argued, but to the weakness of political institutions at the time. Therefore, his elite-persuasion theory rests on the assumption that nationalism is an expression of weak developing democracies, "a disease of the transition" and that "proper" political institutions solve this problem of democratic growth (Snyder 2000, 352).

David Held argued in favor of cosmopolitan democracy, but he admits that nationalism was a critical force in the development of the democratic nation-state. According to Held, nationalism has been closely linked to the administrative unification of the state *because* the conditions involved in the creation of nationalism were often also the conditions that generated the modern state. Contrary to Snyder, who argues that mature democracies overcome the problem of nationalism, Held notes that "the importance of nation-state and nationalism, territorial independence, and the desire to establish or regain or maintain 'sovereignty' does not seem to have diminished in recent times" (Held 1995, 94). This is, in his view, connected to the fact that even liberal democracies, or perhaps liberal democracies most of all, need to maintain a common national identity in order to ensure the coordination of policy, mass mobilization and state legitimacy.

Two other important questions should be discussed here: is national consciousness a derivative of nationalism, or is the reverse the case? The "modernist" claim that nations were invented to meet the need of industrial society for a culturally homogeneous and literate environment logically implies that national identity is a consequence of this invention. However, as Philip Schlesinger notes, "Nationalism ... tends to carry the sense of a community mobilized in the pursuit of a collective interest." However, national identity "may be invoked as a point of reference without necessarily being nationalistic" (Schlesinger 1987, 253).

There are, of course, historical periods when the construction of a national identity may be part of a nationalist program; however, national identity is not necessarily identical to nationalism as such. In other words, national identity and nationalism are different aspects of a more general phenomenon. It would be logical to assume that nationalism is only a part of national identity and that the latter does not have to be nationalistic. Just as national identity may contain other beliefs and myths, it can contain nationalism as a political principle or, as "modernists" would insist, nationalism as a myth. For instance, Gellner claims that:

> Nationalism—the principle of homogeneous cultural units as the foundations of political life, and the obligatory cultural unity of rulers and ruled—is indeed inscribed neither in the nature of things, nor in the hearts of men, nor in the preconditions of social life in general, and the contention that it is so inscribed is a falsehood which nationalist doctrine has succeeded in presenting as self-evident. (Gellner 1983, 125)

Primordialists would argue, however, that the basis of nationalism is much more deeply rooted in the human belief of common ancestry (territorially defined) and destiny. For instance, Smith argues that: "Though nationalism as theory and ideology is quite modern (dating from the late eighteenth century in Europe), the identities on which it feeds and builds are either ancient and persistent, or preserved in memories and symbols that, given the right conditions, can serve as models for nation-creating nationalism" (Smith 1984, 289). In some sense, the set of these identities, memories and symbols can correspond to the belief system that we call *patriotism*. Gellner recognized nationalism as a species of patriotism distinguished by a few very important features: homogeneity, literacy, and anonymity (Gellner 1983, 138). However, as Morris Janovitz has pointed out, patriotism is as old as settled communities (Janovitz 1983).

It is also the case that nationalism as an ideology and doctrine habitually employs various myths as a means of subjugating the masses. As Hobsbawm notes: "Nationalism requires too much belief in what is patently not so. 'Getting its history wrong is part of being a nation (Renan)'" (Hobsbawm 1990, 12).

Nationalists themselves are conscious of their usage of myths. For instance, Benito Mussolini argued that "Our myth is the greatness of the nation."[1] The same idea was expressed by the founder of Ukrainian integral nationalism, Dmytro Dontzov, who wrote in 1923 that each nation has and needs a myth for its own reinforcement (Dontzov 1966). We can conclude therefore that myth in nationalist ideology is required as a tool of mass mobilization. This function is not consistent with either modernist or primordialist conceptions of the transition to the era of nations and nationalism. As Anthony Smith has argued:

> There can be no real 'nation' without its tacit myth of origins and descent, which defines the fictive kinship basis of the nation and explains the network of affective ties and sentiments. Indeed, together with the historical memories of successive generations of members, myths of descent furnish the cognitive maps and mobilizing moralities of nations as they struggle to win and maintain recognition today (Smith 1988b, 14).

When Habermas argues in favor of constitutional patriotism as an alternative to nationalism, he does not develop the idea of American civic patriotism as a "civic religion." However, it is revealing that he defines (American) patriotism in terms of religion. In fact, one might consider religion a myth or belief system. In arguing that nationalism does not have to be ethnic, many scholars equate the civic belief system of the United States with civic nationalism. Therefore, we can conclude that nationalism as a belief system can and usually does include a set of myths as an essential part of its doctrine. At the same time, the structural and functional difference between nationalism and myth should be stressed. Insofar as a myth is included in nationalism as an ideological doctrine, it can be adequately included in national identity. In national identity, however, not only nationalists` myths but also other kinds of myths concerning the nature of nationhood and national belonging can be represented, even a cosmopolitan one. However, a belief about a cosmo-

---

[1]   Benito Mussolini, speech at Naples, 24 Oct. 1922, in *Scritti e Discorsi*, ii.345, quoted in *Nationalism: A Report by a Study Group of Members of the Royal Institute of International Affairs* [1939]. Reprints of Economic Classics. New York (1966).

politan unity, as opposed to a national one, would have to develop in the evolution of the individual worldview within his/her national identity until a break with national belonging takes place.

The possibility of creating a cosmopolitan, non-national or even global democracy poses a serious challenge to the existing world order of nation-states. If Held is right in arguing that the universal political unification of the world into a system of nation-states was a result of European expansion in order to further its commerce and trade, it suggests that if the European Union replaces the nation-state principle with a supra-national principle, this will eventually became a world-wide movement. In other words, the development of the EU could be a test case for the future of the nation-state precisely because its development is driven by the logic of post-industrial economic development, just as the creation of the nation-state was driven by the logic of industrialization and modernization. Those who discount this possibility argue that, in fact, the national principle of state building may not be displaced by the successful integration of Europe. The European Union might become a super-power-type nation-state similar to the United States. A "United States of Europe" might become another civic nation similar to the American one, but based on a single European culture. Liah Greenfeld argues that potentially even a "United States of the World" would not necessarily depart from the principle of nationalism if sovereignty were vested in the population of the world and its various segments were regarded as equals (Greenfeld 1992).

Although the potential transformation of the EU into a single political unit is not likely to happen in the near future, it is possible to predict that such a federal Europe of countries, but not nation-states, would encounter the problem of developing a common identity capable of mass mobilization to the extent that national identity is capable of this within nation-states. However, as Anthony Giddens asks, would not a globalized democracy, featuring representative assemblies, meet with the same problems of apathy or hostility encountered at the national level? According to Giddens, "cosmopolitan democracy is not only about the movement of governance towards a world level, but about diffusion downwards to local regions" (Giddens 1998, 146). Again, the main reason states might devolve power upwards to institutions of global governance is not idealism but, according to Giddens, because it is in their interest to have the global economy managed more effectively. The latter is equally one of the guiding principles of the emerging EU alternative in the East of Europe—The Eurasian Economic Union (EAEU).

The economic necessity for states to form supra-national or cosmopolitan democratic governance does not, however, provide the answer to the question as to whether national identities will disappear completely, merge into a cosmopolitan identity, or become merely regional components of a supra-national identity. In fact, humans enjoy a multiplicity of identities and new ones do not have to replace the old ones. This, however, does not necessarily hold in the case of nationalism as a political principle, according to which a separate national state is essential for the development of a national culture. In fact, the end of the Cold War manifested newly emerging ethno-national revivals and social identities that rapidly challenged national borders on the continent. US president Donald Trump reflected similar rising sentiments in his electoral base when he used his address to the UN general assembly (2019) to deliver a nationalist manifesto, denouncing "globalism" and illegal immigration and promoting patriotism as a cure for the world's ills:

> "The free world must embrace its national foundations. It must not attempt to erase them, or replace them," Trump said. "The true good of the nation, can only be pursued by those who love it, by citizens who are rooted in its history, who are nourished by its culture, committed to its values, attached to its people."
> (Quoted from the Guardian https://www.theguardian.com/us-news/2019/sep/24/donald-trump-un-address-denounces-globalism)

Trump went on to underline the role of patriots, a self-selecting group of citizens uniquely able to interpret national interest in the globalized world: "Patriots see a nation and its destiny in ways no one else can. Liberty is only preserved, sovereignty is only secured, democracy is only sustained, greatness is only realized by the will and devotion of patriots," the president said. It is these groups of patriots that were a matter of preoccupation for scholars of national revivals at least since the 1960s.

1.2. Nationalist Revival, National Identity and Security

The emergence of nationalist revivals[2] in Eastern Europe after the fall of Communism stimulated debate in a number of social science disciplines. Identity, generally, and national identity in particular, became central to scholarly debates on the nature of nations and nationalism. In the 1990s scholars began to explore identity politics and the role of inter-national relations as opposed to inter-state ones, in order to explain the disintegration of the multi-national Soviet state, and inter-ethnic violence in the post-communist world.

Increased attention given to the problem of national identity and nationalist revival in recent years appears to have resulted, according to some scholars, in an "over-production of theories,"', i.e., in the introduction of new theoretical concepts, but ones insufficiently based on empirical and comparative research. The objective of this work, therefore is, first, to compare existing theories of nations and nationalism in the Western and Eastern (Soviet) European traditions in order to develop a synthetic perspective on nationalism and nationalist revival; and, second, to provide empirical grounding for this synthesis.

As previously discussed, nationalism as an ideology and a political movement is often a major cause of inter-group violent conflict. James Kellas (1991) has argued that the principal task of any theory of nationalism is to find out what kind of force makes people go for "the highest sacrifice" and die for their nation (1991, 170). Yet, nationalism is also a largely unavoidable element of nation building in modern European societies. It is therefore crucial to find out the

---

[2]   The term "nationalist revival" rather than "national revival" is used here to stress the political nature of the former. As Chapter 5 will illustrate national revivals in Eastern Europe became a form of belated nationalist project of economic and social modernization that developed into political movements. "National" and "nationalist revival," therefore, are equal terms in a wider sense; however, national revival is not always political in the initial stages and therefore not always nationalist in the more narrow sense.

conditions under which individuals form nationalist groups according to one or another nationalist project.

Modernist theories of nationalism do not explain why individuals decide or happen to choose ideological movements that are new
to them and not rooted in their existing cultures. The only systematic
research in this direction was done by the Czech scholar, Miroslav
Hroch. Hroch enquired into why and under what circumstances
individuals move from a simple awareness of national belonging to
an active national identity or patriotism. Although Hroch's *Social
Preconditions of National Revival in Europe* was written in 1968, this
question remains unanswered, although new comparative research
was published involving case studies from around the world (See
Maxwell 2012).

Hroch (1985) identifies three main phases of national revival:
Phase A—the period of scholarly interest; Phase B—the period of
patriotic agitation; and Phase C—the rise of a mass national movement. As Hroch (1998) points out:

> We know of a number of cases in which the national movement remained in
> Phase B for a long time, sometimes down to the present: here we may point to
> Wales, Brittany, Belarus or the Eastern Ukraine. How can these differences be
> explained? ... The question of the 'success' of the national movement cannot
> be posed in the abstract, but concretely within the individual phases of the na-
> tional movement. ... The first level of the problem [Why did some of the patri-
> ots from Phase A decide to begin national agitation? In other words, why did
> Phase B begin?] has so far been accorded scant attention in empirical research.
> ... This is a serious weakness of my work of 1968—which, however Gellner
> overlooks. But even from this model we cannot explain why some individuals
> decided in favour of the new identity and embarked on national agitation.
> (Hroch 1998, 98, 105 n. 14)

Lack of knowledge about the reasons why individuals sacrifice
their lives for an "imagined community" not only limits our understanding of national phenomena, but also makes it extremely difficult to predict what will motivate individuals to sacrifice their or
others' lives and what, therefore, can potentially be a security threat,
e.g., Chechen suicide bombers in Russia or a Breivik-style attack in
Norway.

Hroch explored the creation and development of new national
movements in Europe during the nineteenth century and suggested

the importance of considering the concept of "groups of patriots," those most actively promoting a national project and who are not nationally known leaders. A "patriot" for Hroch is a person who consciously and continuously devotes his time and effort to the success of a national project. Self-sacrifice and even risk count as a measure of such patriotic activity rather than money or other forms of contribution. In this way Hroch includes in the category of patriots, not only the ideological leaders of national movements, but also those people who assist leaders and make their work possible. Hroch's concept helps to direct research on early modern nationalism not only to known historical figures, but also to the collective identity encompassed by the term "patriotic." Since scholars generally agree on the time frame of European nation building, it is possible to study the probable content of the national identity possessed by specific groups of "patriots" at a specific time. This time is defined not chronologically, but according to the phase of nation-building, defined at least with respect to the so-called "new" nations in Europe, when "patriots" are the main actors of new national projects and are ready to become "national activists" and the most enthusiastic adherents of a new national consciousness (Hroch 1985, 13).

For most of the "new" nations in Europe the first stage of national revival belongs to the end of the eighteenth and beginning of the nineteenth centuries, when little sociological data was available on collective identities. However, historical analogies enable us to investigate the national identity of "patriots" today in a nation experiencing the first stages of nation building. Hroch suggests that historical analogies can be applied both diachronically and synchronically (horizontally). He explains these comparisons as follows:

1. A diachronic comparison in the narrow sense of the word involves the comparison of different historical processes occurring in different countries at the same time.

2. A synchronic comparison according to analogous historical situations. If we can establish that the objects of comparison passed through the same stages of development, we can compare these analogous stages, even if from the standpoint of absolute chronology they occurred at different times. We can only apply this procedure if we are certain that the societies under comparison have passed through roughly equivalent periods of historical development (Hroch 1985, 14-15).

A synchronic comparison allows us to study contemporary identities of "newly" emerged political nations similar to those of early modern nationalisms.

Ukraine is often referred to as a "newcomer" nation-state. It has full achieved independence only with the collapse of the USSR and its political as well as national identity remains undecided. The "nowhere nation" or "unexpected nation," as it has been labelled by some scholars (e.g., Wilson 2000), was characterized as having an incomplete national revival by both Western and Ukrainian historians in the early 1990s (Formuvannia ukrainskoii natsii..., von Hagen 1995). It was noted the, that all three phases of national revival (A — the period of scholarly interests; B — the period of patriotic agitation; C — the rise of mass national movement; Hroch 1985), overlapped in Ukraine subsequent to its achieving independence in 1991.

The empirical research described in Appendix 1 suggests that Ukrainian Cossack organizations that appeared after 1991 represent groups of patriots whose aim is to foster a national "revival" in Ukraine. National activists in Ukraine have chosen the name "Cossacks" because, in their opinion, it is Cossacks, free warriors of the steppe, who represent a positive image of the Ukrainian nation. To promote the Cossack idea and, if possible, to turn all the people of Ukraine into Cossacks is the project. The aim is to create ideal Ukrainians, and this is a typical discourse during Hroch's Phase B of national revival. We have a unique chance to compare synchronically by sociological methods (such as participant observation or in-depth interviews) the national identity constructs of patriots with those of patriots who lived elsewhere two hundred years ago.

There is no satisfactory explanation in the sociological literature for the shift from simple national identification and group allegiance to the action-oriented national identification that typifies "patriots' groups." Identification theory suggests a possible explanation of why individuals might decide to join a "group of patriots." It suggests that people seek positive group identification to obtain psychological security. This is the central argument of all "psychologically" oriented approaches (e.g. Billig 1995; Bloom 1990).

According to identification theory, human beings have a natural tendency to form groups with shared similarities and to distinguish themselves in this way from "the Other." What remains unclear, in the case of Cossacks, is the relationship between psychological security based on positive group identification, and the readiness to engage in self-sacrifice. A plausible explanation could be based on the social identity theory of Henry Tajfel (1981). Tajfel argues that when exiting from a group or category is not possible and self-esteem cannot be protected in this way, a person may seek to induce social change. Such social change would involve the individual in efforts to influence the relative power and status of the group concerned. By achieving greatness for a group one cannot escape, one achieves a reflected grandeur for the self. Tajfel and others have suggested that this may be the spur to the creation of new militant subgroups, the development of new rhetoric, and various forms of social activities.

Glynis Breakwell argues that identity is "a dynamic social product," residing in psychological processes, which "cannot be understood except in relation to their social context and historical perspective" (Breakwell 1986, 9, 36-39). Following her suggestion, our analysis focuses on:

1. Cossack identity over time (nationalist memories, myths, stereotypes — i.e., components of self-perception);
2. the identity processes and the principles of their operation (e.g., transition from pre-Cossack to Cossack and sometimes to a post-Cossack identity);
3. the social context of identity (Cossack revival, perception of Cossacks by their wider social communities);

4. the effects of social change upon identity (transformation of Cossack identity under pressure from other social actors and processes, such as alternative Cossack movements and/or state policies);

5. The relation of identity to action (relation between self-images and real actions).

Despite the official and unofficial support of political elites it is clear also that the Cossack revival is a "bottom-up" movement, i.e., it originates in local, regional initiatives that are supported, at a later stage, by officials. The empirical data also shows that there have often been economic interests directly involved in stimulating the growth of Cossack organizations. Cossack claims to revive "traditional" trades such as beekeeping or, indeed, military service suggest that economic factors form at least part of the explanation for the successful revival of Cossack nationalism. Although economic nationalism was developed as a category to be applied to inter-state relations (Burnell 1986; Hieronimi 1980; Johnson 1967), there is good reason to apply it to small-scale (inter-group) social interrelations if competition for limited resources is present in social discourse.

Research undertaken for this monograph shows that the new nationalist movements that constituted the Cossack revival have had two clear paths of development. The first path is toward the further elaboration of an ethnic model of Cossack and wider Russian (supra-)community, as is happening predominantly in the Russian Federation, Kazakhstan and North Caucasus; the second path has led to the reinvention of a civic model, as in mainstream Cossack organizations in Ukraine. The research suggests that much depends on how the revival of ethno-geopolitics in the region of the Former Soviet Union (FSU) succeeds in promoting economic nationalism and whether this proves beneficial to ethnic and/or national communities. Yet the choice between an ethnic and civic model will have to be made at a cost that is reasonable in terms of nationalist identity, that is, so as not to threaten the societal security of a given national community.

The concept of "societal security" is useful for analyzing violent expressions of nationalism. Traditional state-as-actor theories that predominate in the field of International Security failed to predict the inter-ethnic violence that accompanied the collapse of the USSR and Yugoslavia. The empirical findings clearly illustrate that war preparations among nationalist elites in Russia and Ukraine began practically since 1991. Russia's nation-building project aims at the re-creation of a larger inclusive state within boundaries that historically are associated with the Russian (Tsarist or Soviet) empires. The Ukrainian "irredentist" nation-building project requires the inclusion of all minorities in order to be viable. This, however, contradicts the logic of Russian supra-state expansion that must incorporate most if not all of the Ukrainian nation-state territories. The fact that neither nation-building project is ethnically exclusive does not prevent inter-group violence, as is clearly demonstrated in Donbas, where armed conflict began in 2014. The ethnic composition of fighters on both sides of the conflict is not dissimilar; all nationalities of the former USSR are represented to various degrees and Russian was initially the dominant language of instruction in both militaries.

Scholarly optimists in the 1990s believed that liberalization of developing democracies and the acceptance of extensive non-territorial federal arrangements could be the two factors that would turn the "no war community" of Russia and Ukraine into a "security community" where war is inconceivable. However, Putin's government opted for an armed solution of its upgrading neo-imperial Eurasianist project and made Ukrainians fight for the survival of their nation-state. The logic of the self-determination principle will endure for the foreseeable future; and the better we understand the mechanisms of mass mobilization for violence, the safer that future will be.

1.3. Plan of the Study

The next chapter (Chapter 2) will review theories of nations and national and ethnic identity/consciousness and will suggest a synthesis of Western and Eastern (Soviet) approaches that can help with understanding the dominant perspectives in nationalism studies.

The crucial disagreements among various approaches have to do with the actual role of ethnicity in nationalism. Chapter 2 argues that ethnicity is important to national identity only in some cases. Generally, modern identities, including national ones, absorb elements of ethnic history in the form of common narratives (e.g., myths and stereotypes), transforming the ethnic component to suit new purposes. A continuity of ethnicity from pre-modern history is, therefore, not essential for modern societies as it (ethnicity) can always be (re-)introduced like other cultural borrowings from the past. A clearer understanding of how ethnicity functions in modern societies can help to resolve debates about the degree to which ethnicity is reinvented or is perennial in character (while incorporated into national identity).

Chapter 3 analyzes the connection between nationalism and war as ultimate expressions of insecurity and destruction. Although it is commonplace to blame nationalism for war, few studies have examined the conditions under which nationalism causes violent conflict and war. The main conclusion drawn from the literature reviewed in this chapter is that a new, societal sector of security is a useful lens — along with a state's military, political, economic and environmental security — that can foresee the potential for violent conflict in a given society.

Studies of regional security and nationalist conflict inevitably take researchers into the larger domain of inter-state relations. There is a need, therefore, for methodological clarity concerning levels of analysis, similar to the concern central to International Relations theory. This study traces nationalist conflict from the individual and group level (Cossack movements) to the level of nation-state bureaucracy (governments) and then to sub-system (nation-sates) and system levels (security community of nation-states). These levels are further delineated and discussed in Chapter 3.

Chapter 3 also focuses on the New European Order as an expansion of the European Security Community and its threat to the emerging national identities of Eastern Europe. The enlargement of the EU and NATO, as well as the more assertive policies of Russia toward the countries of the former USSR, has made countries such as Ukraine a buffer between East and West. The re-emergence of "cold peace" rhetoric in place of the former Cold War rhetoric has relegated Ukraine, a country once called a "lynchpin of European security," to the uneasy role of geopolitical buffer. At the same time, hybrid war waged by Russia on Ukraine as a nation-state since 2014 magnifies the threat to societal security as well as state security. With Ukrainian public opinion divided regarding the ability of power-holders to achieve victory and peace because of perceived corruption, the threat of a re-integration with the Eurasian Economic Union and the Russian supra-state nationalist project is existential.

The formation of new political and national identities in Ukraine must therefore be examined in the context of the establishment of a new European order hailed by the West and the new "multi-polar," "post-West" world order promoted by Putin's Russia. In Ukraine, profound popular disappointment with debt-fueled, market economic reforms favoring the oligarchic clans more than the relatively poor majority, and the implications of the customs restrictions that accompany EU enlargement may pose a threat to the Ukrainian national identity. To what extent do myths of a Ukrainian "Golden Age" harmonize with the idea of a "People's Europe" if they do not bring jobs and prosperity?

On the one hand, pro-independence, nationalist elites promote the idea of the EU and NATO integration as a part of the Ukrainian national idea; on the other hand, some studies suggest that threats to Ukrainian national identity from a nationalist (neo-imperialist) Russia and the lack of a real prospect of joining the security community of the NATO-led Western Alliance escalates the security dilemma in Ukraine and might even lead to resolution in policies of nuclear deterrence, following the examples of India and Pakistan.

Threats to national identity threaten "societal security" which, as previously mentioned, is a dimension of state security linked to collective identity. Chapter 3 describes the identity process of the Ukrainian political elite, analyzing the election manifestos of presidential candidates as well as strategic documents relating to Ukrainian military doctrines and national security. This is related to existing studies of both Ukrainian mass national consciousness and possible future directions of the development of Ukrainian national identity. The analysis addresses the question of whether the legacy of Soviet thinking about nation/state-building and the new Western political and military dominance in Europe influences the way Ukrainians think of their future, in terms of national dignity, well-being, and security.

The concept of "societal security" was introduced originally by a group of scholars from the European Security Group at the Centre for Peace and Conflict Research in Copenhagen (1993). It was designed to draw attention to the significance for International Relations theory of identity politics:

> Security studies have traditionally been concerned about relationships amongst collectivities, and we have shown that one can remain within this tradition and yet include completely new dynamics and insights through the elevation of society to the status of a referent object beside the state (Buzan et al 1998, 186).

In general, the issues raised by notions of societal security reflect threats to or influences upon social identity: it is about situations in which societies perceive a threat in identity terms. The authors admit that although a national identity is not necessarily dominant among other constructions of social identity, in specific situations it mobilizes and organizes the other identities around itself. These are first of all situations of threat, either real or imagined.

The concept of societal security is interlinked with the older concept of "security community" introduced by Karl Deutsch (1970). Deutsch's "security community" is a community in which, over a long period of time, war becomes unimaginable or implausible among its members. The creation of a "security community" depends to a large extent, therefore, on social perceptions. A community in which war is not likely, but where preparations for war are nevertheless made as a precaution is called a "No War Community." The notion of "societal security," it is argued, is useful for monitoring conditions under which nationalism might call for war. These include migration, horizontal and vertical competition among peoples of the same region, and depopulation of a country. The political rhetoric and the actual policies of ruling elites, however, are still a decisive factor, as war is only one among many available policy options.

Together, Chapters 2 and 3 will clarify how theories of nations and nationalism developed in the FSU, and how they have affected nationality policy in the Newly Independent States (NIS) of the FSU, particularly in Russia and Ukraine, the two biggest countries of the region. A strong inclination toward primordialism in post-Soviet scholarly works as well as policy planning led to the dominance of *ethno-geopolitics* in the academic and political circles of some countries of the former USSR. Just as the theoretical notion of "societal security" was meant to draw attention to the lack of understanding of relations among societies, as opposed to states, in the West, ethno-geopolitics draws attention to relations among "imagined" ethnic communities in Eastern Europe.

Chapter 4 examines how ethno-geopolitics developed within the discipline of Soviet Ethnography, and how it continues to influence thinking among post-Soviet scholars and policy makers in Russia and Ukraine. Soviet Ethnography, which reached its zenith under the "leadership" of academician Yulian Bromley in the 1970s and 1980s, is now largely ignored in the West. However, it still provides an important framework for Russian and Ukrainian academic thought and policy planning.

The "socio-spherical" approach that dominated Soviet Ethnography was close to the "modernist" paradigm in the Western tradition. But it also featured elements of "primordialism." "Modernist" and "primordialist" approaches in the Western tradition encompass other schools of thought such as "instrumentalism," "functionalism," "constructivism" and "perenniallism," and logically could be related to what in Soviet terminology was called "socio-spherical" and "bio-spherical" approaches.[3]

As the current literature on nationalism in Eastern Europe emphasizes, Soviet ethnography was not only an academic discipline, but also a tool to justify and fortify Soviet nationality policy. It might be seen as having directly influenced the creation and "constitutionalization," not only of numerous Soviet nationalities, but also ethno-

---

[3]   Sotsiologicheskiye teorii natsionalisma: nauchno-analiticheskiy obzor. AN SSSR. (Moskva: Nauka, 1991). Also: B. Popov, A. Shkliar, eds., *Etnos I sotsium* (Kyiv: Naukova Dumka, 1993).

national borders from the oblast level up to the republic or, in the case of Russia, the federation level. The heritage of such academic thinking and policy is now often deemed responsible for the ferocious conflicts in the Northern Caucasus and, even, for the disintegration of the Soviet Union as a whole. Yet there has been little research on the extent to which Soviet Ethnography continues to influence current academic thought in Russia and Ukraine. The influence of Western theories in this area has been limited and academic traditions today in Russia and, to a lesser degree, Ukraine are influenced by the "bio-spherical" theories developed by Lev Gumilev and the "new Eurasians." The latter only dramatized the old Soviet paradigm and, to a great extent, led to the revival (or creation) of ethno-geopolitics.

Chapter 4 examines the relationship between Soviet Ethnography and Soviet nationality policy, and compares it to the current vision of Russian and Ukrainian policy makers and scholars. It also examines the methodological foundations of ethno-geopolitics as a theory, and the implications of ethno-geopolitics as a policy concept.

The Cossack revivals in Russia and Ukraine will be the focus for examining inter-ethnic conflicts within the FSU. Chapter 4 therefore provides a historical background of Cossack movements in Russia and Ukraine. In doing so, it illuminates the relationship between ethno-geopolitical discourse, paramilitary movements and the assertion of national identity.

One of the reasons for the growth of the Cossack movements, as some scholars have indicated (Dawisha and Parrot 1994; Plokhy 1993), is the direct and indirect interest of national elites in using these movements in political and military discourse. Presidential decrees in the NIS established a semi-legislative basis for Cossack activity where the Cossack revival has developed most of all, that is, in Russia (1992 and 1996) and Ukraine (1995, 1999, and 2001). In both countries there was a tendency to subordinate Cossack units to the military authorities despite the Cossacks' historical tradition of autonomous self-government. The active participation by Russian Cossacks in armed inter-ethnic conflicts in the territories outside of the Russian Federation (Moldova, Georgia, Bosnia, Chechnya, Donbas,

etc.) shows the potential danger for regional security.[4] This is especially true if one takes into account the danger of involvement by
regular armies, as has happened, for instance, in Abkhazia, Trans-
Dnestria and Donbas. Another important factor is the direct involvement of security forces and intelligence services in Cossack
leadership via retired officers.[5] A central question with which this
research is concerned is the influence of the ruling elite rhetoric on
the development of the Cossack revival, and vice versa.

A comparison of the distinct Cossack revivals in Russia and
Ukraine also emphasizes how different theories of nationalist
movements can underpin different national policies and, ultimately,
different socially constructed realities. Theory and practice in re-
gards to nation and nationalism still go hand in hand in territories
where historical revivals, typical in other regions of Europe in the
nineteenth century, have only now emerged. So, for instance, in Russia, a Cossack movement established Russian Cossacks as an "ethnic
community" with a tendency toward, on the one hand, local self-
government and, on the other, Russian supra-state expansionism.
Clearly, the dominant perceived threat to Russian Cossacks is the
one directed against them as an ethno-cultural community, in addition to other threats directed against Russia as a Supra-ethnos Russian civilization.

The post-Soviet Ukrainian Cossack movement evolved as a
public organization and did not develop an ideology separate from
that of a moderate Ukrainian nationalism. As a result, Ukrainian
Cossacks perceive any external or internal threat directed against
Ukraine as one directed against them. The co-existence of Russian
and Ukrainian Cossack movements, often in the same geographic
and political space, has led to confrontation and nationalist conflict
between them. This is a consequence of the inter-nation-state conflict
on a regional scale that became clear from Russian designs on Crimea starting in the early 1990s.

4   G. Mashtakova, "Ih snova khvataet v sherengah po vosem," in: *Moscow News*,
      no.16, 21-28 April 1996, 4.
5   Lola Topchieva, "The Renaissance of Red Russia," in: *Independent*, 9 June 1996, 6-
      7; "The Cossacks," in: *Eastern Europe Newsletter* 6, no. 15, 20 July 1992, 5-7.

The empirical research undertaken for this study, and detailed in Appendix 1, demonstrates the utility of the notion of societal security for explaining the reassertion of national identity in Ukraine, in a situation in which Russian and Ukrainian national projects are competing for the same target audience at the same time. It traces the Cossack revival in Ukraine as a form developing both a national identity and a social structure to fill the void of civil society in post-communist space, and explores social phenomena related to societal security tensions.

The mobilization of people into "patriots' groups" around the idea of revived Cossackdom suggests that there was a threat to societal security in Ukraine practically since the achievement of formal independence in 1991. Yet the usefulness of the "societal security" concept is that it puts the state-society relationship in a new light, by showing that the security concerns of these two do not necessarily coincide. This theoretical assumption allows this study to compare the different ideological orientations of Cossack groups to each other and with respect to state ideologies, showing the existence of different discourses of societal (in)security or (in)securities in the region.

Chapter 5 suggests the outlines of a normative theory of nationalism and the issues it might address. Some of the basic assumptions of such a theory would include the following:

1. Although often based on pre-modern cultures, *nationalism is a distinctly modern political principle that links society and polity* in a nation-state;
2. distinctions drawn among varieties of nationalism, such as "cultural" and "political," "civic" and "ethnic," "liberal" and "conservative," while not without some merit, do not in fact constitute real alternatives; *nationalism is a political principle used by many ideologies and is not necessarily an ideology of its own;*

3. once nationalism is universally recognized as an organizing principle of self-determination, attempts to limit the right of self-determination will be normatively self-defeating; *nationalism is embedded in national identity and is based on the belief that mankind is "naturally" divided into nations* and nation-states and that this division is important to human development; it is this quality of national identity, of combining rational and irrational or emotional beliefs that makes the denial of national sentiments so explosive.

Yet nationalism is of great importance even for modern liberal democratic societies, as it functions to secure state patriotism in a world of competing nation-states. As European integration illustrates, a post-nation-state world is not impossible. Until, however, nationalism is deconstructed and un-invented, federalism and civil society an only ease the negative excesses of this political principle. Chapter 5 also explores how federalism, together with civil society institutions, is capable of modifying extremes of the internationally enshrined right to self-determination, keeping together peoples within the same polity and easing inter-ethnic (national) confrontation until the possible development of new non-territorial identities solve the dilemma of competing nationalist projects. Finally, Chapter 5 summarizes the arguments and evidence for using the concept of societal (identity) security as a means of understanding the security concerns of societies, as opposed to states, as well as threats insufficiently evident in existing theoretical frameworks. This is then applied to the existing conflict of Ukrainian and Russian nationalisms and its likely resolution.

2   Theories of Nation and National Identity: Comparing Soviet (Russian, Ukrainian) and Western Perspectives

There is a good deal of ambiguous terminology in the study of national and nationalist phenomena not only in the Western tradition, but also in the Eastern European tradition heavily influenced by the Soviet Ethnography. This chapter clarifies key terms, including "nation," "*ethnie*" or "ethnic community," "national" and "ethnic" consciousness. It conceptualizes national consciousness as a complex system of beliefs of rational and emotional origin, whose development is a constant dynamic process that reflects a group's social existence. Terms drawn from cognitive psychology make it possible to conceive national consciousness as a myth while at the same time showing how myths and stereotypes are crucially important to the functioning of national consciousness. This chapter therefore establishes a common ground necessary for further exploration of nationalism as an ideology behind the nationalist revival and reveals its socio-historical dimension. It also compares major Western and Soviet (Post-Soviet Russian and Ukrainian) perspectives on national identity. The analysis identifies the key arguments of each school of thought, and, then suggests a possible synthetic approach to achieve clarity of analysis.

2.1. Major Elements Within the Genesis of Nation, Ethnie, National and Ethnic Consciousness

Comparative research illustrates that despite little academic exchange between Western and Soviet social scientists, understanding of national identity was substantially similar. For instance, Anthony Smith's argument about the nature of national consciousness is closer to the position of the Soviet theoretician Yulian Bromley than to the purely modernist approaches that currently predominate the western social sciences. On the other hand, Eastern European theorists, such as Miroslav Hroch or Valeriy Tishkov have developed modernist or "constructivist"[11] approaches.

The key terms explored are "nation," "ethnic community" (*ethnie* or *ethnos*), "national consciousness" and "ethnic consciousness." The term "identity" in this monograph is distinguished from "consciousness" in the following way. Identity represents consciousness at a certain period of time and qualitatively defined by this period. *Consciousness is therefore a process; identity is a part of it.* Identity is related to the past and future of consciousness as a process. In this way the term "identity" will be related, for instance, to a subject (bearer) of consciousness at a moment of time in a specific location. The reason for making this distinction is to capture such phenomena as situational identity, as distinct from consciousness as a process, a constant activity that one can lose rather than change (Waver 1993, Drobizsheva 1985). Where reference to a specific subject, time or place is irrelevant, or the process itself is the focus of discussion, the term "consciousness" will be used rather than that of "identity."

2.1.1 "Nation": Modernist vs. Primordialist Perspectives

The word "nation" acquired its contemporary meaning after the French Revolution (1789-1794). As Liah Greenfeld (1992) has argued, "nation" originally referred to parties of student within medieval universities; later it was used to reflect on the social stratification of cities. Only at the end of the eighteenth century did the term acquire a political meaning: to identify the whole of the "revolutionary" people of France. It was only after the end of the Napoleonic wars and the second restoration in France (1815-1830) that "nation" acquired an association with ethnicity. In the English-language literature on nationality, "nation" is given two meanings: nation as a state, and nation as people. Therefore there were suggestions to introduce different terms — "state nation" or "nation-state" as well as, separately, "people" or "ethnic nation" (Riggs 1990, 12). In the Eastern European tradition, "nation" was usually understood as "people," i.e., it directly corresponded to the word "*narod.*" It is often the case that depending on the first (state-nation) or second meaning (people, *narod*) different concepts are derived and theories are created.

Among Western scholars, the perennialist (modified primordialist) approach advocated by Smith is more receptive to the influence of the modernists than vice versa. Generally, primordialists like Smith (1986) and Llobera (1994) agree with Gellner`s model of social transformation from agrarian to industrial society. They recognize that nations are a *modern* phenomenon, precisely because of what they require—a unified jurisdiction, unified economy, fairly compact territory, "political culture," all so crucial in modernist theories. Yet, Smith noticed that even though there are common characteristics which form the basis of modern nations, these do not make the world of nations homogeneous.

Smith distinguishes at least two models (Western and Eastern) that emphasize different aspects of nationhood. The first places importance upon territory, a system of laws, institutions and civic culture. The second emphasizes ethnic descent and cultural ties. It is the latter type of nation that led the author to his conclusion about the ethnic origins of nations. This point is clearly reflected in his book *The Ethnic Origins of Nations* (1986) where he argues that, historically, the *first nations were formed on the basis of pre-modern ethnic cores:*

> A nation can be defined as a named human population sharing a historic territory, common myths and historical memories, a mass, public culture, a common economy and common legal rights and duties for all members (Smith 1991, 14).

According to primordialists, a perennial process of ethnic development leads to the emergence of nations. Thus, ethnic links are of central importance to the development of nations. This challenges the modernist assumption that ethnic links within contemporary nations are artificial, and, therefore, unimportant. This view is not widely supported, even by proponents of the Western model of nations[6] since, according to primordialists, nations are inconceivable

---

6   Usually, the Western model of nations is defined by the tradition of individual membership based on civic and territorial citizenship as opposed to the ethnic characteristics of the Eastern nations. This would, however, place Germany into

without some common *myths* and *memories* of territorial home and these can be based only on prior *ethnies*. Whether this process of adoption is natural or artificial is not of fundamental importance and reflects the peculiarity of historical development within a particular nation. Natural or not, in all cases an ethnic element is of substantial importance as it provides the character or "soul" of the people. However, scholars are in accord that *ethnies* and nations are different social units and represent different historical formations.

Modernists stress the artificial connections of ethnic heritage in nation-building. Much attention in their theories is paid to the role of mass education (universal, standardized and generic). Hobsbawm and Ranger (1983) pointed out the importance of printing for mass education and the homogeneity of cultures. The term "invented traditions" (Hobsbawm 1990) became a catchphrase, to stress the fact that the national idea was an innovation at a certain period of social development. Ernest Gellner, on the other hand, emphasized the importance of the new division of labor required for industrial development. Both these factors led to a mobile and anonymous social organization as well as to the homogeneity of modern society, something reflected in Benedict Anderson's term "imagined communities" (Anderson 1991). According to this author, the very fact that nationals count people, whom they have never met, as belonging to "their" nation, underlines the subjective, "'imaginary" nature of national communities or nations. The question here is: why did these "imagined communities" or nations appear among homogenous industrial societies? Gellner puts forward two possible explanations: regional development of industrialism and development of nationalism as an ideology. The former leads to the appearance of new social units (nation-states) and the latter determines the *national* character of these new social formations. Gellner explains the phenomenon of nationalism through the peculiarities of high culture development during the transition from agrarian society to industrialism. There is a possible contradiction within this argument because, as Smith`s *The Ethnic Origin of Nations* (1983) demonstrates, "the peculiarities of

---

the Eastern rather than Western pattern, which is debatable. (See: Hunt 1984, Kohn 1967, Seton-Watson 1977, Smith 1984 b).

the high culture" are *always* (naturally or artificially) based on the ethnic heritage. However, for modernists, such ethnic, and therefore rather socio-cultural explanations, are unacceptable, since for them it is *socio-economic* factors that are central to the development of nations. This is why modernists cannot accept arguments about the ethnic (i.e., *socio-cultural*) origins of nations. To some extent, this is also the philosophical problem of the primacy of idea or matter. In this sense, modernists and primordialists argue from different paradigms and therefore it is unlikely that any compromise could be reached.

Both Soviet and contemporary Ukrainian and Russian scholars attempted to solve similar theoretical difficulties. Soviet Ethnography, which was almost alone among other disciplines in dealing with these problems, insisted on both paradigms: it defined socio-economic factors as the initial condition for nation-building, while insisting on the ethnic nature of modern nations (Bromley 1990, Kuznecov 1989). So, for instance, the fundamental feature of Bromley`s concept is the unity of ethnic and national development which is evident in his definition of nation as an "ethno-social organism." This author's terminology for dealing with national and ethnic phenomena can be easily applied to the logic of terms used by Western scholars. For instance, his term *ethnicos* has generally the same definition as Smith`s *ethnie*. Yet, as *ethnicos (ethnie)* can represent not only ethnic and territorial unity but also a socio-economic unity (historically dependent on concrete socio-economic formations such as feudalism, capitalism, socialism, etc.), Bromley has invented the term "ethno-social organism," which is wider than simply *ethnicos (ethnie)*, and as a result more flexible. Nation, for instance, is referred to in these terms as an ethno-social organism during the period of "capitalism" and "socialism," i.e., during industrial and post-industrial society.

Table 1.   Ethno-Social Organisms (ESOs)

Stages of human social development	Forms of ethno-social organization	Socio-economic formations
Tribe	*Ethnicos*	Primitive or Slavery
Narodnost'	*Ethnicos*	Feudalism
Nation	*Ethnicos*	Capitalism/Socialism

Only in the widest sense did the author suggest using the term "ethnos" to cover all periods of both ethnic and socio-economic development. In this way, we have a synthetic attempt to take into account (at least on the level of terminology) the socio-cultural as well as the socio-economic nature of national phenomena simultaneously. Bromley`s approach does not contradict either Smith`s or Gellner`s theories, the former because the two sets of terms almost overlap, and so simply complete each other, and the latter because Gellner`s periodization of human history (pre-agrarian, agrarian and industrial society) is reflected in the classification of ethnos (in the wider meaning of the term) according to the three historical types (tribe, *narodnost`* and nation), where the main criterion is socio-economic. All of the above suggests that Bromley`s, and the wider Soviet, terminology offered the possibility of a synthesis of "perennialist" and "modernist" approaches to understanding national phenomena. But first of all it makes sense to find out why the contradictions exist in the first place, and why the links between pre-modern ethnic communities and modern national communities are so crucial in these debates.

2.1.2 Ethnic Community, Ethnie, Ethnos

The terms "ethnic community," "ethnos" or *"ethnie,"* like "nation," have different meanings depending on the conceptual approach. "Ethnos" (in Greek, tribe, people) has been used since the beginning of the nineteenth century both in ethnography and social anthropology. It was applied, first, to small collectivities or groups that were the subject of anthropological research. Later on it was also applied to bigger communities. In the Western tradition it is not broadly used. More common are the terms "people," *"volke,"* *"ethnie"* and so on. "Ethnos," though, has been a key term for Soviet Ethnography since 1970s. But the term "ethnic community" has wider acceptance within different national traditions and therefore will be used further as a working term. A brief survey is necessary to establish in which context this, and other terms, are to be used.

The term and concept of *"ethnic community"* is understood by Anthony Smith as a type of cultural collectivity which emphasizes the role of myths of descent and historical memories, and which is recognized by one or more cultural differences, like religion, customs, language or collective institutions. The author lists six main attributes of ethnic community or *ethnie*:[7]

1.   A collective proper name;
2.   A myth of common ancestry;
3.   shared historical memories;
4.   One or more differentiating elements of common culture;
5.   An association with a specific "homeland";
6.   A sense of solidarity in significant sectors of the population.

The combination of these attributes can be, and usually is, different; but the more of these attributes a given population possesses, the more closely it approximates the ideal type of an ethnic community or *ethnie* (Smith 1991b, 210). This would be a common definition of the ethnic community as it is accepted in the English-language literature.[8] In this way, *ethnie* is a culturally defined community that dominated in pre-modern political entities with a hierarchical structure. Smith assumes that to exist in modern times, *ethnie* must be politically suppressed by other nations, as in the case of the Basques. In the Soviet tradition, the term *"ethnie"* corresponds to the term *"ethnicos,"* or to the narrower meaning of the term "ethnos." The

---

[7]   Smith notices that there is no special term for the concept of "ethnic group" or "ethnic community" in the English language. In his view, the French term *"ethnie"* is the most appropriate for this concept because it unites an emphasis upon cultural differences with the sense of a historical community (Smith 1986, ch. 2).

[8]   Johnston, for instance, wrote that "ethnic group" can be defined as a distinct category of a larger population whose culture is different from its own (Johnston 1989, 108) The members of the group share, or think they share, common ties of race, belief, nationality or culture (Richmond 1988, 188, quoted in Kinnear 1992, 7).

latter was defined as a stable human community that has historically formed on a certain territory and possesses common (relatively temporary) specific features of language, culture and psyche, as well as an "awareness" of its own unity and distinctiveness from other similar communities (self-consciousness) which was fixed in a self-given name (ethnic name—"ethnonym") (Svod, 49).

Smith and Llobera stress the socio-cultural nature of ethnic communities, as they are defined by religion, customs, language and collective institutions. Primordialists believe that it is these factors which are most important for nation-building, since new nations receive their crucially important collective myths and memories from a prior ethnic heritage. They also accept that *subjective* factors are crucial for nation-building.

"Modernists" do not consider "ethnic communities" as central to the nature of nations, and underline the purely functional role of ethnic elements for nation-building. For Gellner, previously existing pre-modern cultures are only randomly turned into nations by the force of nationalism. Although previous ethnic boundaries could be important for the social and political security of the new national states, modernists stress that "ethnicity" turns into nationalism only when cultural homogeneity and continuity is conditioned by the economic fundamentals of social life. In other words, "modernists" highlight the *objective* (socio-economic) aspects in the relationship between ethnic communities and nation-building, where ethnicity is a situational or even random element.

The Soviet term "ethno-social organism" or ESO creates, to a certain extent, some logical order within the framework of the debates described above. ESO was considered to be an *ethnicos* (*ethnie*) within a certain socio-economic unit (historically dependent on concrete socio-economic formations). In this way, *ethnicos* can exist within different socio-economic formations, while ESO exists always within a defined formation. Nation, for instance, is firstly an *ethnicos* or group of *ethnicoses*, and secondly an *ethnicos* which is included whithin a "capitalist" socio-economic unit. Only in the widest sense was it suggested to use the term "ethnos" to cover all periods of both ethnic and socio-economic development. In this way, we have a synthetic attempt to take into account (on the level of terminology) of the socio-cultural as well as the socio-economic nature of the national phenomenon, also taking into account the fact that, in the wider meaning, ethnos is a *dynamic system* and therefore a *process*. Soviet scholars stressed two main developments of this process. The first is "ethno-transformation," where ethnic identification and membership is shifting or changing. The second is "ethno-evolution," where ethnic identification persists. Soviet ethnosociology argued that the ethnosocial dynamic in the modern world has tendencies toward both the formation of new ethno-national units, and toward ethnic integration and internationalization. Simultaneously, it stressed the importance of diachronic (as well as synchronic) informational bonds between generations of *ethnicos*, generally seen in the context of ethnic history as the result of the common historical practice of a series of human generations (performed in specific material as well as spiritual attributes and fixed in their consciousness). Soviet terminology suggested the possibility of a synthesis of "perennial" and "modernist" Western approaches on the level of concepts and terminology, without ignoring their differences. This is possible partly because, in the Soviet terms, the ethno-social (cultural) as well as socio-economic aspects of ethnogenesis were equally reflected in a unifying manner.

Dominant as it was, Soviet Ethnography had an alternative school of thought represented by the "bio-spherical" concept of Lev Gumilev and his theory of *passionarnost'*. Gumilev claimed that his theory was groundbreaking, and therefore claimed to have created a new direction in the social sciences, in fact a new science— "ethnology" (Gumilev 1993, 293). He denied the social origin of nations and insisted on their origin from nature. In a way, this could be considered similar to the "primordialist" approach, but Gumilev's idea was more far-reaching. He tried to study the nature of "ethnos" by means of the natural sciences, and only additionally via a correlation with history.[9] Since Gumilev's theory has had a profound influ-

---

[9]   As Gumilev said: "Within the boundaries of social doctrine (either Stalin's Marxism or Levi-Strauss` structuralism) the distinctions of one ethnos from another were considered in some amount of social characteristics. ... The alternative ap-

ence on nationalist thinking in Russia and Putin's Eurasianism, it is important to consider the main points of Gumilev's approach, which are the following:

- From the point of view of geography as a science, *mankind could be considered an anthroposphere*, i.e., one of the few spheres of the Earth. This sphere consists of a special substance — Homo sapiens.

- An anthroposphere, with all its ethnic subdivisions, is a part of the Earth's biosphere. Since there are constant biochemical fluctuations and changes within the latter, ethnogenesis should be considered as a part of this natural process.[10] In other words, *ethnogenesis is a natural process or fluctuation of the biochemical energy of a biosphere`s living substance*.

- The start of *ethnogenesis*, according to Gumilev, *can be caused by an impulse of biochemical energy* which, hypothetically, together with social psyche, creates a mutation that is the beginning of a new ethnicity. As he describes it:

    The burst of this energy (*passionarnyi* or drive impulse) creates movement which depends on the set of circumstances in a certain region of the planet — the geographical one, which influences the economic activity of ethnos; social and historical ones, which influence via the received traditions from previous ethnogeneses. <...> This formulation excludes the possibility to of identifying ethnoses with racial types because races

---

proach is based on the usage of the natural sciences for historical materials" (Gumilev 1993, 178).

[10]   The fact of "the role of bioenergetic source" in ethnogenesis as a theoretical supposition was recognized by other Soviet scholars already at the beginning of the 1970s (Yefremov 1971, 79; Bromley 1973, 163); however, only Gumilev produced an attempt to develop the supposition on the basis of Vernadsky`s discovery. To illustrate this discovery Gumilev quoted in his fundamental work the following passage from Vernadsky: All living being is constructed from the summation of organisms, i.e., living substances which are interconnected in different ways, perpetually changing and undergoing an evolution over geological time. This original dynamical balance aspires to a static balance in time ... The longer it [balance] exists in time (if there is no adequate phenomenon which is oriented in the opposite direction) the closer a free energy will be to zero. i.e., the energy of a living substance which acts in a direction which is opposite to entropy. Because the action of a living substance creates a development of free energy which can do work. (V. I. Vernadsky, *The Chemical Structure of the Biosphere of the Earth* [1965], 284-285).

are biological taxons and located on a level higher than historical time (Gumilev 1993, 78).

- For Gumilev, there was not and cannot be an ethnos with only one ancestor. All ethnoses have two or more ancestors. "Ethnic substrata, i.e., components of a forming ethnos in the moment of fluctuation of the biosphere's living substance, are combining and creating a joint system that is a new, original ethnos" (Gumilev 1993, 84).

- Along with the social model of the nature of ethnos, *Gumilev rejected the importance of collective (ethnic) consciousness as a determining factor for ethnogenesis.* "The basis of ethnic relationships lies outside of the sphere of consciousness" (Gumilev 1993, 299). The author claims that the roots of these relationships are on the level of emotions: sympathy and antipathy; love and hatred. Furthermore, in the author's view, antipathy and sympathy are strictly predetermined by unconscious feeling — *complimentarnost`* — which was formed on the basis of a natural stereotype of behavior.

- Gumilev identified the following phases of ethnogenesis: 1) a burst of creative activity caused by *passionarnost`* impact.[11] At this stage, the new ethnos is born from substrates of the remains of previous ethnoses, which become a basis for a new ethno-social system; 2) an *acmatic* phase, an increasing development of ethnos which can lead to a break or even collapse of the ethnos but is usually transferred to a phase of inertia; 3) an inertial phase or, one could say, a period of "civilization." The *passionarnost`* is decreasing smoothly; 4) a persistent phase, i.e., a transition from dynamic process to homeostasis. The ethnos can be regenerated or become a relic. Gumilev identified a life-span for ethnos — approximately 1,500 years from the moment of the impact until a final disappearance.

---

[11] *Passionarnost`* is a special kind of biological energy. According to Gumilev the equivalent for this energy is a concrete historical work of the particular ethnos, i.e., its achievements and defeats.

Table 2. Ethnogenesis according to Lev Gumilev

Phases of ethnogenesis	Energy	Life-span of ethnos
Origin	Burst of *passionarnost'*	New ethnos is born from Ethnic Substrata
Acmatic Phase	Active flow of *passionarnost'*	Expansion of ethnos
Inertial phase	*Passionarnost'* decreases	"Civilization age"
Persistent phase	Transition to homeostasis or regeneration	Ethnos becomes a relic or disappears

- Practically, *passionarnost`* functions within *ethnic fields* which, according to Gumilev, exist in nature as electromagnetic, gravitational and other fields. "The fact of the presence of ethnic fields can be observed not in individual reactions of particular persons but in the collective psychology which influences people" (Gumilev 1989, 301). The rhythms of these fields create the unconscious feeling of *complimentarnost`*, which vary with different ethnoses.

The majority of Soviet scholars were critical of the original theory, while post-Soviet scholars of the CIS countries tend to take this theory into account and even use it as a basis for further development (Tishkov 1997, 26). In Russia, this is generally connected with the revival of a popular and politically defined idea of Eurasianism, "*Yevrasiystvo*," that later developed into "neo-Eurasianism" and evolved into the pseudo-scientific neo-imperialist semi-official state ideology of Putin's regime (Putin's Eurasianism). Considering that neo-Eurasianism is crucial to understanding Russian state ethno-geopolitics it will be analyzed separately in Chapter 4.

In post-Soviet Ukraine, Gumilev was initially considered to be valuable probably because of the pendulum effect: everything which was discouraged in the Soviet time must be worth considering. A celebrity edition of *Short Encyclopedia of Ethno-State Science* (Nationhood and Statehood), by the National Ukrainian Academy of Science

(NUAS) was a good example. A whole set of entries in this Encyclopedia dealing with ethnic and national phenomena reflect to various degrees the conceptualizations of Gumilev. In some cases there is no reference to Gumilev; his terminology is used out of context and employed to illustrate the authors' own positions. Such approaches were often incoherent, since Gumilev's terms cannot exist outside his bio-spherical theory (Mala 1996).

Generally speaking, we can state that there is a certain consistency among various approaches and types of terminology when we consider such phenomena as "national" and "ethnic community." So, for instance, the meaning of the term "nation" (as a group of people which become distinct within industrial society) for most of the English-language literature coincides with the meaning of ESO (within capitalist/socialist/post-communist society) for the Soviet tradition and much of the current Ukrainian and Russian academic literature. The term "ethnic community" is understood as a large group of people with a collective name, self-identity, distinct language, culture and territory. But from a political and international (legal) status, it is often defined as *'ethnie'* within the English- and French-language literature and *'ethnicos'* within Soviet and post-Soviet social sciences. Debate more often concerns the content of these terms and their character, such as "natural" or "imagined." The key concept for such debates is one of "national consciousness" or "national identity."

2.1.3 National Consciousness as a Complex System of Beliefs

The conceptualization of the terms "national consciousness" and "national identity" is widely used in debates about the nature of national phenomena. As John Shotters points out: "identity" has become the watchword of the time (Shotter 1993a, 188). Michael Billig notes that "the watchword should be watched, for frequently it explains less than it appears to" (Billig 1995, 60).

Social identity theory has been called "the most ambitious contribution to the exploration of social processes" (Eiser 1986, 316). The theory was conceived by Henry Tajfel, later developed into what is called "self-categorization theory" (Abrams and Hogs 1991; Taylor and Moghaddam 1994; Turner 1984; Turner and Giddens 1987). Though Tajfel's theory was designed to explain national group identity, it was effectively used to explain the fundamental psychological principles of group identity in general.

Social identity theory holds that psychological principles are central to collective behavior, assuming that it is personal identifications that form a group out of free individuals. Tajfel was concerned specifically with national groups or in other words "nations." According to the theory, this is the main means of categorization into human groups and communities. These categories therefore unavoidably divide people into "we" and "the other." In answer to the question about what makes people categorize themselves, Tajfel explains that human beings naturally look for a positive self-concept or positive social identity. This search for positive self-identity leads individuals to categorize themselves into groups. Yet, to achieve a positive group identity, groups have to compare themselves (according to certain characteristics) with contrast groups — "the other," and this leads to the emergence both of positive self-stereotypes and negative stereotypes of :the other." The building up of positive self-stereotypes creates a positive group identity.

Both "primordialist" and "modernist" traditions adopt the basic assumptions of social identity theory. They differ, however, in respect of the content and ideological, social and political functions of national consciousness or identity. For "primordialists," national identity is based more on a unity of history and culture rather than, for instance, ideology. That is why national identity, according to Anthony Smith, for instance, consists of a number of interrelated components — ethnic, cultural, territorial, economic and legal-political. We can distinguish two sets of dimensions — the first civic and territorial, the second ethnic and genealogical. In relation to these dimensions, Smith identifies external (territorial, economic, political) and internal functions of national identity. If the former connect the social unit with a concrete location within social space, then the latter work instead on the individual level of consciousness, defining, locating and socializing individual selves in this social unity. In this context, Smith argues that individual identities tend to be more situational or even optional, while collective identities are more pervasive and persistent.

Smith's view of national identity is determined, *first*, by his concept of the ethnic origins of nations and, *second*, by the recognition of national identity as a part of the multiplicity of contemporary social and historical identities. This, again, situates the "primordialist" position on national identity much closer to the Soviet and, more generally, Eastern European tradition than the Western "modernist" one.

"Modernists" recognize the dual nature of the origin of national phenomena. According to Gellner, the appearance of nations was predetermined by socio-economic conditions during the transformation from an agrarian society to an industrial one. However, people's loyalties and solidarity, *which exist in social consciousness,* determine the real boundaries of national units. Gellner sees nationalism as appearing first (on the basis of specific development of previous high cultures), and only then, as a result of its existence, are nations created. Gellner also stresses that nationalism as an ideology creates an artificial and false national consciousness (because of mythical inventions). However, according to the author, this pervasive national consciousness plays a *functionally* determinative role in nation-building. "Modernists" do not agree that national consciousness adopts myths and memories from previous *ethnies*. It is assumed that nationalist myths only profit from the defense of traditional folk culture, when in fact they are forging a new high culture. In this way, national consciousness is functionally important but "genetically" artificial.

Soviet Ethnography distinguished two meanings of the term "national consciousness," according to the ethno-social and socio-economic content of the national essence.[12] In the narrow meaning, national consciousness was equal to ethnic consciousness (Bromley suggested calling it ethno-national) and includes: ethnic identity, along with some knowledge of national history, national territory and the national state system. In a wider meaning, national con-

---

[12]   Again, according to Bromley's theory: nation = ethnicos + socio-economic unity = ESO (ethno-social organism) during capitalism.

sciousness was considered as the whole social consciousness of the nation (Bromley suggested the term "ethno-social consciousness of the nation"), which should include political, moral, aesthetic, religious and philosophical forms of reflection and awareness of the existence of the ethno-social organism.

Here it is necessary to mention that all Soviet social scientific inquires into the nature of group identity had to build on the "official" theory of Soviet Marxism, namely, the "theory of reflection." This assumes that consciousness is a natural way in which individuals relate to the world via a system of knowledge which evolves as a social product and is fixed in language, in all its meanings. Consciousness "is the highest form of *materia's* reflection" (Filosofskyi 1986). Support for the view was found in Engels and Marx (e.g., *The German Ideology*) as well as in the works of Russian psychologists like I. Sechenov and I. Pavlov (Zubkov 1990, 112), and remained unchallenged. Consciousness, therefore, was generally understood as a characteristic of "highly organized *materia*," i.e., the human brain, with the main function being to "reflect" or create "subjective images of the objective world," and in the Marxist tradition was to be considered as "nothing else but awareness of being" (Marx V.3, 24). Philosophers stressed that consciousness is a product of historical social practice, giving the answer in this way to the "main philosophical problem" (i.e., what is primary *materia* or consciousness). Sociologists believed that general elements of individual consciousness reflect "social existence" and, by adding to each other, build up a consciousness of society, which is already a separate spiritual system and not the simple sum of individual identities. "Consciousness of society" or social consciousness implements itself via philosophical, scientific, artistic, moral, legal and political ideas and expressions. In this way, social consciousness was considered to be relatively independent of individual identities as well as of social existence as such (Grushin 1987, Mikhaylov 1990). Psychologists defined consciousness in empirical terms as a multiplicity of constantly changing sensuous and cognitive images that appear to individuals as their "inner experience," and are prior to their practical activity (Psikhologiya 1990, 369). This approach became so widely accepted that "the gnoseological aspect of consciousness as a concept was considered the least problematic" (Shkliar 1992, 62). However, a more critical review shows that this approach is not sufficient to understand the phenomenon of national consciousness. "Reflection theory" does not provide the answer as to how, when and why collective (national) identities appear.

For Soviet social scientists generally, the concept of national consciousness always included ethnic identity (as in the "primordialist" concept), and in the narrower meaning of the term, was even equal to ethnic consciousness (Likhachev 1945; Dashdamirov 1983). This might lead to the incorrect conclusion that Soviet Ethnography, on the issue of national consciousness, is incompatible with the "modernist" position. This is not entirely so. In cases where ethnicity has played a substantial role within a particular high culture, which creates nationalism, i.e., national consciousness, Gellner, for instance, tends to use the terms "ethnic" and "national" consciousness interchangeably. This means that there is a certain coincidence at least on the level of terminology between the theories of Gellner and, for example, Bromley. Moreover, when both authors work in a materialistic paradigm they are in absolute agreement that national (like any other) consciousness is a consequence of socio-economic conditions (that is Gellner's main claim). The difference is that Gellner or Anderson assume only an occasional, random overlapping of ethnicity and national consciousness, whereas for Bromley such overlapping was naturally systematic. One of the possible ways of explaining this difference in their position can be found in Hroch`s identification of Western and Eastern models of nations, with different levels of emphasis on ethnic and civic determinants. Gellner recognized that China, for instance, is an exception to his theory. In any case, the preceding conditions illustrate that there is a high enough degree of similarity in the common understanding of national identity phenomena to claim that between "modernist" and "primordialist" theories, on the one hand, and the Soviet tradition, on the other, there is a common ground which provides adequate understanding of the same concepts.

Ukrainian scholars developed their own view on the matter after 1991. Zhmyr defined *national consciousness* as "a kind of group consciousness, which is based on social values, norms which define a person as belonging to a national community. National consciousness has the characteristics of a group consciousness and reflects the division between 'we' and 'the other' and in this way functions as a means of national integration. National consciousness should be considered as a higher level in comparison to ethnic consciousness" (Zhmyr 1991, 104).

National identity is understood by the Ukrainian scholars in a cultural context as all norms of "ethnosocial behavior." It is assumed that "national" means "ethnic" in the wider sense, as it was considered in the framework of Soviet Ethnography. *The Short Encyclopedia of Ethno-State Science* states that "national identity assumes that a group of people share the feeling of a common past, present and future as well as a certain consensus concerning the principal issues of economic, political, cultural and social life, the current development of the state and its policy' (Mala 1996, 98). The article on national self-consciousness by Pustotin (Mala 1996, 103), and the article on different levels of national self-consciousness by Rymarenko (Mala 1996, 103-104), among others in the encyclopedia, illustrate that generally Ukrainian scholars throughout the 1990s remained within the boundaries of the Soviet "sociospheric" concept, and worked within a framework of "reflection theory" from a methodological point of view. Despite some discussion of this problem (Hryb 1997), this was the dominant paradigm in Ukraine for explaining the processes of national identity. Gradually, however, such scholars as Heorhiy Kasyanov, Yaroslav Hrytsak and Mykola Ryabchuk introduced Western modernist theories of nations as "imagined communities" and national identity as a "daily plebiscite" (Kasyanov 1999). Ryabchuk arrives at the conclusion that Ukrainians formed two types of national identity: one of a modern political nation in Western Ukraine and another of Little Russians (*malorosy*) in Eastern Ukraine that mostly consists of a '*surzhyk*'-speaking population that neither embraces Ukrainian high culture nor belongs to the Russian ethnos (Ryabchuk 2011, 6). Hrytsak similarly argues that nation-building in Ukraine is defined by competition of different models of civic national identity based on language (Ukrainian and Russian) rather than the competition of Ukrainian and Russian national ideas (Hrytsak 2011, 60). Myroslav Popovych concludes that the Ukrainian national idea exhibits a contradiction between an "ethnic" and a "political" understanding of the nation and, therefore, the political nation in Ukraine could only be multicultural and inclusive of various nationalities (*bahatonatsionalna*) (Popovych 2005, 10). Vadym Bondar arrives at the conclusion, based on Ukrainian historiography, that a liberal, civic and inclusive form of nationalism has a fairly good chance of success in Ukraine despite inevitable competition from more narrow ethnic nationalism (Bondar 2012, 330).

2.1.4 Ethnic Consciousness — Optional or Crucial?

"Primordialists" consider ethnic identity as similar to a national one, belonging to the multiplicity of contemporary and historical identities. Llobera observes that, for the greater part of human history, the twin circles of religious and ethnic identity have been very close and have sometimes overlapped with each other (Llobera 1994, 217). This, presumably, is one of the reasons why mythical imagination is as important for ethnic as it is for religious consciousness (Smith 1991a; Shkliar 1992, 217). Smith also considers the perennial existence of ethnic consciousness in the social development of mankind and its great importance for the formation of national consciousness. According to this approach it is ethnic identity that *as a rule* (first of all through its myths and memories) creates a basis for the formation of national identity.

"Modernists" do not assume any strict connections between ethnic and national consciousness. Gellner claims that only *sometimes* can ethnic consciousness be transformed, under pressure of the transition to industrialism, into a national one, but even in this case it substantially changes its nature according to new socio-economic conditions. This is almost the only crucial difference between the two visions.

Gellner argues that ethnic consciousness belongs rather to historical identities and survives into the industrial epoch only in marginal forms. That is why the destination of ethnic identity in modern times can proceed mainly in two directions. *First*, it can construct (through its loyalties and affiliations) the basis for the social consciousness of a new type. Then the substantially transformed and developed ethnic consciousness becomes a national one. *Second*, and more likely, ethnic consciousness mostly or totally disappears and dissolves into other identities of the new era.

On this subject the difference between "primordialist" and "modernist" is how they *estimate the role* of ethnic consciousness in nation-building. For the latter, ethnic consciousness is only an occasional substrate for the creation of the new identity needed for industrial society. For the former, ethnic identity is an active agent of new national identity as well as a new important element for the consolidation of national unity.

In this sense, the Soviet Ethnography approach, and the predominant current views of the Ukrainian scholars, is definitely in agreement with "primordialists." First, ethnic consciousness (using the wider meaning of term) is considered to be an attribute of ethnos. Second, ethnic consciousness (in a narrow meaning) is not imagined to be excluded from a national one. According to Bromley, ethnic consciousness, as the other modern form of social consciousness, possesses its reflexive level not only on an individual, but also on a social level. This means that ethnic consciousness not only does not dissolve but actually develops. This statement is determined by a vision of ethnos as a dynamic system, i.e., a process, which was common for the Soviet tradition and is preserved by contemporary Russian scholars.[13] An individual ethnic self-consciousness is believed to have its expression in reflexive ethnic affiliation and awareness of one's own actions, motives and interests in this context. Collective imaginations about typical characteristics and achievements of the community represent the self-consciousness of ethnos. The latter can be fixed not only through personal expressions but

---

[13]   In the previous account it was mentioned that ethnic (national) processes can be evolutionary and transformational, but this is not contradictory. Gellner also mentioned that, for instance, changes of symbols within a national consciousness of national unity are national processes (Gellner 1983, 58) but in the case of ethnic consciousness he tends to treat them only as merging.

also in impersonal ones, i.e., in other objective forms of social con-sciousness — language, folklore, art, scientific literature, norms of morality and law (Chesnokov 1991; Ionin 1996, chs. 4-6). The most formal expression of self-consciousness on the social level is consid-ered to be a common ethnic name.

Ukrainian scholars consider ethnic consciousness on the indi-vidual level as a multitude of knowledges, attitudes and aspirations about the culture, tradition, values and self-identification with a group and within the context of other groups. The individual ac-quires this consciousness during the process of "ethnization," i.e., personal or group experience. The structure of ethnic consciousness includes ethnic or national character, customs, ethnocentrism, ethnic feelings, ethnic self-consciousness, self-identity, and so on. Each of the elements is considered to be "quite a complicated psychological phenomenon with its own structural forms of expression, principles of functioning" (Mala 1996, 41). It seems that such a reference to a "psychological phenomenal nature" is an attempt to avoid further explanation of what all these concepts consist of, and in a way this is a common "escape" used by sociologists in general, not only Ukrain-ian scholars. Billig stressed the opposite tendency of social psy-chologists to explain the nature of human consciousness by reference to "sociological and cultural factors," which can lead to a situation where there is a mutual and agreed misunderstanding between both sociologists and social psychologists (Billig 1995).

Ethnic identity is defined in the context of "Social Identity The-ory," i.e. as a form of self-categorization by individuals (Mala 1996, 35) or as a result of a set of similar identification processes (Boldetskaya 1996, 53). Ethnic identification is considered an im-portant component of ethnic consciousness. It is understood as self-affiliation or acceptance of likeness to some ethnic group. This pro-cess develops by way of the individual adapting himself to the roots and fundamentals of an ethnic group (Mala 1996, 41). In this way, the differentiation of the two terms "ethnic identity" and "ethnic identification" is incomplete and not fully convincing, since social psychologists argue that individual ethnic identity does not always imply identification with a group in a cultural sense. Psychologists differentiate therefore between ethnicity as interrelation between ethnic groups and ethnic identity as a part of an individual's wider identity process (Liebkind 1989, 28). This lack of coherence was partially admitted by another Ukrainian scholar, Olena Donchenko, who agreed that the "process of mass identification is a social phenomenon which is not entirely understood by sociologists" (Donchenko 1994, 167).

Summary

We can draw at least two synthetic conclusions from the discussion so far. First, authors generally agree that changes of national consciousness should be considered as *dynamic processes*. However, "modernists" recognize this only indirectly as, for instance, Gellner does when writing that changes of symbols within national consciousness are national processes (Gellner 1983, 58). Second, the "primordialist" tradition, as well as Soviet Ethnography and contemporary Russian and Ukrainian scholars, recognize the substantially important role of ethnic consciousness for the creation of national consciousness and of the nation as a whole. "Modernists" insist that ethnic consciousness has a random role, if any, for national phenomena and stress "objective" social and economic determinants.

From the analysis above we can sum up the similarities and differences of the main Western and Eastern European approaches to the concepts of nation, ethnic communities, national and ethnic consciousness. Although, on the one hand, synthesis is possible, it is important to stress that the common concerns expressed by different traditions do not imply a similarity of conceptual approach: often different authors reached similar conclusions as a result of different methods and means of enquiry.

Although "primordialists," Soviet and post-Soviet scholars in Russia and Ukraine generally agree on the ethnic origins of nations and the crucial role of consciousness in their genesis, in fact their primary assumptions were substantially different. "Primordialists" developed their conclusions as a result of the assumption that consciousness is an immanent and inseparable condition of the appearance of nations, which was illustrated by the studies of world ethnic history and concrete historical and contemporary identities. Within Soviet and post-Soviet traditions, such an assumption would be unacceptable because of the materialistic paradigm in which they developed. Nevertheless, historical analysis of concrete national identities led both schools of thought to agreement, in principle, as to the role and functions of ethnic and national consciousness for the existence of national phenomena.

At the same time, although "modernists" and Soviet/post-Soviet ethno-sociologists based their theories on historical materialism, they disagree on several important issues. The former argue for the importance and functionally occasional role of national/ethnic consciousness in the appearance of national-social units during the foundation of industrialism. They claim that national consciousness is a consequence of nationalism and therefore originally initiated by the new socio-economic conditions which created the concrete boundaries of nations. The real causes of the nations' genesis, then, lie in the development of the productive forces. In this scheme, ethnic consciousness is not necessary, so "modernists" logically conclude that substantially it is unimportant. The climax of such logic is the recognition of the fact that the appearance of "national" units itself was accidental in the development of human society during the industrial epoch (Gellner 1994).

The materialistic concept of Soviet Ethnography also states that the creation of nations is strongly bound up with the socio-economic development of human society at the stage of industrialism or "capitalism." Consciousness here is a consequence of social reality. However, unlike "modernists," Soviet scholars believed that national consciousness is a reflection of its nation. In this case, national consciousness is not a "creator" of the boundaries of national unity (as Gellner claimed), and is not an immanent condition of a nation's appearance (as Smith argued), but is an internal attribute of the nation that serves an important function. It is striking that the description of these functions is quite similar within all concepts. What is difficult to harmonize is the correspondence between national and ethnic consciousness. "Primordialists," Soviet and most of post-

Soviet ethno-sociologists are together in their sense that national consciousness inherited, naturally and evolutionarily, ethnic consciousness, whereas "modernists" insist on the accidental relationship between ethnic and national consciousness.

Scholars list the following elements of national consciousness that are common to all traditions: awareness of a common historical territory ("homeland"); self-given name ('*ethnonym*'); a common culture in its private and civic expressions; a common state order; and a socio-economic organization. Most of these categories reflect rational elements that are relatively easy to study using sociological research tools. However, it is the emotional elements of consciousness able to reflect the relationship between ethnic and national consciousness that are the least explored. And it is this relationship that evokes the most disagreements among scholars of different schools.

2.2. Ethnicity and Its Place Within National Consciousness

The fact that the majority of scholars agree on the importance of ethnicity for national consciousness, but have different opinions as to the role it plays, requires a closer look. As previously described, "primordialist" Western as well as Soviet and post-Soviet traditions have stressed the continuing or perennial role of ethnic components in the transformation from ethnic to national consciousness. But what exactly are these components?

Smith pointed out that ethnic myths and collective memories locate a new, already national, community within a historic space and legitimize it, providing the status of an "ancient" one. Similarly, Bromley argued that diachronic information links between generations are extremely important for the existence of an *ethnicos*.[14] Both

---

[14]   Bromley stresses that the dual nature of ethno-social communities established the necessary internal bonds. On the one hand, these are information links (synchronic and diachronic) reflected within ethnic self-consciousness; on the other hand, these are also social and political bonds. "It is hardly possible to avoid mistakes if we do not take into account the differences between these two types of social bonds and their specifics during various levels of historic development" (Bromley 1983, 385).

authors include among these elements self-stereotypes of typical characteristics of a community, self-stereotypes of a common historical destiny (myth of origin, according to Smith), and images of a "homeland" or common territory of such a community. Ukrainian scholars tend to include here cultural archetypes which national consciousness inherits from the previous historical development of a community (Yaniv 1993; Mala 1996). In light of the above discussion, it is worth considering the following elements of ethnic heritage that are deemed to be important for national phenomenon: myths, self-stereotypes and cultural archetypes.

2.2.1 Myths of National Consciousness or National Consciousness as a Myth?

The problem of the correspondence between such phenomena as myth and national consciousness continues to be the subject of intense debate and contradictory approaches to the nature of the problem abound. On the one hand, one can claim that a myth is an unchangeable part of national consciousness, and sometimes has a different appearance and meaning. On the other hand, some scholars seem to be sure that national consciousness is itself an invented myth and a consequence of nation building. We shall compare different approaches to the nature of myth and national consciousness in order to draw a picture of this phenomenon.

First of all, it is necessary to concentrate on the description of myth as a social and cultural entity as well as on possible ways to investigate myth. Then the relationships between myth and national consciousness/identity will be explored through a psychological complex, such as a belief system, i.e., a cognitive structure consisting of separate beliefs and their particular components. Also, it is important to take into account the concrete historical circumstances in which these relationships take place, and their dynamic. This means that the only way to analyze the nature of these phenomena correctly is to treat them as historically continuous.

On the whole the notion of "myth," while it indicates one of the intrinsic attributes of human society, remains a concept which social scientists still prefer not to consider as a fundamental issue. This can be explained by the difficulties connected with the dual meaning of the term; for a long time it had an entirely religious context, and only relatively recently has it possessed a wider conceptualization and implementation. Although Claude Lévi-Strauss skeptically characterized the situation in the study of myths as "chaotic, because of the lack of a commonly assumed approach to the phenomenon" (Levi-Strauss 1983, 207), we can distinguish two main approaches toward the problem of myth, namely, the functionalist and the phenomenological. The former points out the social function of myth, putting the emphasis on those myths that serve as definite goals of the social group; whereas the latter considers the appeal to the past, treating origins as the intrinsic essence of myth.

For instance, Anthony Smith considered that "myths are neither illusions nor mere legitimation, they may perhaps be regarded as widely believed tales told in dramatic form, referring to past events but serving present purposes and/or future goals" (Smith 1988b, 2). Lévi-Strauss suggests a similar definition: "myths are actually *a posteriori* attempts to construct a homogeneous system on the basis of disparate rules. This hypothesis would also imply that, sooner or later, mythical thinking conceives of these rules as so many possible answers to a question" (Lévi-Strauss, 1983, 159). As a working definition therefore, the notion of "myth" further will be used in its wider context, namely, as a widely shared social belief, related to a particular event in the historical past and bound up with the present and the future. The concepts of "belief" and "belief system" are used as they were developed by Rokeach (1968, 1969) and are widely applied in cognitive psychology.

On the one hand, scholars usually agree that myth is a special means of information transfer, that "myth is the part of language where the formula *traduttore, tradittore* reaches its lowest truth value" (Lévi-Strauss 1983, 210). We can add that myth is a particular kind of language that consists of symbolic information in allegorical form. On the other hand, when scholars start to discuss the practical functioning of this special kind of language, their viewpoints become contradictory. For instance, Benedict Anderson estimates the role of this language in the nature of nationhood: "from the start the nation was conceived in language, not in blood, and that one could be 'invited into' the imagined community. ... Through that language, encountered at the mother's knee and parted with only at the grave, pasts are restored, fellowships are imagined, and futures dreamed" (Anderson 1991, 145,154).

Harald Harman, who works on sociolinguistic problems, stressed "the relativity of language as a symbol" of national identity in itself (Harman 1986, 258). The importance of language for the national phenomenon was stressed also by Fishman (1973), though in his work language does not have such a defining role. Soviet (Russian and Ukrainian) scholars stressed that language powerfully differentiates people into "we" and "the other" (Bromley 1981; Gumilev 1989; Guboglo 1979; Nikitina 1989; Shkliar 1991), but the experience of Slavic and other national histories shows that language could well be in the shade as a national marker. There are cases when different national groups share the same language but use it for different national discourses (like Serbs and Croats, Romanians and Moldavians, Americans and Canadians, not to mention the English who "leased" their language to so many people in the world). So, it seems that to consider myth as a special kind of (national) language is not enough.

Lévi-Strauss suggested a few rules for the interpretation of the role and meaning of myths in order to encompass the opposition of different approaches. According to him: 1) a myth must never be interpreted on one level only. No privileged explanation exists, for any myth consists in an *interrelation* of several explanatory levels; 2) a myth must never be interpreted alone, but in its relationship to other myths which, taken together, constitute a transformation group; 3) a group of myths must never be interpreted alone, but by reference: a) to other groups of myths; and b) to the ethnography of the societies in which they originate (Lévi-Strauss 1983, 65).

To illustrate the last point, we can take the example of the myth of common ancestry that is very common in different ethnic communities. The listed rules suggest we analyze this particular myth not only in the context of other similar myths but also in relationship to other main attributes of the ethnic community (*ethnie*), which

Smith, for example, identifies as 1) a collective proper name; 2) shared historical memories; 3) one or more differentiating elements of common culture; 4) an association with a specific "homeland"; and 5) a sense of solidarity in significant sectors of the population (Smith 1991a, 21).

Also, according to Lévi-Strauss, we should take into account that there must be, and that there is, a correspondence between the unconscious meaning of a myth—the problem it tries to solve—and the conscious content it makes use of to reach that end, i.e., the plot. "However, this correspondence is not necessarily an exact reproduction; it can also appear as a logical transformation" (Lévi-Strauss 1963, Vol. 1, 204)

Such an interpretation leads to a completely new view of the nature of myth as a social phenomenon, namely, that the kind of logic in mythical thought is as rigorous as that of modern science, and that the difference lies, not in the quality of the intellectual process, but in the nature of the things to which it is applied. As Lévi-Strauss put it: "What makes a steel ax superior to a stone ax is not that the first one is better made than the second. They are equally well made, but steel is quite different from stone" (Lévi-Strauss 1963 Vol. 1, 230). Or, as Leszek Kołakowski said, the difference between scientific knowledge and narrative (mythical) knowledge is that the former uses one universal language, while the latter usually uses different ones (Kołakowski 1990). By analogy, if we follow the logic of Lévi-Strauss "the same logical process operates in myth as in science, and ... man thinks equally well in both. The improvement lies, not in an alleged progress of man's mind, but in discovery of new areas to which it may apply its unchanged and unchanging powers" (Lévi-Strauss 1963 Vol. 1, 230). The Russian philosopher Aleksei Losev stated something similar when he defined myth as "poetic estrangement given as a thing." Losev wrote: "Science, morality and art are *intelligent* constructs while mythology *realizes in fact* these or other constructs" (Losev 1991, 163). Therefore it is important to differentiate our understanding of the usage of the term "myth" from another possible variant wherein it is implied in wider social concepts, namely, *belief systems*.

For instance, John Talmon (1981) used the term in this way:

> The French Revolution bequeathed a colossal myth, which continues to have an incalculable effect as an inspiration and example all over the world: the vision of a people's revolutionary war, in which patriotism and ideological revolutionary ardor became fused. The defense of native land then became identified with the struggle for a political-social ideal; against a counter-revolutionary league of selfish traitors and foreign reactionary powers. "*Patrie*" became synonymous in France with 'La Revolution', revolutionary "Liberté," "La République une et indivisible." Such slogans as "la patrie en danger," "levée en masse," and symbols like the tricolor, the "Marseillaise" and the red cap, came to evoke an almost religious response. In the cases of the Bolshevik, Chinese, Cuban, Vietnamese and other revolutions, the memory and legends of similar struggles have proved to be far more potent and more cohesive influences than social-economic doctrines and innovating aspirations. (Talmon 1981, 5)

In this case, we should speak not about "colossal myth" (too many components and different aspects are included), but about the complexities of a belief system, i.e., a perception of the world order.

The crucial difference between the usage of these two terms, "belief system" and "myth," can be found in the scale of the phenomena. These two terms reflect different levels of self-perception by social agents. A belief system tends to be based on the whole of a human being's self-identity, whereas a myth is instead a particular component of this self-identity. For example, Smith (1984) describes ethnic myths and their components as a particular part of ethnic identity.

The term "belief system" is consistent with both social identity theory as well as with "reflection theory,", since the former is a part of the same framework of the cognitive tradition in psychology, and the latter defines consciousness as a means of relation between the individual and the world (and this relation is defined by the socially developed system of knowledge fixed in language and all its meanings). This system of knowledge is adopted by the individual from early unconscious childhood and is in fact the first belief system to be built upon. Later on, this initial belief system develops and is accomplished with other belief systems, creating altogether a complex of beliefs or, in other words, an individual worldview, i.e., a cognitive scheme of the world.

In this way a myth as a particular kind of social belief can be a part of a belief system not only as a particular component, but also in the form of a transformation group of myths, as mentioned above. The dynamic between belief systems as a whole and their components remains debatable; however, it is important to stress the inherent differences which exist between them.

As pointed out earlier in this Chapter, national identity usually consists of national myth in the form of an ethnic myth or a complex of ethnic myths, because nations certainly built upon a preexisting "ethnic mosaic" in Europe and, mostly, outside. As Smith observes: "Myths of national identity typically refer to territory or ancestry (or both) as the basis of political community" (Smith 1991, viii). According to the author, the main features and characteristics of these myths vary. For instance, myths of ethnic descent can include, in different combinations, myths: 1) of origins, both temporal and spatial, telling us when we were born and from where we came; 2) of migrations and/or liberation (charting our wanderings and our road to freedom); 3) of descent proper, with a special emphasis upon the nature of our ancestors; 4) of the heroic age, which is an idealized past, a golden age when the community was great and glorious, when our national genius flourished and men were heroes; 5) of communal decline and, perhaps, conquest and exile; 6) of rebirth, a reawakening of the community which involves a summons to political action.

Myths usually exaggerate and dramatize historical events in order to make necessary conclusions more obvious. The Ukrainian philosopher N. Hamitov stated that national mythology is "the way to solve the tragic contradictions of the nation, which are not to be solved in an 'ordinary' life" (Mala 1996, 100) and one can only add that the "tragic" character of its perception could be well conditioned by the mythology itself. The function of myths in national (social) consciousness therefore is in mobilizing social opinion and social action. "The myths not only inspire, and even require, certain kinds of regenerative collective action; they answer the all-important questions of identity and purpose which religious tradition no longer seems able to resolve. In the shape of ancient heroes, they give us our standards of collective morality ... By 'replacing' us as links in an unbroken chain of generations, the myths of descent disclose our national destinies" (Smith 1984b, 115-123).

At the same time, Gellner argued: "nationalist ideology suffers from pervasive false consciousness. Its myth inverts reality..." (Gellner 1983, 125). In response to this, one can say that a myth of national identity represents reality in another dimension by another language. In fact, a myth successfully performs a real mobilizing function within the national community. If so, it might mean that either reality is already inverted (that is, unreasonable) or that myth is a special form of this reality.

We can apply this consideration not only to nationalist myth but also to all kinds of myths. For instance, Smith writes: "we might well see the emergence of a new European identity and community forging its own myths and symbols, and unifying itself around common values and memories out of the many cognate traditions to hand" (Smith 1988, 25). The basic assumptions for a belief system of European identity are much more amorphous and bleak than for a nationalist one;[15] however, its belief system is rather successful. This means that where the nature of myth and its successful functioning are concerned, it is not necessary to follow rational knowledge.

"Under normal circumstances, most human beings can live happily with multiple identifications and enjoy moving between them as the situation requires" (Smith 1991b, 59) But, sometimes, one or another of these identities can come into confrontation with external reality, or enter into conflict with another individual identity. In this case it is a myth that very often can make confrontation less painful for the individual. Myth can become a kind of irrational medicine in order to encompass, or at least to simplify, contradictions within national consciousness. This mechanism is also applica-

---

[15]   Smith described the problem of European cultural identity as following: "Such a culture must be consciously, even artificially, constructed out of the elements of existing national cultures. But existing cultures are time-bound, particular and expressive. They are tied to specific peoples, places and periods. They are bound up with definite historical identities. These features are essentially antithetical to the very nature of a truly cosmopolitan culture" (Smith, 1991b, 66-67).

ble to social identities where conflicting knowledge can be encompassed through forgetting:

> All profound changes in consciousness, by their nature, bring with them characteristic amnesias ... As with modern persons, so it is with nations. Awareness of being imbedded in secular, serial time, with all its implications of continuity, yet of "forgetting" the experience of this continuity—product of the ruptures of the late eighteenth century—engenders the need for a narrative of "identity." (Anderson 1991: 204-205)

On the other hand, the virtue of a social consciousness is that it can assist in maintaining collective myths much longer than would be possible for an individual consciousness:

> Collective identities, however, tend to be pervasive and persistent. They are less subject to rapid changes and tend to be more intense and durable, even when quite large numbers of individuals no longer feel their power. This is especially true of religious and ethnic identities, which even in pre-modern eras often became politicized. It is particularly true of national identities today, when the power of mass political fervour reinforces the technological instruments of mass political organization, so that national identities can outlast the defection or apathy of quite large numbers of individual members. (Smith 1991b, 59)

We can now summarize some conclusions from the previous description of the relationships between national identity and myth. Contrary to the assumption of some "modernists" that national identity within a nation-state was created by industrial society and would be overcome with the establishment of post-industrial society, Philip Schlesinger has precisely noted that such assumptions have failed to conceptualize *national* identity, as opposed to the identities of emergent collectivities within established nation-states: "*The parameters of the nation-state are taken for granted.*" Schlesinger concludes that national identity "is to be understood as a particular kind of collective identity. In other words, it is an identity constituted at a given strategic level of a society" (Schlesinger 1987, 260-264).

Another important aspect here is that an individual internalizes reality ("national relationships" as it was called in Soviet Russian or

Ukrainian terminology)[16] in the context of the cultural and historical conditions of a particular society. In other words, an individual perceives and adopts national relationships not separately but in the context of other theoretical and practical aspects of reality.[17] This complex determines the specifics of an individual consciousness. That is why we can easily observe that the conditions of social life, which become more intensive in societies during some transformations and especially in a period of national revival, cause meaningful changes within national consciousness. Sometimes these changes can provoke a confrontation between the multiple identities of an individual and his or her different loyalties. And it is myths that play an important role in overcoming this confrontation.

On the social level of national consciousness, a myth (ethnic, national, etc.) can also serve the important function of mobilizing public opinion and collective action in order to solve contemporary contradictions in social (national) development. The fact that the importance of myths increases mainly during periods of social transformation only underlines the importance of these mobilizing functions.

In an ideological sense, a myth as part of different, broader cognitive schemes (as a part of a complex belief system) is required to reconstruct the connections between the past, present and future in social consciousness if, for instance, the chain of historical self-perception is destroyed or broken. The Ukrainian scholar Oksana Zabuzhko stressed that the mythologization of national life is a result of "weak or uncompleted national worldviews" (Zabuzhko 1993, 51). At the same time, a myth itself can also successfully initiate a new chain in the process of social organization, and this is the case of so-called "invented communities." Nationalism as an ideology and doctrine habitually employs different myths in order to subjugate the masses. As Eric Hobsbawm notes: "Nationalism requires

---

[16]   National relationships are seen as a particular area of social relationships where the social agents are nations, national groups, and individuals who are members of these nations or national groups.

[17]   Ukrainian scholars would argue that the most important aspects of such reality are personal experience on the individual level (Shkliar 1992, 66) and social, political and "regional" factors on the collective level (Boldetska 1996).

too much belief in what is patently not so. 'Getting its history wrong is part of being a nation' (Renan)" (Hobsbawm 1990, 12). Even nationalists themselves are conscious of their use of myths. For instance, Mussolini, one of the founders of fascism, said: "Our myth is the greatness of the nation." The founder of Ukrainian integral nationalism, Dmytro Dontzov, in his main work *Nationalism*, wrote at the same time (1923) that each nation has and needs a myth for its own reinforcement (Dontsov 1966). So, we can sum up that myth within nationalist ideology is supposed to play a certain functional role such as mass mobilization or reinforcement of "weak national," or rather nationalist, worldviews.

It is important to stress the extreme ability of myths to survive under any conditions and the hopelessness of attempts to deny a myth from a rational point of view. This situation of mythical thinking continues to exist in the present and, as Leszek Kołakowski said, contemporary people believe in absurdities no less than ancient people did. Individuals may deny myth for themselves, but not for other people. "Through life in a myth people become aware of transcendence, and in this encounter the objective and the subjective are inseparable; thus it is as impossible to find scientific truth in a myth as to reduce a myth to its personal, existential content" (Kołakowski 1990, 102). This must be what Losev meant when he wrote in his "final dialectical formula of myth" that myth is "a miraculous personal history given in words" (Losev 1991, 169).

Kołakowski also believed that narrative knowledge, to which some myths belong, is, in fact, much more positive for mankind than one can imagine. This point can be illustrated by the following passage:

> When I try ... to point out the most dangerous characteristic of modernity, I tend to sum up my fear in one phrase: the disappearance of taboos. There is no way to distinguish between "good" and "bad" taboos, artificially to support the former and remove the latter; the abrogation of one, on the pretext of its rationality, results in a domino effect that brings the withering away of others. Various traditional human bonds which make communal life possible, and without which our existence would be regulated only by greed and fear, are not likely to survive without a taboo system, and it is perhaps better to believe in the validity of even apparently silly taboos than to let them all vanish. (Kołakowski 1990, 13).

Of course, Kołakowski does not mean that myth should remain a core of the modern worldview as it was in ancient times; but, presumably, as he suggests, it does make sense to restore, reluctantly, some of those irrational values, in order to survive, and thus to deny our rationality, thereby proving that perfect rationality is a self-defeating goal.

In the concept of nation a myth has not only a mobilizing and ideological function but also transfers its own ability to be perennial (if not endless) to national belief systems. This suggests two main conclusions: on the one hand, that any approach which oversimplifies the role of myth in national consciousness is destined for failure (such an approach would not take into account the fact that internal, irrational logic is as successful for myth as rational logic is for science); and on the other hand, myth is a necessary element of a complex belief system for an "orderly" group outlook, i.e., a cognitive schema of the world or worldview. For the latter, myth is required as a legitimizing factor under conditions when other legitimacy is not available. Psychologically, this is possible because the fundamentals of belief are "deeper than knowledge or thinking" (Psikhologia 1990, 50). Belief precedes knowledge and thinking precisely because the latter both rely on it. And since belief comes first it is stronger than knowledge and thinking.

Another important element of the human cognitive schema is stereotyping. It also has a complex relationship with rational knowledge, and therefore requires somewhat detailed consideration within the context of national phenomena.

2.2.2 Stereotypes and National Consciousness

The term "stereotype" was introduced by Wasserman Lippmann in his 1922 book *Public Opinion* (Lippmann 1998, 79). Usually, but not always, the term applies to stable, simplified characteristics of certain social groups which are the results of the general life experiences of an individual, as well as the learning of certain cognitive schemes prevalent within a given society. The latter are often full of prejudice and Lippmann considered stereotypes as to the opposite of rational thinking, as they precede critical thinking and ignore any evidence that challenges them. Tajfel later showed that stereotypes, in fact, could find some justification in reality, but they do so via mechanisms of selective perception of new experience (Tajfel 1981). Lippmann called this phenomenon a "blind spot" in human consciousness, but also stressed the positive aspects of stereotypes since they create a comforting feeling about the world which is familiar and therefore manageable (Lippmann 1998, 104-115).

Social psychologists and sociologists have developed three main approaches in the study of stereotype: 1) motivational, e.g., represented by Theodor W. Adorno (1950) and Allport (1954); 2) cognitive, represented by Bar-Tal (1989) and Tajfel (1981); 3) rhetorical, represented by Billig (1991).

The first approach places the emotional experiences of an individual at the core of stereotyping. Adorno developed this approach within the context of an authoritarian personality type and defined stereotypes as a core of ethnocentrism. The latter was considered to have a dual nature: 1) as an ideology within society (or a kind of culturally defensive provincialism); 2) as a psychological attitude. Adorno suggested the following structure of ethnocentrism:

1. Denial or rejection of individuals from the "other" group
2. Random choice of criteria to define or characterize the "other" group, i.e., lack of rationality
3. Undeveloped ability to identify oneself with somebody else
4. Perception of "the other" as dangerous, threatening and in some way inferior
5. Tendency to generalize individual experience as characteristic of the whole group of "the other"
6. Judgmental tendencies to label "the other" with negative characteristics
7. Idealization of one's own group when "negative characteristics" of the "other" group are considered automatically positive for "our" group
8. Belief that there is "natural" order, authority and hierarchy among groups (often based on valuation of what is a superior and inferior culture or race)

9.   Conviction that there is a definite way that conflicts between groups should be solved (usually expressed in a certain strategy of preserving "our" group and remaining in control).

Adorno stressed the role of parents in the education of the "authoritarian personality" and argued that the roots of ethnocentrism are in the universal human ability to divide social groups according to categories of "we" and "the other."

Allport considered stereotypes as a form of human prejudice. The latter he defined as negative emotional attitudes toward a group or an individual that are the consequence of misunderstanding, and which result from that psychological discomfort. This is why Allport stressed the cognitive, emotional and behavioral components of prejudice, where emotion has a leading role. Because of the latter, Allport was skeptical about Lippmann's hopes of eliminating negative human stereotypes and prejudice by means of education, since the latter does not have much power over human emotions. Prejudice and stereotypes, according to Allport, are functionally important because they fulfill certain psychological needs and in this context have five major forms of expression. These are: 1) speech (as a rule in negative expressions about the subject of prejudice); 2) avoidance of someone or a group as a whole; 3) discrimination of rights; 4) physical attack but not premeditated assault; 5) systematic physical persecution.

Other social psychologists, such as Tajfel (1969, 1970), considered stereotypes in cognitive but not emotional dimensions. Tajfel pointed out the ways in which people perceive and interpret information, and therefore stressed the role of language. He defined the following functions of stereotypes:

1.   A cognitive function that provides for "economical thinking," i.e., minimum intellectual efforts to work out an orderly image of the world in general, and social groups in particular.

2. An instrumental function that provides the ability to take decisions and action in daily life on the basis of already existing knowledge, i.e., without additional considerations.
3. A subordinate ideological function when an individual or a group accepts the cognitive schemas of the world worked out by dominant existing ideologies.
4. A positive identification of someone's own group in relation to a "contrast" group. For this purpose positive self-stereotypes and negative stereotypes of "the other" are chosen via mechanisms of selective perception for the groups that are accordingly defined as "we" and "the other."

Some scholars define also a fifth "defensive" function when the task is not so much establishing "our" own positive image as it is dissociating from the "negative" group of "the other" (Chalasinski 1935, 61).

Another approach to the nature of stereotypes is known as the "theory of a scapegoat," and implies the aggressive transfer of someone's frustration onto someone else. Stereotypes enter the game when there is a need to justify such a transfer. Similar to this is the "theory of establishing justice," where there is a similar aggressive transfer. Other theories include the theory of conflict, group socialization, the role of mass media, cultural tradition, and so on. What is important is that most of them agree that stereotypes are learned and adopted by individuals, starting from early childhood, within a given social surrounding.

Different theories provide various explanations as to why stereotypes are such persistent phenomena in social life, as none seem to be universal. But for the purpose of this study it is sufficient to bear in mind that stereotypes and self-stereotypes, in particular national stereotypes, are products of socialization. This provides the possibility of studying when, how and what kind of stereotypes an individual internalizes from his or her social surroundings concerning his or her national or ethnic group. Generally, all students of national consciousness stress the important role of such self-stereotypes for the national phenomenon. Most scholars agree that there are certain cognitive schemes typical for each national identity, such as "visions" of who are "our people" (Bromley 1987; Anderson 1991; Hobsbawm 1990), images of what is "our homeland" (Smith 1984b; Bromley and Podolnyi 1990; Shkliar 1991), behavioral ethno-stereotypes (Gumilev 1993; Shkliar 1992) or self-stereotypes and stereotypes of the other (Vyrost 1989; Malewska 1994).

Ethnic and national stereotypes can be studied on three levels. Firstly, the level of language, where samples of text are examined for the presence of open and hidden stereotypes. The Discriminatory Speech Act theory, created by Graumann (Graumann and Moscovici 1987), could be considered one of the most successful in this. Grau-mann suggested methods to uncover open and hidden forms of ste-reotypical speech where the main five functions of stereotypes are distinguished as follows: separation (we — the other); distancing (they, such and such, etc.); exaggeration (when negative features are highlighted); diminishing (e.g., using pejorative endings); fixation (e.g., "they will be always like that"). Hidden stereotypes should be studied within the context of cultural meanings that are functional within a language.

The second level of analysis is to study stereotypes of behavior. Gumilev insisted that it is stereotypes of behavior that define belong-ing to this or the other nation, as well as differentiating nations among themselves. Although Gumilev's theory stands on its own within this subject, some other scholars referring to ethnographic studies stress that it is patterns of behavior (like folklore traditions such as dancing, games, family relations) that can preserve distinct features of different social groups and peoples (Skliar 1992, 38-50).The third level of analysis of stereotypes would be concerned with material culture (types of buildings, tools, arms, types of cut-lery, etc.).

In sum, stereotypes are internalized by individuals from early childhood and change during the course of adult life. This makes it possible to explore which ethnic and national stereotypes are adopt-ed by individuals, and at which age, in various cases.

Conclusions to Chapter 2

The analysis of this chapter suggests that national consciousness is a system of beliefs of rational and emotional origin, which develops as a constant *process* reflecting group social existence. National identity is a part of this process taken at a certain moment of time, i.e., in a particular setting.

Analysis suggests that the origin of national consciousness is bound up with the development of industrialism and the new social organization that followed. Most of the analyzed schools of thought agree in their description of the historical conditions under which national phenomena first appeared. The importance of socio-economic factors is stressed by the majority of scholars.

It seems there is also a consensus as to the importance of ethnic consciousness for the development of national identity and of a nation as a whole. As a rule, ethnic identity is represented within national consciousness via adopted and transformed ethnic myths and collective memories, although some scholars insist that such adaptation of ethnic heritage is artificial and optional. If ethnic memories are present within national identity they are best preserved on a collective level (group consciousness), where they tend to be more stable and are not easily undermined by rationality.

The crucial disagreement among the various approaches has to do with the actual role of ethnicity in national phenomena. "Primordialists" and most of those in the Eastern European tradition tend to emphasize the continuity of pre-modern ethnic and modern national development, while "modernist" discourses insist on the discontinuity of such developments, or at least their crucially different nature. The latter also stress that, even if sometimes ethnic heritage is represented within national consciousness, it still has to be totally transformed and reflects mythical aspects of national existence.

Yet the analysis in Chapter 2 suggests the possibility of a synthesis of existing approaches. It seems possible to explore, using sociological techniques, the most debated elements of national identity, such as ethnic myths and collective memories, and to define their role in each particular case. The latter is important since it is clear that often it is myths and collective memories that make national identity so enduring. Moreover, national identity based on such myths could become the main worldview defining belief systems for individuals. This is because myths and collective stereotypes, as elements of belief systems, are necessary for the creation of group cognitive schemas and an "orderly" world-perception. Psychologists are not completely certain as to why human nature requires such simplified, stereotyped "order" for individual and group consciousness. One reason, perhaps, is that humans have to deal with increasing numbers of different people around them and one way to process information on an increasingly complex human terrain is to sort "other people" into "types." Unfortunately, such simplification, however efficient in the short term, creates distortions in human minds as to each other's nature. So, the initial goal, to manage contacts with "the other" in the most efficient way, is achieved only partially. Therefore, it happens that mutual understanding (or in fact often misunderstanding) is not efficient enough and even easily formed stereotypes are not sufficient to reach the compromise in inter-group understanding or positive group self-perception. In this case, irrational myth is the only symbolic language able to explain certain contradictions in a collective self-perception without actually solving them. Myth, in this way, is a social phenomenon that, due to its symbolic language, is accepted by belief rather than by thinking processes such as, in this case, rational explanation. Like stereotypes, myths are effective because they encompass contradictions in collective histories and therefore have an emotional, existential function. Precisely because of this, people believe in myths and do not need to understand or reason them. Somehow myths "make sense" of the outside world where reasoning is not helpful. This lack of reasoning makes myths and stereotypes stronger rather than weakening them.

National identity in this context could be understood as a complex belief system that consists of a set of lower-scale belief systems and beliefs of both a rational and irrational/emotional nature. To what extent these kinds of beliefs are inherited from a previous ethnic social development could be more specifically defined by the empirical study of a specific culture, since there has been no universal principle established by social scientists. Verification of the existing theories with new empirical evidence can, in this way, encompass differences in scientific discourses.

Chapter 3 focuses on nationalism as a political principle that requires that the nation be congruent with the state, and thus provides guidance for the nationalist movements aspiring to "educate" as many people as possible in the spirit of a corresponding national identity.

3 Nationalism and Societal Security

As was suggested in Chapter 2, the ethnic or civic content of national identity constructs is usually defined by the concrete circumstances of the social, economic and political history of a region. There are, however, some universal features of nationalism as a political movement that always threaten the existing social order by suggesting a different organization of the state. In the post-Cold War environment, nationalism was perceived as the most common cause of most conflicts with the exception, possibly, of those caused by religious fundamentalism. Yet, historically, nationalism has been an organizing principle for the European nation-states, and it has not been abandoned by the member countries of the European Union. British exit from the EU is, to a large extent, an attempt to preserve British culture within sovereign state boundaries that would be once again controlled by the national government as oppose to suprastate legislation.

This chapter considers the relations between nationalism, war, and security. Its particular concern is to explore the dynamics of security dilemmas within and between states and societies threatened by nationalist movements. To do this, it uses the notions of "security community" (one in which no war preparations are made), and "societal security" (where a threat to a dominant identity can lead to war preparations).

3.1. Nationalism, War, and Security

The literature on nationalism refers frequently to its explosive and violent potential and the need to contain it through the building of democratic institutions and civil society (Snyder 2000; Kaldor 1999). Politicians often refer to nationalism as a political evil and a cause of war. In the context of European integration it is often suggested that the nationalism and war that characterized the European past can be avoided by pan-European unification, and that this is the only road to a peaceful and prosperous future. This was the theme expounded by François Mitterrand in a speech to the European Parliament in March 1995:

> . . . if we fail to overcome our past, let there be no mistake about what will follow: ladies and gentlemen, nationalism means war! War is not only our past, it could also be our future! And it is us, it is you, ladies and gentlemen, the Members of the European Parliament, who will henceforth be the guardians of our peace, our security and our future! (Mitterrand 1995, 51).

This simple equation of nationalism with war is politically expedient but intellectually problematic on a number of levels. War predates the age of nationalism and so cannot be fully explained by nationalism. The equation remains problematic even if we restrict our focus to World Wars I and II, which was what the French president had in mind, as it is not universally agreed that these wars were caused by nationalism as a political principle: "one culture, one state." WWI was fought mostly by the European (multinational) empires to start with. Historians refer to a variety of economic and political causes, from colonial revisionism and the struggle for new markets between established capitalist states, to the rise of a particular kind of racist ideology within German militarism before World War II. Although Nazi ideology and nationalism are frequently equated, demonizing nationalism, the German national socialism of the 1930s cannot be explained by nationalism alone. As Ernest Gellner put it, even in the era of nationalism, the horror of Nazism and Fascism is optional (Gellner 1997, 56).

Just as there is no single theory of nationalism, there is no single explanation for what causes war. And yet, academics, as well as politicians, connect the two. What they frequently argue is that the most salient cause of conflict in the twentieth century was the struggle for self-determination and inter-ethnic conflict between various minorities seeking political autonomy or a state of their own. Although wars of self-determination are not always seen as negative, because of an international consensus favoring the right of national self-determination, the inter-ethnic violence that often accompanies them is usually widely condemned, and rightly so.

In fact, most studies of nationalist violence are concerned with inter-ethnic conflicts and thus with *ethnic* nationalism. However, as argued above, the distinction between ethnic and civic nationalism is largely theoretical, and tells us more about history and geography than about the nature of nationalism. Indeed, if we accept the "modernist" assumption that ethnicity survives in the modern age only in the form of nationalism, then ethnic conflict is nothing else but nationalist conflict *per se*. That takes us back to the discussion of "bad" (ethnic) and "good" (civic) nationalisms, when in fact none are inherently more or less violent. The latest research in military anthropology indicates that human culture does not cause war but can only legitimize armed conflict:

> A far right system of ideas does not cause people to act; it merely makes it socially more acceptable to act in particular ways to which they had already been motivated. ... Ultimately, group violence is emotive and subconscious, rather than the product of conscious reasoning. (Martin 2018, 213)

According to Mike Martin, claiming that culture causes violence and homicide relegates humans to passive recipients of social forces and removes human agency (which is required by most definitions of homicide, in the concept of intent). "It is a similar argument to the one stating that religion causes war, or ideology causes people to blow themselves up" (Martin 2018, 63).

And yet, the literature reviewed in Chapter 2 suggests that some forms and phases of nationalism are more likely to cause conflict and war than others. So, for instance, the nationalism of the early industrialized countries in Western Europe "satisfied" the political principle of "one culture, one state" and thus did not generate problems that were impossible to solve by nonviolent political means. Separatism in Northern Ireland and the Basque country seem to be exceptions and likely resolved with the expansion of the suprastate European community. However, nationalism in countries of the Former Soviet Union still faces the Habsburg dilemma of conflicting high cultures competing for their own states on territories with mixed populations.

It is here that the principle of self-determination threatens to lead to ethnic cleansing, because competing nationalisms are focused on disputed territories and there is therefore no clear solution as to how to satisfy what is accepted as the natural right of self-determination. The vicious circle of territorially-bound nationalisms in Eastern Europe was only partly solved after World Wars I and II by the policy of resettlement and exchange of population and territories. So, for instance, Bulgaria, Greece and Turkey solved territorial disputes by exchange of populations in the 1920s, while the Polish-Ukrainian struggle over control of Eastern Galicia was resolved by the resettlement of populations in the 1940s. Conflicts in Nagorno-Karabakh (and in Cyprus) have been effectively frozen after warring sides created minority-free territorial enclaves. The conflict in Kosovo is likely to subside with the exodus of Serbs and Roma from Albanian-dominated territories, which may lead to the creation of an ethnically (nearly) pure Kosovo.

Russian attempts to repeat a "Kosovo-style liberation" of South Ossetia and Abkhazia in 2008, however, met with worldwide condemnation. Yet, if the right of people to self-determination continues to exist, it is difficult to imagine other ways in which the nationalist projects inherent in the conditions of modernity might be satisfied in cases of territorially competing nationalisms. The example of Kosovo proves that military intervention is capable of changing the balance of forces in a conflict area, but it is not capable of solving the Habsburg dilemma. So, is there a nonviolent solution to nationalist aspirations even when nationalisms are competing? Although nationalism and war are thought to be inter-related, there has actually been little research or general analysis of security issues in which the nation is the object, as opposed to the state.

Stephen van Evera offers nine hypotheses on the relationship between nationalism and war that help to identify, more or less dangerous nationalisms, the conditions which might lead from nationalism to war, as well as those in which nationalism may actually work to "dampen" the risk of war (Evera 1994). The hypotheses concerning what approximates or provokes war include the following:

1. The greater the proportion of state-seeking nationalities that are stateless, the greater the risk of war.
2. The more those nationalities pursue the recovery of the national Diasporas, and the more they pursue annexationist strategies of recovery, the greater the risk of war.

3. The more hegemonic the goals that nationalities pursue toward one another, the greater the risk of war.
4. The more severely nationalities oppress minorities living in their states, the greater the risk of war.

Of the four conditions that might provoke war, the last three can potentially be eliminated by liberal democratic governance and the rule of law. If, as is widely assumed, democracies do not fight wars with each other, it is logical to project, as well, that democracy would eliminate these nationalism-related causes of war. The first hypothesis is conditional, as not all nationalities seek states of their own. Van Evera therefore suggests the additional, structural, and political/perceptual factors necessary for this situation to operate as a proximate cause of war. The structural factors are identified in the following additional hypotheses:

1. Stateless nationalisms pose a greater risk of war if they have the strength to plausibly reach for freedom, and the central state has the will to resist their attempt.
2. The more densely nationalities are intermingled, the greater the risk of war.
3. The greater the defensibility and legitimacy of borders, and the greater the correspondence between these political borders and communal (ethnic) boundaries, the smaller the risk of war.

Two additional hypotheses focus on political/perceptual factors:

1. The greater the past crimes committed by nationalities against one another, the greater the risk of war.
2. The more divergent the beliefs of nationalities about their mutual history and their current conduct and character, the greater the risk of war.

The structural factors in this scheme suggest that the immediate cause of nationalistic war depends not so much on the quantity of state-seeking nationalities within the given territory, but upon their ability to struggle for actual self-determination. In reality the number of potential state-seeking peoples is much larger than the number of peoples struggling for self-determination, meaning that the majority of potential nationalisms never reach the stage of becoming political. On the other hand, the structural factors that Van Evera points to suggest that the more "ethnically" (i.e., culturally) homogeneous nation-states are, the less the risk of war. In other words, "satisfied" nationalisms are in fact the most peaceful and/or "liberal" nationalisms, although the process of gaining "satisfaction" often causes nationalisms to produce conflict and wars. Van Evera comes to the conclusion that Western powers with "satisfied" nationalisms should use their economic leverage with those new Eastern European states containing "hungry" nationalisms, so that the latter conform to a code of peaceful conduct that precludes the sort of policies that make nationalism dangerous.

The code to which he refers includes six elements: (1) renunciation of the threat or use of force; (2) robust guarantees for the rights of national minorities to include, under some stringent conditions, a legal right to secession; (3) commitment to the honest teaching of history in the schools, and to refrain from the propagation of chauvinism or other hate propaganda; (4) willingness to adopt a democratic form of government, and to accept related institutions — specifically, free speech and a free press; (5) adoption of market economic policies, and disavowal of protectionist or other beggar-thy-neighbor economic policies toward other Eastern states; (6) acceptance of current national borders, or agreement to settle borders promptly through peaceful means (Van Evera 1997, 58).

Apart from general points about tolerance and the adoption of a market economy, the code is concerned with the state's sovereign right to use force, the stability of borders, and the right of secession. With regard to this last point, Van Evera argues, in a footnote, that the West should support the right of secession of minorities in those Eastern states where governments are not willing to guarantee minority rights. While this might be effective in the case of states that are willing to collaborate with the West, it has two fundamental problems. The first problem is that it has the potential to lead to privileging some minorities over others. For instance, the armed liberation struggle of the Kosovo Albanians was considered to be a "terrorist" activity until the Milosevic government finally turned its back on the West; it was only then that NATO went to war to protect the rights of the Albanian minority in Kosovo. Although independence has not yet been granted to the Albanians of Kosovo, this national minority is clearly in a better position to achieve self-determination or ethnic reunification in a "Greater Alabania" than, for instance, similar minorities in Chechnya or Kurdistan.

The other fundamental question is: which international organizations can or should actually enforce minority rights and be allowed to violate the sovereignty of "abusing" states that refuse to collaborate on this issue with the West or with the UN? It is often stated that international organizations are cumbersome and indecisive and cannot respond rapidly and efficiently to "national" crises of this nature. Moreover, it is also argued, as Mary Kaldor has noted, that major international organizations "are often dominated by the most powerful nations, and therefore do little more than disguise colonialism"; and, as Kaldor goes on to point out: "These arguments do have substance ...Was the objective of Nato's mission in the crisis in Kosovo to save lives in Kosovo or to maintain the cohesion and credibility of the institutions?" (Kaldor et al 2000, 192).

Van Evera's hypotheses on nationalism and war therefore provide insight not so much into nationalism and war, but into the wider issues of the relationship between nationalism and democracy, democracy and minority rights, state sovereignty and human rights, the stability of borders and geopolitics. They say little, however, about why and when war becomes inevitable. For this, we must look to theories of war.

Broadly speaking, there are two major schools of thought about war and the wider condition of international security: the realist and the idealist/constructivist. The dominant perspective is the realist one. While this perspective considers war on the individual and societal levels, it considers the international level, that of nation-states, to be most determinative in decisions to engage in war (Waltz 1959; Waltz 1989).

Focusing on the state and, more specifically, state governments, the realist approach explains nationalism as a cause of violence by

reference to the rational policies of ruling elites who choose nationalist mass mobilization because of a lack of democratic institutions
and practices. For instance, Jack Snyder has applied this argument to
Eastern Europe: "the sophisticated Czechs were able to invent a
working civil society almost overnight" while the "less sophisticated" Georgians were eager to establish an exclusive ethnic identity
for their new state, one that led to war with the Abkhaz minority
and the division of the country (Snyder 2000, 72).

What this argument fails to notice is that the "sophisticated"
Czechs achieved a relatively homogeneous society *after* the ethnic
cleansing of Germans from their territory at the end of World War II
and separation from their Slovak federal partner, as well as from
large Hungarian and Ruthenian/Ukrainian minorities, in 1993. The
argument also fails to notice that the "exclusivist" Georgians actually comprise numerous ethnic groups with a dominant Kartli cultural
component, including Svans and Megrels speaking distinct languages (Tishkov 1997, 14.). In fact, "Georgian" is the collective name
of a civic national project dating back to the nineteenth century,
which has included various ethnicities, with a dominant group
called Kartveli. It is precisely the attempt to include within the
Georgian nation the historically close people of Abkhazia (similar in
origin, but different in religion), who were militarily supported by
Russia, that led to the 1993 war.[18] The Russo-Georgian war took
place over Abkhazia and South Ossetia 15 years later, despite the
strong democratic institutions built in Georgia over that time and
recognized as such by the West.

Although there have been many neo-realist attempts to modify
the state-as-actor approach and to build a more comprehensive theory of war, the major criticism of such approaches, from the point of

---

[18]   By the spring of 1993 President Shevardnadze described the Abkhazian war as a
conflict between Russia and Georgia, writes British historian Jonathan Aves: "The
failure of any foreign country to offer peacekeeping forces to monitor the cease-
fire in Abkhazia, and the introduction there of a purely Russian contingent in
May 1994, was the final nail in the coffin of Georgia's attempts to use Western
countries as a counterbalance to Russia. Georgia thus had no choice but to enter
into a close partnership with Russia which imposed real limitations on its sovereignty" (Aves 1998, 184).

view of the other, idealist, perspective, is that, in a new globalized world, territorial nation-states are eroded and therefore wars are no longer launched by states for ideological or geopolitical reasons but, rather, are based on identity politics. These "new" or postmodern wars are fought not between state-organized armies, but by armed groups against an unarmed population (Kaldor 1999). Low-intensity conflicts, or "terrorist" wars, are only a few examples of this new type of warfare, which is often associated with nationalism and inter-ethnic violence.

There are numerous paradoxes associated with these, new, "postmodern" wars. Here are a few noted by Chris Hables Gray:

1. The main moral justification of war is now peace.
2. The main practical justification for repression is the fight for freedom.
3. Security comes from putting the very future of the planet in grave risk.
4. The battlefield is really a battlespace. It is now three-dimensional and ranges beyond the atmosphere. It is on the "homefront" as much as on the battlefront.
5. Politics are so militarized that every act of war needs political preparation and justification. Wars can only be won politically. Through military means the best that can be accomplished is not to lose.
6. The industrialized countries want colonialism without responsibility (neo-colonialism); people in the nonindustrial and industrializing regions want Western technology without Western culture; others want both; others want neither.
7. War itself proliferates into the general culture.

According to Gray, postmodern war is held together not structurally but rhetorically as a discourse system. Hence a gloomy prediction: "If war is impossible, if peace seems to make sense, make ready for the most impossible war — nuclear" (Gray 1997, 170).

The main difference between realist and idealist approaches to theorizing war is not so much in the description of the problem as in the suggested solutions. Statistically, nuclear attack, at least on a regional level, is most likely to happen sooner or later because of continuing arms proliferation, and because of the cultural differences on a global level that are even more acute due to what is called identity politics. Therefore, some neo-realists claim that a clash of civilizations is inevitable.

Samuel Huntington has argued that the arbitrary intervention of Western civilization into other parts of the world (Iraq but not Palestine, Bosnia but not Chechnya, etc.) evokes strong resentment:

> The West won the world not by the superiority of the ideas or values or religion (to which few members of other civilizations converted) but rather by its superiority in applying organized violence. Westerners often forget this fact; non-Westerners never do.
> Separately, terrorism and nuclear weapons are the weapons of the non-Western weak. If and when they are combined, the non-Western weak will be strong. (Huntington 1996, 51, 188)

Huntington therefore concludes that the Western belief in the universality of its culture is "false, immoral, dangerous, and results in imperialism," and that "only respect for other civilizations can safeguard us from a world war." Ironically, it is Russian attempts to build a so-called Eurasian civilization, based on a culturally Russian world (*russkiy mir*) within old imperial borders, that caused the postmodern undeclared "hybrid war" on Ukraine and prompted the new Cold War with the West.

Western idealists cannot accept the legitimacy of territorially based political entities based on cultural identities and argue instead for a cosmopolitan form of governance based on *humanism* as a source of legitimacy. Moderate idealists argue for the development of "a global civil society in which the globally vulnerable will be well represented" via "globalist campaigning organizations" (Shaw 1996, 182). More "radical" idealists argue in favor of "cosmopolitan law-enforcement," "transnational pacification" "under the umbrella of NATO, including Russia, the OSCE, or the United Nations" (Kaldor 1999, 149). Idealist criticism of "realists" stresses that there is no place for nation-states in the global world, so the very concept of nationalism, where each culture has its own political space, i.e., state, is outdated. National identity must pave the way to a cosmopolitan identity, and nations should be "replaced" by non-territorial cultural communities of a neo-medieval type. Realists fight back by dismissing the concept of cosmopolitan governance as lacking legitimacy and therefore being non-viable.

Debates between realists and idealists inevitably involve more philosophical assumptions concerning Natural Law and Universal Reason. As Sabrina Ramet points out:

> both liberal idealists and liberal realists value both legitimacy and order. The difference is that, where idealists believe that civic order is a consequence of system legitimacy and that legitimacy is, in turn, measured in terms of the system's harmony with certain values and norms, realists construe legitimacy as but the face of civil order, however achieved. Machiavelli, still a central reference point for the realist tradition, or what is left of it, had no objection to legitimacy as such but placed his emphasis on the *appearance* of legitimacy ... Idealists tend to be universalists, that is, to treat human reason as the final arbiter, and to believe that it is appropriate to judge laws according to standards set by Natural Law or some other external standard, as well as by normative covenants such as the Universal Declaration of Human Rights (Ramet 2000, 68, 70).

Whatever the outcome of this centuries-long philosophical debate, as long as nationalism provides a source of legitimacy for nation-states, realism will prevail in politics, and therefore in decisions about whether or not to go to war.

So far, attempts to launch wars in support of or against nationalist political claims have depended on the perception of what constitutes *national* security threats or *international* security threats, where "international" is largely understood as *inter-nation-state*. The decision by liberal democracies whether or not to fight nationalist aspirations outside the West has been made on the basis of their own political, economic or environmental interests, i.e., their *national* interests. The fact that the Kosovo NATO campaign was proclaimed to be the first war fought on humanitarian grounds only stresses the postmodern nature of contemporary war, where the "main moral justification of war is now peace." This is not to say that humanitarian considerations were not involved in the decision to start the Kosovo campaign. However, the decision to start a war campaign in Kosovo and not in Chechnya, Kurdistan or Palestine, etc., had a political/realist and not a moral/idealist basis. It was Western and non-Western identity politics that clashed in Kosovo, and the victory, as it is in postmodern wars, could not be anything but *political*. Neither Albanians nor Serbs in Kosovo/Kosova could be satisfied with the outcome, because the nationalist principle driving the conflict toward ethnic cleansing was not fulfilled for either side, even though the pattern of violence was reversed and, according to the UN refugee agency, at least 230,000 Serbs and Roma had to leave their homes in order to save their lives.[19]

Here it is important to consider the international environment as a condition within which wars are fought and nationalisms are pacified. As mentioned earlier, movements for self-determination within Western states with "satisfied" nationalisms do appear, but they seem lightened, if not resolved, by the expansion of the EU, which has acquired more and more supra-state functions while member states have surrendered a number of their functions. Could this be a model for solving the problems of Eastern European nationalisms if most FSU states are accepted into the EU?

In theory, the answer should be in the affirmative, although in practice those states would not be accepted *unless* they first established liberal market-democracies of their own. However, the modernization of industrializing societies requires cultural homogeneity and mobility, something associated with nationalism as an organizing principle for a nation-state (one culture, one state), as well as the source of legitimacy for a democratic mass mobilization. Under these conditions of competing high cultures, known as the Habsburg dilemma, this would inevitably mean "satisfying" some nationalisms while "pacifying" others.

The realist approach to war and peace might give an accurate understanding as to why "satisfying" nationalism during this transition can cause war, i.e., it may lead to an understanding of structural causes; however, the political and perceptual causes of warmongering nationalism are better understood via the idealist/constructivist approach. Though the two approaches are methodologically different, they might usefully be combined to better

---

19   The UN Refugee Agency Website (2002) "Federal Republic of Yugoslavia: Kosovo." (http://www.unhcr.ch/cgi-bin/texis/vtx/balkans-country?country=kosovo)

identify the conditions that cause nationalism to lead to war, conditions which might otherwise be missed by either of the perspectives on its own.

The first attempt to achieve such a methodological combination was made by Karl Deutsch, who suggested considering political communities separately from security communities. Political communities, usually states or groups of states, according to Deutsch, are those where social transactions are supported by both enforcement and compliance. In a situation in which compliance is, for some reason, diminishing, civil war might possibly result. Security communities are those that are integrated to the extent that a common sense of community develops, that are accompanied by formal or informal institutions or practices, sufficiently strong and widespread to resolve conflicts of interest by peaceful means. War is not imaginable among members of a security community and no war preparations are made. We can say, therefore, that in these communities a collective defense identity unites its members. What application to practical research can such a distinction have? Deutsch suggests three broad questions relevant for every geographical area and historical period that might be studied:

1. How much transaction is there among political communities?
2. How much integration has been achieved?
3. How much probable security is there under these conditions?

The third question, Deutsch says, is deliberately phrased to avoid the realist assumption of determinism. Rather, it is about the subjective decision-making process by politicians:

> Something more human than mere reliance upon anonymous "forces of history" is involved here. Whatever such forces are believed to be, whether inflation or Islam, excessive emphasis on them tends to divert attention from the role of human decisions in the politics of history. Yet, politics notoriously is both the making of decisions and the art of the possible. To judge political performance is to appraise the exercise of this art by living men and women. To do so it is necessary to assess the range of data, resources, and opportunities available to those who make the crucial decision at given moments of time. (Deutsch 1970, 42)

In other words, politicians are capable of making decisions that either increase the capabilities of security communities in respect of stability and/or decrease the capabilities of secessionist or separatist regional governments. This leads us to a consideration of the problem of nationalist aspirations for self-determination, and the possibility of "satisfying" such aspirations within the parameters of either a single political community or a security community of states.

3.2. Security Communities and Societal Security

In clarifying under which conditions nationalism "means war," i.e., the ultimate form of individual and collective insecurity, we have also established that the creation of a "security community" represents a vehicle of maintaining peaceful co-existence as it provides a sense of security to people, rather than to states.

However, the creation of a common defense identity necessary for the formation of a security community is unlikely where at least one social group has aspirations to national self-determination. Theoretically, there is always the possibility that such aspirations will develop; however, not every potential new nation-building project will reach a political stage. Moreover, even if the identity of an ethnic minority conflicts with that of the majority, secession will not always be desirable as, for instance, in cases where liberal guarantees are provided by the state majority. For instance, ethnic Russians in Estonia have better living standards and a wider range of liberties than across the border in the Russian Federation, so are unlikely to mount a political secessionist movement. The Estonian majority is keen to ensure that ethnic Russians enjoy the same standards of living and have the same opportunities as long as they accept the culture and language of this majority in compliance with the EU's democratic framework.

However, in other FSU countries social groups find themselves without an efficient mediating party (e.g., government or supra-state EU institutions) that can guarantee agreements among them. James Fearon (1998) illustrates this situation with respect to post-Soviet Eastern Europe where, in his view, there exists a "commitment problem." This arises in situations in which ethnic majorities are unable to commit not to exploit ethnic minorities in newly created states. The author suggests that this "commitment problem" explains, as realist "security dilemma arguments cannot, why groups in conflict cannot bargain to a settlement and, instead, prefer to engage in a costly war" (Fearon 1998, 121).

According to security dilemma arguments, conflict results from mutual uncertainty about the other side's intentions, when all assume the worst. Barry Posen (1993) defines this "security dilemma" as follows:

> Relative power is difficult to measure and is often subjectively appraised: what seems sufficient to one state's defence will seem, and will often be, offensive to its neighbours. Because neighbours wish to remain autonomous and secure, they will react by trying to strengthen their own positions. States can trigger these reactions even if they have no expansionist inclinations. This is the security dilemma ... (Posen 1993, 28)

The notion might be useful in analyzing inter-state security; however, it is used as an "internal security dilemma" or "ethnic security dilemma" when applied to groups within a state or society. Indeed, Peter Wallensteen has argued that solutions to the ethnic security dilemma, at least in some cases, might be found by creating separate political units that permit the self-determination of the groups involved. Wallensteen points to the demilitarization and democratization of societies confronting ethnic security dilemmas as a means of avoiding the creation of new ethnically based units, but admits that "often such solutions are open only to stable democratic societies" (Wallensteen 2002, 197).

Dan Reiter and Allan Stam challenge the notion that democracies are less likely to launch wars, especially against other democracies. They argue that:

> Democracies do initiate wars, and they do so when it is seen to be in the national interest (as defined by the people) — and not as only a last-ditch effort to preserve the national defence when diplomacy failed. Further, they initiate wars against weaker foes, they initiate imperialist wars, and they sometimes use genocide in warfare (Reiter and Stam 2002, 198-199)

Reiter and Stam argue that what leads democracies to wage wars less frequently, and to win them more frequently than other states, can be explained by "temporary consent" or "electoral punishment" models. These focus on public consent for government policies. The authors point out that studies of international relations overlook public consent. The perception of what is consistent with the national interest at a given moment, they argue, is a critical factor in the choice of a conflict solution strategy.

As Bill McSweeney points out, the importance of perceptual factors in (ethnic) security dilemmas has led realist theorists to take into account the concept of identity as an independent object of security analysis (McSweeney 1999, 78).

One concept that takes into account the security of national groups, as opposed to that of nation-states, has been suggested by a group of scholars from the European Security Group at the Centre for Peace and Conflict Research in Copenhagen. This group was concerned to update traditional realist regional security complex theory[20] by introducing an additional *societal* sector of security. The authors[21] argue that apart from traditionally defined political, military, economic and environmental sectors of security that are centered on the state, there is a societal sector that reflects threats to the identity of a community or a nation. The authors proposed a "reconceptualization of the security field":

> Instead of talking about five parallel sectors all held by state security, we shall work with a duality of state security and societal security, the former having sovereignty as its ultimate criterion, and the latter being held together by concerns about identity. Both concern survival. (Waever et al 1993, 25).

Such a distinction helps to respond to the idealist criticism that state-centered approaches are not useful at a time when territorial nation-states may, in fact, be starting to disappear, at least in the countries subscribing to the EU integration model.

Focusing on societal security allows us to see threats to national communities that are not related to threats to the state as a whole,

---

[20]   On security complex theory, see Buzan 1983; and McSweeney 1999, 63-65.
[21]   See Waever et al 1993; also Buzan et al 1998.

i.e., those concerning, primarily, state sovereignty. Recognizing identity-based communities as self-constructed "imagined communities," the authors conclude that societal security, i.e., identity security, involves the perception of threats to a concept of "we" such that the reproduction of "us" might not be possible. Four major issues are seen as threats to societal security:

1. *Migration* – X people are being overrun or diluted by influxes of Y people; X identity is being changed by a shift in the composition of the population.
2. *Horizontal competition* – although X people are still living here, they will change their ways because of the overriding cultural and linguistic influence from the neighboring culture Y.
3. *Vertical competition* – people will stop seeing themselves as X, because there is either an integrating project (e.g., Russian Eurasia or the EU) or a secessionist-"regionalist" project that pulls them either to a wider or a narrower identity.
4. *Depopulation* – whether by plague, war, famine, natural catastrophe, or policies of extermination. Depopulations threaten identity by threatening its carriers.

The authors believe that EU integration does lead to the diminishing importance of the territorial state, the disappearance of borders, and the shift from a modern to a postmodern state with the desecuritization of most kinds of political, social and economic interactions, although not the disappearance of actual nations.

According to such a logic, the New Europe should become a civic polity with state-like superstructures, while nations decoupled from their states would retreat into some form of cultural self-cultivation (*Kulturnation* without *Staatnation*). Cultivation of national cultures without politicizing them would be the best security policy. "Simplistically, one can say, a sound relaxed national identity is the best guarantee against nationalism, against reactions of fear and defence" (Waever 1993, 70). (It remains to be seen whether the relative success of the UK's exit from the European Union might trigger a similar trend among EU member states to reassert territorial control over nation-state borders or stimulate further continental integration.)

However, until nationalisms are "satisfied" and national identities become "relaxed," the understanding of societal security, i.e., "identity security" will provide a good framework for the analysis of "new wars" that are based on identity politics.

Recent developments in international relations show the desirability of integrating sociological analysis into theories of international relations. The consequences of omitting sociological analysis, MacMillan and Linklater argue, are illustrated by the importance, simultaneously, of processes of globalization and fragmentation. They argue that:

> Realism sought to explain the survival and redrawing of boundaries by focusing upon the struggle for military power and the impact of inter-state war upon human society. But there is almost no analysis of how the members of a society understood the social bond that united them within the bounded community and separated them from the remainder of the world, and there are few resources in the realist approach for analysing the current challenge to political boundaries. (MacMillan and Linklater 1995, 13).

Transformations in the nature of political communities across the world due to the influence of globalization and fragmentation require the modification of traditional approaches to International Relations. This has put the levels of analysis problem in International Relations back on the agenda. Neither systemic nor subsystemic arguments have provided a definitive solution.

Barry Buzan (1995) suggests distinguishing, in a more precise way, sources of explanations and objects of analysis, so that levels can be understood as different types or sources of explanation for observed phenomena. The table, below, does this for the present analysis:

TABLE 1. Objects of analysis and sources of explanations

Objects of analysis	Sources of Explanations	
	Structure	*Process*
System	Security Community	New European Order
Subsystem	Nation-States	Nation-building
Societal Unit	National community	National mobilization
Bureaucracy	Governments	Nation-building
Individual	Cossacks	National agitation

This schema will serve as an approximate guide for the analysis of subsequent chapters of this study. More specifically, it will be used to identify the main conceptual issues involved in how the extension of the EU-NATO security community to include Central European states has influenced the societal security of Ukraine.

There is only one group of states in Europe that can qualify as a "security community" in Deutsch's terms: the NATO countries and their allies. The relationship between Russia and the FSU countries, initially highly interdependent, included collaboration on security issues. For instance, the Russian Federation was one of the signatories of Budapest Memorandum (1994) that assured Ukraine's sovereignty and territorial integrity. However, even before armed conflict over Crimea and Donbas started in 2014, these countries did not belong to a security community. They were at best a "no war community," i.e., a community whose member states are not likely to go to war but where war preparations are made just in case.

The following section explores the utility of the concept of societal security for analyzing the dynamics that arise between "satisfying" a majority's nationalism in order to legitimize democratic nation-building, and inter-state security dilemmas. It does so by examining the societal security of Ukraine in the context of the establishment of a new European order, the Eurasian Economic Union, Ukrainian nation-state-building, and the rise of Cossack ideology as a reflection of these changes.[22]

---

[22]   A detailed analysis of Cossack groups in Ukraine as revivalist "groups of patriots" at the stage of national agitation and mobilization is elaborated elsewhere (see Chapter 1, and Appendices 1 and 2 describing fieldwork methods, procedures and analysis involved in the study of the Cossack revival).

Societal security is understood here as an additional dimension of state security, expressed in terms of a threat to the Ukrainian identity as it is perceived by Ukrainian elites, the population as a whole, and by "groups of patriots" — Ukrainian Cossacks. This threat has arisen in the context of perceived injustice and corruption at the state level, external Russian armed aggression in Crimea and Donbas on the inter-state level, and the inability to join the EU and NATO security community on a systemic level. It is connected with the confrontation of nation-building polices in Ukraine with projections of ethno-geopolitics from Russia (a detailed analysis of ethno-geopolitics in Russia and Ukraine is presented in Chapter 4).

In addition to a discussion of societal security in Ukraine, the next section will describe the main tendencies within the contemporary identity process of the Ukrainian political elite, based on the analysis of election manifestos by presidential candidates, as well as of strategic documents and recent research on mass national consciousness in Ukraine. It also considers to what extent the new global reality of Western political and military dominance in Europe and a resurgent militant Russia influence the ways Ukrainians think of their future in terms of national dignity, well-being, and security. Central to this issue is the interaction between the emerging national "mythology" of the Ukrainians as people of the new independent state, loss of territorial control over Crimea, and protracted armed conflict in Donbas.

Some studies suggest that threats to the new emerging national identity of the Ukrainians, involving an existential threat from a neo-imperialist Russia (officially defined as an aggressor state in Ukrainian law) or from the NATO-led Western Alliance (in the case of the Russian minority in Ukraine), or both, can lead to an escalation of the security dilemma in Ukraine and its resolution through policies of nuclear deterrence. This section, together with fieldwork findings summarized in Appendix 1.2, shows how societal security discourses operate on different levels of analysis: in the inter-state system (system level), in the state (sub-system level), in Cossack movements (societal unit level), and governmental structures (bureaucracy level), and among Cossack leaders (individual level). In this way, sociological and international relations analysis are combined, and show how studies of security communities and societal security at different levels of analysis are complementary to studies of political communities and inter-state security.

3.3. The Security Community of EU-NATO and the Societal Security of Ukraine

The Yugoslav crisis was a landmark in the post-Cold War European order with important long-term consequences. The bombing of Belgrade by NATO allies to prevent the worsening of the humanitarian catastrophe in Kosovo, showed not only the military strength of NATO, but also dented the self-perception of Russia as a global power, crucial for decision-making in what it considers its nearby sphere of interests.

It was symbolic that the Kosovo operation occurred simultaneously with the enlargement of NATO to Central Europe, including Hungary, the Czech Republic and Poland, and despite strong objections from Russia. The Russian reaction was to test similar tactics of "peace-enforcement" internally.

It took only a few months for Russia to repeat, on a smaller scale in Dagestan and Chechnya, some tactics of NATO's new strategy of peace-enforcement, though with different outcomes. Rules seemed to be clarified and accepted. The US offered to provide Russia with intelligence assistance to fight "terrorism" on its legitimate soil and Russia accepted the presence of American troops in Central Asia and the Caucasus.

The terrain seemed to be also divided into ex-socialist states seeking integration into the EU and the rest of the FSU countries that have not made up their mind. This time, the division was based on existing national borders and national identities and therefore seemed to be fair. Those who have not made up their mind had only themselves to blame. Ukraine under President Kuchma, once referred to by the US as a lynchpin of European security, found itself among those undecided with so-called multi-vector foreign policy. The oligarch-dominated Ukrainian governments combined pro-

Western rhetoric with constant political and economic trade-offs with Russia, actively integrating themselves in the extensive FSU network of the shadow economy.

The New European Order that was proclaimed after the disintegration of the USSR, followed by NATO and EU enlargement in Eastern Europe, put Ukraine directly between the hammer and the hard place. The New European Order is a term used to define the security situation in Europe since the unification of Germany and collapse of the Warsaw Pact, as well as the end of the Soviet Union. It was characterized by the lack of ideological confrontation along the old division, but was also full of ambiguities in terms of security arrangements in Eastern Europe. The role of NATO was often perceived as keeping Russia content while enlarging the organization to the east, and at the same time keeping Eastern Europeans hopeful that their interests will be taken into consideration (Carr and Iffantis 1996). Diplomatic language or "pleasant semantic policy" was employed for this reason, when the enlargement of NATO was presented as an "opening of NATO" by means of programs like "Partnership for Peace" and the inclusion of Russia in a NATO council with separate status.

The bombardment of Yugoslavia in 1999, which coincided with a welcoming ceremony for the new NATO member states, clearly defined the new rules of engagement. The initial, furious, response from a humiliated Russia was joined by negative responses from Belarus, and to a lesser extent Ukraine, but also by such important international actors in Eurasia as China and India. This made it obvious that the construction of the new Europe's security framework did not have a coherent policy, based on the mutual trust and consensus.

As Grudzinski and van Ham put it, the postmodern approach to foreign policy issues within the Western community was combined with a tough, realistic approach toward "non-West" third parties. In other words, "the well-intentioned and widespread desire to see military force eliminated as a means of settling international disputes has proved to be realistic only for a part of Europe, but certainly not for Europe as a whole" (Grudzinski and van Ham 1999,

148). Western Europe is associated with a liberal-institutionalist understanding of security, while Russia and many other Eastern and southeastern European countries are dominated by a realist, state-as-actor mindset. The reason primarily is that the economies of Western European countries are increasingly interdependent and influenced by globalization, while Western state structures are becoming more fragmented and dominated by EU policies and legislation.

The widely shared view behind the process of European integration is that the challenge of globalization can be effectively met in the contemporary European context only by institutional inter-state and inter-societal integration that replaces previous modern national divisions, creating a collective European entity within a single economic and political framework. Apart from the transnational economy, another key component of integration is the development of a transnational civil society, ensuring that purely state interests do not dominate societies. It is also assumed that civil society processes possess effective mechanisms for dealing with social and state security issues. Precisely for this reason, liberal democracies do not go to war with each other (Kaldor 1999). This is not the case, however, with developing democracies and those societies where civil society is weak or non-existent. It is also clear that newly established democracies in Eastern Europe had to rely on nationalism as the integrating force of their national, as well as foreign, policy (Prizel 1998, 413-417).

For most Central and Eastern European countries this situation continued well into the twenty-first century, despite the fact that their free-market economies have eventually integrated into the EU and the wider global economic community. Conservative center-right governments came to dominate Poland, Hungary and the Czech Republic from 2000 onwards, while the Baltic countries chose a deliberate policy of limiting the voting rights of their respective Russian-speaking minorities from the early days of their independence.

For some Eastern European states, including Ukraine and Moldova, with weaker economies, being a buffer between a resurgent Russia and the EU/NATO led to a similar realist stance in their foreign policies. Russian threats of a "Cold Peace" and redeployment of SS-20s in its European territories, even before the Kosovo crisis, were the first signals, ignored by the West, before Putin's rise to power. A large part of the Russian elite considered NATO enlargement to be a "demonstration of certain cruelty" and a "mistake on a world-historical scale" (Gadzshiev 1998, 323). Within a decade, Russia would invade Georgia with President Putin directly quoting the Kosovo example as a blueprint for an "independent South Ossetia and Abkazia."

All attempts by the Ukrainian leadership to avoid a buffer-zone scenario, either via the Central European Security Zone (1993), or the Nuclear Weapons Free Zone (1996), initiatives that would bind Ukraine to Central Europe, did not bring desirable results. The reason why Ukrainian leaders were so concerned with Russian resurgence in the 1990s cannot be explained by state-centric security theories alone. Ukraine concluded multilateral agreements with Russia, obtaining guarantees of territorial integrity in exchange for nuclear weapons, and possessed a large army equipped with some of the best Soviet hardware and well-trained security forces. Despite all of Moscow's reassurances, successive Ukrainian governments courted NATO, something that could be better explained by the inherent threat to the societal security of Ukraine.

As mentioned earlier, the concept of societal security was developed by the European Security Group at the Centre for Peace and Conflict Research in Copenhagen to reflect on the structural transformation in European Security at the end of the Cold War. Society is considered to be not simply another sector of state security with the other sectors traditionally defined as political, military, economic and environmental. The authors argue that society is a distinctive referent alongside the state, so it needs to be considered through the duality of societal and state security. This could be especially important where nation and state do not coincide. In these situations, the security of the nation may increase the insecurity of the state by generating insecurity among minorities (Brubaker 1996). In this way, societal security is to be understood as the security of a social agent which has an independent reality and which is more than and different from the sum of its parts.

Indeed, Ukrainian state security could only benefit from the presence of the powerful military and economic alliance on Ukraine's borders as a stabilizing factor, as well as from the EU's financial assistance. "The concept of the National Security of Ukraine," adopted by the parliament on 16 January 1997, in fact considered integration into the European and world community a priority, above other national interests.

This, however, was not the case for societal security, where a fragile balance of national consensus was put at risk. Ukraine had an eclectic national identity in which the post-Soviet population did not initially share a common national mythology, or even a common language (Wilson 1997). When the overwhelming majority of the population in Ukraine voted for independence, they did so more on the basis of economic considerations, rather than out of cultural nationalism, hoping for a more prosperous independent Ukraine. It is this unfulfilled dream of prosperity in the independent Ukraine which will suffer most as a consequence of the acceptance of Ukraine's immediate Western neighbors into the EU, and the subsequent new visa restrictions for Ukrainian citizens. This concern was openly voiced by the Minister of Foreign Affairs of Ukraine, Borys Tarasyuk, in 1998:

> Drastic changes in the current trade, customs, and visa regulations on the bilateral level will lead to a worsening of the economic situation in those countries left outside the EU. The gap between the levels of involvement of different countries in the European integration process will widen, and it is already resulting in the re-emergence of new dividing lines in Europe, and the appearance of new threats to its stability and security.[23]

The extension of the European Security Community to include Ukraine's immediate Western neighbors (Poland, Slovakia and Hungary), a change at the systemic level of analysis, was perceived in Ukraine (sub-system level) as leaving it exposed and vulnerable to

---

[23] Bory Tarasyuk, "Ukraine in the World," in Lubomyr A. Hajda, ed., *Ukraine in the World. Studies in the International Relations and Security Structure of a Newly Independent State* (Cambridge, MA: Harvard University Press, 1998)

increasing Russian influence. Ukrainian ruling elites, coming mostly from the Russian-speaking Eastern industrial heartland, chose a civic nationalist model for independent nation-states and granted full rights to Russian-speaking, non-ethnic Ukrainians who lived in the territory of Ukraine when the Soviet Union dissolved. This inclusive model was chosen partly because of the Soviet legacy, when Russians were a privileged minority, but also partly because of the weakness of ethnic Ukrainian nationalism (outside of Western Ukraine). Therefore, the Russian minority along with culturally Russian-speaking Ukrainian oligarchs retained disproportionally high influence over Ukrainian internal and foreign policy. All attempts by the Ukrainian state expert-led institutions to advance national security through deeper integration with the EU and NATO were sabotaged by the pro-Russian ruling elite minority. At the same time, Russian pressure to move the Ukrainian state toward re-integration would trigger massive street protests by the Ukrainian majority. Such massive protests happened at least three times in less than 25 years of independence and became known respectively as the student Revolution on the Granite (1990), the Orange Revolution (2004-2005) and the Revolution of Dignity (2013-14). All attempts to increase the security of the Ukrainian state would decrease the societal security of Ukraine by threatening the dominant pro-Russian minority, whose rule defied Ukrainian national interests and subsequently continued to threaten Ukrainian national identity.

With President Putin's rise to power, Ukrainian nation-state-building, based on civic nationalism, increasingly found itself on a collision course with the Russian Eurasianist project that aimed at the inclusion of Ukraine into a bigger Supra-State structure. Parts of the Ukrainian political elite supported the Russian reintegration scenario and promoted it during the parliamentary elections in Ukraine (2002) under the slogan "Towards Europe with Russia." Similar ideas were pushed by the "Russian bloc" in 2007, Party of Regions in 2012, the Opposition Bloc in 2015, and the For Life Bloc in the 2019 elections. The power struggle between the Russian-speaking *pro-Russian minority elites* and the Ukrainian-speaking *pro-Western majority* represented vertical and horizontal competition in

Ukrainian society and increased the societal insecurity of Ukraine. The relationship between the EU-NATO security Community and its influence on Russian and Ukrainian nationalisms can be analyzed by the modeling of various scenario outcomes below.

3.1.1 Presidential Election Campaigns in Ukraine (1999-2019) as Reflection of Societal Security Concerns

Ukraine's frustration with its inability to manage the struggling economy and the wait-and-see attitude of the EU was reflected in the 1999 presidential elections in Ukraine, where most of the candidates were racing to put the blame on the incumbent President Kuchma and his multi-vector foreign policy. Rival candidates concerned themselves not only with the corruption scandals in Kuchma's close circles, but also with the inefficient and wasteful management of Western financial help.

The most influential rivals from the left, such as communist leader Petro Symonenko, and the leader of the Progressive Socialists, Nataliya Vitrenko, rejected the idea of Western aid and called for collaboration with Russia and Belarus as well as economic self-reliance. Other more moderate contenders from the left, Oleksandr Tkachenko and Oleksandr Moroz, called for the review of programs with the IMF and World Bank. Criticism of the way in which previous Ukrainian governments had handled collaboration with Western financial institutions was expressed by other, less influential candidates, such as the leader of the Slav movement in Ukraine, Oleksandr Bazyliuk, who believed that the geopolitical relationship with the West should be based on a Slav Union, the CIS and a broad-based coalition of anti-NATO states including China, India and others. Bazyliuk supported the idea of

> a reasonable combination of market and state economy, but not in a way that current government does it, rushing about in search of a way out of the deadlock, heeding Western advisors like the IMF and the World Bank, impoverishing Ukraine and drawing it into the trap of debts...[24]

---

[24] "Program of Ukrainian Presidential Candidate Oleksandr Bazylyuk," in *Holos Ukrainy*, 15 September 1999.

Even pro-Western candidates, such as the leaders of the two *Rukh's* organizations, Yuriy Kostenko and to a lesser degree Henadiy Udovenko, criticized government economic policy. The former Minister of Justice and presidential Candidate, Vasyl Onopenko, who joined Kostenko in the proclaimed Union of national-democratic forces, said: "In Ukraine government and power are as corrupt as in Moscow where different clans rule."[25] Another influential pro-Western presidential candidate, Yevhen Marchuk, former Prime Minister and head of the Ukrainian Security Service, almost openly led a campaign against the corruption of Kuchma's government. During his visit to Odesa, Marchuk accused the incumbent president of betraying the national interests of Ukraine by freezing the oil terminal project to please Ukrainian and Russian oligarchs. According to Marchuk, Odesan projects were not only Ukraine's bridges to Europe, but also significant factors in the weakening of Ukraine's dependence on Russia.[26]

Criticism of the Ukrainian government and, indirectly, of Western institutions, seemed to be so widespread that President Kuchma himself could not help but join the critical voices. He criticized the Foreign Ministry for being incapable of persuading the European Union to take a more favorable stance on Ukraine, and he also criticized the EU. During a visit to Salzburg for the World Economic Forum in 1999, Kuchma accused the West of hypocrisy and neglect with respect to Ukraine. Asked by Reuters if he was satisfied with the level of support Ukraine was receiving from the West, he replied:

> "In fact, there is none. There is just talk, nothing else. We have promises. Could you explain the strategy of the European Union towards Ukraine? When we ask such a question, we do not understand the answer." Referring to criticism of the slow pace of reform Kuchma added: "When the West starts to discuss the pace of reform ... in my view there is a sort of hypocrisy, nothing else. ...We cannot be compared with any other Eastern European country."[27]

---

[25]   "Onopenko ne vykliuchaye mozshlyvosti zaprovadzhennia v Ukraini nadzvychaynoho stanu," *UNIAN*, 14 September 1999, 4.

[26]   Yevhen Marchuk, "Odeski proekty — nashi mosty v Yevropu, hoch Kuchma zviv yihniu sut' do habariv baronam," in *Den'*, No. 171, 1999 (electronic version).

[27]   *Reuters Financial.* Economy-Ukraine-Kuchma. By Richard Murphy, July 1, 1999.

Neither critical rhetoric, nor reference to his 145 economic decrees could help President Kuchma explain to the Ukrainian people why the country was not doing better. In fact, two thirds of the population recognized that they lived on the edge, or under the line, of poverty. Officially 4% and unofficially up to 30% of people of working age were practically unemployed (formally often on unpaid leave). Every second family in the small towns survived, at the end of twentieth century, by working plots of land on which they grew vegetables.[28] However, the perception of the causes of the worsening situation in the country was not directly reflected in public opinion. According to Valeriy Matvienko, president of the Ukrainian-American Center of Strategic Communication, only 39.6% of people in Ukraine believed in 1998 that it was the president who was responsible for the situation in Ukraine, while around 44% expressed the Soviet stereotype of there being "a plot by world imperialism against Ukraine and the other CIS countries."[29] President Kuchma successfully exploited these sentiments as well as state administrative resources to get elected for a second term in office. He became the only president in Ukraine to serve two full terms in the post.

3.1.2 Influence of the EU-NATO Security Community Expansion on Russian-Ukrainian Relations

The Ukrainian National Institute of Strategic Studies noted at the end 1990s that the key difference in opinion polls between the intellectual elite and the general public related to the possibility of a military alliance for Ukraine. The first clause of the "State program for Ukraine's collaboration with NATO till the year 2001" stated that full-scale integration into European and North-Atlantic structures, as well as participation in the pan-European security system, is a strategic goal of Ukraine. The program was approved by a presidential decree in November 1998. In fact, the majority of Ukrainian experts supported this document at the time, while only one third of the

---

28 Lvivshchyna—98. Sotsialnyi portret v zahalnoukrayinskomu konteksti. Lviv (NANU, 1999): 213-224.

29 "Samovidchuttia hromadian Ukrainy za rik do prezydentskyh vyboriv," in *Den'*, No. 209, 1998 (electronic version).

population considered collaboration with NATO as a positive factor. About the same number could not make up their minds, and the majority of the public listed collaboration with NATO as a much lower priority than collaboration with Russia.[30]

At the height of NATO's bombing in Yugoslavia, 54% of the population, according to the polls conducted by the Kyiv Center for Political Research and Conflict Studies,[31] believed that Ukraine should halt (32%) or stop (22%) cooperation with NATO. 41% wanted President Kuchma to condemn NATO's military operations, while 49% of respondents thought that the Ukrainian president should not give an evaluation of NATO's action but should issue peacekeeping initiatives. In this way, events in Kosovo stimulated those undecided to make up their mind. As Sherr and Main noted:

> It [the campaign in Kosovo] has exposed Ukraine's impotence and its dependence on the geopolitical calculations of others. In practical terms, NATO's policy over Yugoslavia has injured the standing of a pro-Western President on the eve of an electoral contest against reactionary, vengeful and very anti-Western opponents … Pressures for Ukraine to re-examine its core foreign policy assumptions are now considerable. (Sherr and Main 1999, 2)

The fear in Kyiv was that enlargement of the EU and NATO under such conditions would freeze divisions within Ukrainian society and make it impossible for the political elite to promote closer cooperation with the West. Indeed, President Kuchma chose to dismiss his openly pro-Western and pro-NATO Foreign Minister, Borys Tarasyuk,[32] in September 2000 and nominated the old Soviet diplomat Anatoliy Zlenko to lead Ukrainian foreign policy once again, altering the balance between Russia and the West. Opinion polls showed that negative attitudes concerning NATO expansion toward

---

[30] "Dodatok. Sociologichni doslidzshennia zovnishnio-politychnyh I geopolitychnyh oriyentatsiy Ukrainy ta ii polityky u sferi bezpeky," http://www.niss.gov.ua/book/oglj ad/dod.htm, 20.

[31] M. Pohrebynskyi, "Presidential elections in Ukraine: Could Kuchma have a real competitor?", in *Nezavisimaya Gazeta*, 17 August 1999.

[32] Foreign Minister Tarasiuk claimed back in 1999 that the European idea was becoming a Ukrainian national idea uniting the whole society. Tarasyuk believed that a revival of Ukrainian and European identity would be a platform for the integration of Ukraine and the EU (Interfax-Ukraine, 24 November 1999 9:32 gmt).

Ukraine grew to 50.2% by 2001, compared to 46.1% a year before. 56.6% of respondents believed that NATO had no right to intervene by force in sovereign countries to solve humanitarian problems.[33]

The pressure on President Kuchma increased even more after 2000, when he was implicated in a scandal involving the murder of an opposition journalist and alleged illegal arms sales. The presidential security officer who taped Kuchma's conversation with top officials in his office and then made his accusations public took asylum in the USA. President Kuchma and his advisors interpreted this as an attempt by the West to remove him from his post and install in his place the even more pro-Western Viktor Yuschenko, who was Prime Minister at the time. Although it is unclear who instructed ex-KGB Major Melnychenko to tape Kuchma's office and publish numerous accusations, the consequences of this act clearly damaged the relationship between Ukraine and the West.

In this context, Ukraine's decision to apply for NATO membership announced on 23 May 2002 and formally welcomed by the NATO summit in Prague (21 November 2002) seems to be a diplomatic move to "re-brand" President Kuchma's own image in the West. According to the sociological national survey conducted by the Razumkov Center in February 2002, only 14.4% of respondents wanted Ukraine to join NATO immediately and 36.3% at some point in future, leaving 30.5% negative and 18.8% undecided toward NATO membership.[34]

The tape scandal was also used by Russia to increase its influence with the Ukrainian leadership; so, while President Kuchma did not make a single official visit to the West between fall 2000 and spring 2002, he met President Putin at least a dozen times. Kuchma's cold reception at the NATO summit in Prague in November 2002 was presented in Kyiv as a diplomatic victory, but, in fact, looked more like an embarrassment.

---

[33]   Razumkov Ukrainian Center for Economic and Political Studies published this data in *Natsionalna Bezpeka I Oborona*, No. 9 (2001), 1-3.

[34]   M. Pashko, V. Chalyi, "Zovnishnia polityka Ukraiyny pislia parlamentskyh vyboriv: mozhlyvi korektyvy," in *Zerkalo Niedieli*, 16-22 March 2002 (electronic version).

Thus, the initiative in the geopolitical arena was handed to Russia's policies on the "near abroad," which, as Tor Bukkvoll suggested, could develop relations between Russia and Ukraine according to four major scenarios:

1. nationalists in Ukraine and nationalists in Russia;
2. nationalists in Ukraine and moderates in Russia;
3. moderates in Ukraine and nationalists in Russia;
4. moderates in Ukraine and moderates in Russia.

The relationship between the two states under Presidents Kuchma and Yeltsin resembled the most favorable scenario of two moderate executive powers. The situation changed, however, when Vladimir Putin took over the Kremlin in 1999. Russian influence on Ukraine has increased economically via privatization by Russian businesses of some key strategic infrastructure and the exploitation of the weakened position of President Kuchma, whose reputation was tarnished by the tape scandal (known also as "Kuchmagate").

This development shifted the relationship between the two countries toward the third scenario: of moderates in Ukraine and nationalists in Russia, which, according to Bukkvoll, was both likely and quite dangerous, since the Russian elite tend to misinterpret Ukrainian resistance to full reintegration as "disguised Ukrainian nationalism" (Bukkvoll 1997, 88-94). Here it is important that in Bukkvoll's schemes the difference between Russian moderates and Russian nationalists in relation to Ukraine is that the former would refrain from using force to integrate Ukraine back into a single Russian supra-state, while the latter would "consider most means of achieving integration justifiable, including, in the last instance, military force" (Bukkvoll 1997, 89). In other words, the difference between moderate Russian policy toward Ukraine and the more aggressive nationalist policy of reintegration was a question of tactics, as neither moderates nor nationalists in Russia rejected the reintegration model.

Indeed, Moscow mayor Yuriy Luzshkov, who managed to unite a substantial political force into a powerful pre-election political alliance, *Nashe Otechestvo Vsia Rosiia*, not only repeatedly claimed that Crimea and Sevastopol are Russian, but also believed that the majority of Russians supported him, demanding a new tougher policy toward Ukraine. In an interview with Krymskaya Pravda, Louzhkov claimed that it was necessary to return Crimea and Sevastopol to Russia, as they had been "unreasonably" ceded to Ukraine in the distribution of territories.[35] Louzhkov demanded that President Kuchma fulfill previous pre-election promises and provide Crimea with economic independence, dual citizenship, and the introduction of Russian as a second state language.

Reintegration of Ukraine with Russia had cultural, economic but most of all strategic objectives. On the one hand, it was vitally important for Russia to preserve Ukrainian participation in a common air defense system, military-industrial complex production value chains, and to have access to the human resources of high-tech industries located in Southeastern Ukraine. On the other hand, according to military analysts, if Ukraine reunited with Russia, Russia could reduce the imbalance vis-à-vis Western military forces in Europe by at least one-and-a-half to two times, if not eliminate it entirely. "This would constitute a major change in the military-strategic situation in Europe" (Perepelytsia 1999, 195). Russia started reinforcing its military capability in Europe under President Yeltsin. In October 1999 fighter jets of the Russian Black Sea fleet were upgraded from the Su-17 to the Su-24. These were not merely more modern, but also capable of carrying nuclear weapons. According to the former Ukrainian Minister of Defense Veleriy Shmarov, Ukraine did not have the capability of carrying out inspections on the Russian jets in Crimea in order to check whether they complied with the agreement against mounting special devices enabling planes to carry such weapons, or to ensure that no nuclear weapons were deployed on Ukrainian territory.[36]

The military pressure on Ukraine was tempting, since the Russian military believed that "Ukraine, in essence, is literally defenceless against any future Russian intrusion ... both psychologically

---

[35]   *UNIAN*, August 3, 1999 1550 gmt (BBC monitoring).
[36]   Interview by Valeriy Shmarov with BBC World Service (Ukrainian section) on 30 September 1999.

and materially' (Molchanov 1998, 9). The moderates-nationalists scenario, hinted at by Bukkvoll (15 years before it was actually played out) did not exclude a small-scale, military action confined to Crimea. Russian policy initially was limited to covert subversion of the Ukrainian government and state-capture through "active measures" familiar to President Putin as a former KGB operative.

Discredited by an ex-KGB member of his security detail, President Kuchma's attempt to hand over his presidency to a chosen successor, Prime Minister Viktor Yanukovych, in 2004 led to the mass protests known as the Orange revolution. Yanukovych was widely believed to have been recruited by the KGB in his impoverished and violent youth. This was later confirmed by the ex-head of the Ukrainian Security Service Valentyn Nalyvaychecnko, and is the likely explanation for how Yanukovych, an ex-convict, made the smooth and sudden transition from the criminal underworld to being a respected Soviet industry manager, regional politician and finally a prime minister of Ukraine (Nalyvaychenko 2017). On two visits to Kyiv, President Putin took considerable pains to demonstrate that Yanukovych was his preferred presidential candidate in the 2004 elections, therefore lending his clout to a weaker candidate who appeared to be losing to his arch-rival Viktor Yuschenko. When the electoral committee announced victory for Yanukovych, contrary to exit-polls, a million-strong crowd of orange-clad protesters filled Maidan Square in Kyiv and did not leave until the rerun of the second round and victory for the opposition leader Yuschenko in January 2005. This was a major blow not only to Yanukovych, but also to President Putin's self-esteem and geopolitical calculations.

Yuschenko was a liberal former banker, ex-prime minister and, among other titles, an enthusiastic Cossack Hetman whose election symbolized the victory of national-democrats over the ex-Communist nomenklatura, the pro-Russian oligarchy, and the Kremlin's covert meddling. He wanted Ukraine to become both a liberal democracy and a nation-state based on traditional Ukrainian values, including its Cossack traditions of free elections of Hetmans, self-government and strong local communities. Yuschenko's foreign policy meant to take Ukraine toward both EU and NATO membership in order to benefit from the EU-NATO security community, and, initially, it looked like he had every chance of success. Yuschenko was the only foreign head of state in living memory who received a standing ovation in the US Congress during his visit in April 2005 as the embodiment of the victory of Western liberalism in Eastern Europe, the defiance of Russian clandestine interference, and for his personal courage to fight for the presidency after suffering serious poisoning during the election campaign. However, personal health ailments, a chaotic management style, and team infighting did not allow Yuschenko to capitalize on his popularity with EU and NATO leaders and achieve significant progress toward membership in both organizations. Yuschenko's hope of joining NATO was dashed when Russia invaded Georgia in the summer of 2008, and it became clear that the Russian-Ukrainian relationship would develop via the moderates-nationalists scenario much faster than anyone could have envisaged. President Putin was determined to get his protégé in Ukraine, Viktor Yanukovych, back in power, making sure that he kept Ukraine within the Russian orbit and, eventually, the Eurasian Economic Union. Once Yanukovych was elected president in 2010, capitalizing on Russian support and widespread disap- pointment with Yuschenko's presidency, Moscow gradually placed Russian citizens and local reliable cadres in control of the Ukrainian security apparatus. This signified a nearly successful attempt of cov- ert state-capture, leading to significant destruction of the Ukrainian Armed Forces' war fighting capabilities, paralysis of the security forces and change in foreign policy orientation (see *The Struggle for Ukraine* 2017). Instead of signing the long negotiated Ukraine-EU Association Agreement in November 2013, President Yanukovych chose alignment with the Eurasian Economic Union — the Kremlin's platform for integrating former USSR territories under neo-Eurasian ideology. Despite all of the Kremlin's efforts, a mass protest in Kyiv, known as Euro-Maidan or the Revolution of Dignity, led initially to a clampdown by the security forces, and then to the fall of the Yanu- kovych regime in January 2014. President Putin personally instruct- ed the Russian army to begin the invasion of Crimea, which would become the start of a long armed conflict with Ukraine lasting longer than the so-called Great Patriotic War—a foundation myth of Soviet military glory in the twentieth century. With Crimea lost and Donbas in flames, the new president of Ukraine Petro Poroshenko would be elected based on the single electoral promise to end the war within weeks of the June 2014 elections. Poroshenko's victory reflected the hope of Ukrainian society that war with Russia over Crimea and Donbas was a matter of negotiations with the Kremlin; and Poroshenko looked like the best person for the job. A good communicator who spoke fluent Russian and English, a successful billionaire oligarch, Poroshenko was one of the co-founders of the pro-Russian Party of Regions, a foreign minister in Yuschenko's administration and an economy minister in Yanukovych's administration. He had extensive commercial interests in Crimea and the Russian Federation and a reputation as a pragmatic businessman. Before running for the presidency, Poroshenko took advice from another oligarch, Dmytro Firtash, who was widely believed to be linked to Gazprom and, therefore, the Kremlin. Once elected, President Poroshenko indeed seemed to keep the back door open to negotiations with the Kremlin, despite tough official rhetoric in support of Ukrainian independence and against Russian hybrid war on Ukraine. In July 2014, the Ukrainian parliament declared the Russian Federation an aggressor state:

> Since February 2014, Ukraine has been suffering the aggression from a state guaranteeing its independence and territorial integrity. The Russian Federation occupied two regions of Ukraine—the Autonomous Republic of Crimea and the city of Sevastopol—and engaged in active destabilization of the southern and eastern regions of Ukraine. Unsupported by the Ukrainian citizens in the south and east of the country, the government of the Russian Federation started organizing a terrorist war against Ukraine. (*Resolution of the Verkhovna Rada of Ukraine, No. 1597-VII On Measures to Prevent Expansion of International Terrorism Supported by the Russian Federation, 22 July 2014* https://goo.gl/svqdwB).

However, no meaningful negotiations could take place once inter-state armed conflict reached the scale of army-on-army confrontation and ended in the devastating defeat of Ukrainian battle formations near Illovaysk in August 2014. With the mediation of Paris and Berlin, Moscow imposed on Ukraine the so-called Minsk Agreements that would call for a ceasefire between Kyiv and Russian proxy state formations — the People's Republics of Donetsk and Luhansk. In its preliminary report, the Prosecution of the International Criminal Court in the Hague referred to the events in Crimea as an international armed conflict between Ukraine and the Russian Federation, and stated that the situation within the territory of Crimea and Sevastopol factually amounts to an on-going state of occupation (Preliminary Report, November 2016 https://goo.gl/mOEA Vd). NATO's Parliamentary Assembly condemned Russia's military, economic and information *aggression against Ukraine*, and expressed concern about the persistent failure to implement the Minsk Agreements due to the almost daily violation of the ceasefire in eastern Ukraine by Russia and its proxies (Resolution 431 Supporting Nato's Post-Warsaw Defence and Deterrence Posture, 2016 https://goo.gl/ozrOnI). The Parliamentary Assembly of the Council of Europe (PACE) recognized in its fact-finding report that the Donbas conflict is a Russian aggression (Report 14130: Political consequences of the conflict in Ukraine 2016 https://goo.gl/fB3zN2). The UN General Assembly passed a "Resolution on the Situation of human rights in the Autonomous Republic of Crimea and the city of Sevastopol (Ukraine)" that affirms the territorial integrity of Ukraine; the Russian Federation is referred to as the occupying Power and the Autonomous Republic of Crimea and the city of Sevastopol are deemed temporarily occupied territory (December 2016 https://goo.gl/81vUas). Western sanctions were imposed on Russia over the 5 years of the conflict, but it would be Ukrainians who would pay the ultimate price of the continuing war effort, with over 13,000 killed and over one and a half million internally displaced people.

The Russian government consistently denied its aggression against Ukraine and presented this armed conflict internationally as a "civil war" between Kyiv and its separatist regions. The Kremlin's designs on Ukraine did not include the separation of Donbas for the sake of integrating it into the Russian Federation as was the case with Crimea. After all formal and informal negotiations, President Poroshenko stated in the Ukrainian parliament that Russia aims at turning the occupied territories into a so-called "Donbas protectorate, infiltrating it on their conditions into the Ukrainian state in order to undermine us from within ... [W]e will not allow this and refuse to accept it" (President's annual address to Verkhovna Rada, "On Ukraine's internal and international situation in 2016"). Despite genuine efforts to reach an agreement with Russia, President Poroshenko failed in his key electoral pledge and lost his re-election campaign.

The new Ukrainian president Volodymyr Zelensky elected in April 2019 would still face the same challenges without a peaceful settlement acceptable to all parties in sight. The Ukrainian-Russian relationship evolved from a no war community, to a no peace community where war is not declared but conducted via proxy separatist entities under full Russian command and control. Waging this new generation war in Europe became the "new normal" to the extent that the Parliamentary Assembly of the Council of Europe invited the Russian delegation to resume its work without any preconditions in June 2019, despite earlier sanctions linked to the illegal annexation of Crimea and armed conflict in Donbas. Emboldened by such recognition, the Russian authorities in Crimea even announced a compensation claim to Ukraine for underinvesting in Crimean infrastructure of 2.5 billion roubles between 1991 and 2014. President Putin triumphantly declared that the world domination of Western liberalism is dead. (FT interview, June 28 2019)

Russian strategic calculations that Western resolve to counter annexation of Crimea would wither away sooner or later turned out to be realistic. Despite the limited sanctions and Cold War 2.0 rhetoric, Western businesses have not abandoned their quest to capitalize on Russian state procurement programs, a strong indication of intent that the Russian president never fails to mention at international forums. The Russian TV channel Rossiya reported President Trump's words that it was "great honor" to meet President Putin at the G20 summit in June 2019.

Five years of armed conflict in Donbas left Ukrainians impoverished, the economy indebted to international loans, society exhausted by the constant loss of human life on the frontline, and the international community gradually becoming indifferent to the loss of

Ukrainian territory due to ongoing Russian aggression. Kyiv faces the real risk of Russian-led Donbas separatists returning to the Ukrainian parliament as MPs if the Kremlin's plan to reunite Donbas with Ukraine were accepted by the Ukrainian government under pressure from Berlin and Paris, key signatories of the Minsk cease-fire agreements. Considering that the country is awash with weapons and experienced fighters it is not difficult to predict a violent backlash by Ukrainian radicals who would not accept Putin's "peace plan" without a fight. The worst case scenario—a nationalist government in Kyiv and another in Russia cannot be discounted.

A nationalist government in Kyiv would be relatively weak vis-à-vis Moscow and could only rely on asymmetric response to counterbalance a strong nationalist government in Russia. Ukraine's under-funded army is unlikely to prevail against a much larger and better equipped Russian army in case of a full-scale invasion (the ultimate state security threat). Russia's ongoing covert attempt to capture the Ukrainian state from within constitutes an existential threat to its societal security (preventing Ukrainians from remaining as they are under external aggression). Putin's ideology of Eurasianism denies the right of Ukrainians to exist as a separate people outside the larger "one people" (Russian civilization) neo-Eurasian construct. If the worst case scenario looks unavoidable, where both state and societal security are existentially threatened, it is not impossible that a "nationalist" government in Ukraine could revert to the ultimate weapon of the weak, i.e., the nuclear deterrence option. This does not have to mean an expensive, long-term project of nuclear missile production and deployment, although the experience of India and Pakistan shows that "nuclear" pride is a "cheap" way to win national support for the governments.

With the sufficient potential of Soviet-built conventional tactical missiles (e.g., OTR-21, "Tochka"), Ukraine already possesses Soviet produced nuclear artillery systems (e.g., the 203mm self-propelled gun "Pion," the MLRS BM-27 "Uragan," etc.) capable of delivering nuclear projectiles or missiles. Although officially all nuclear artillery shells were removed from Ukraine in the early 1990s, "Pion" is technically capable of delivering an enhanced radiation weapon

(ERW) charge, i.e., a low yield thermonuclear weapon. In fact, a Live Journal blogger published videos in May 2015 showing that such a weapon was allegedly detonated by the Ukrainian Armed Forces in Donetsk on 8 February 2015, at the same time as the crucial Debaltsevo battle against Russian-led separatists (https://ermalex76.livejournal.com/706254.html). With no independent corroboration, these videos could represent an attempt at military nuclear deception while playing a weak hand (not necessarily by a state actor). Ukraine's technical capability of producing such charges, however, has not been disputed.

At the same time, Ukraine inherited Soviet technology for building conventional medium-range missiles, although the ability to produce strategic nuclear missiles (SS-24s) was most likely lost during the nuclear disarmament process of the 1990s. The sentiments of the Ukrainian leadership regarding the loss of Ukrainian nuclear potential were expressed at the highest level, and Ukrainian experts never excluded reconsideration of this option under certain circumstances. President Kuchma said in Sevastopol back in 1999: "I am very sorry that we have split and do not have nuclear weapons, because the nuclear shield was forged in Ukraine."[37] Manzhola and Galaka thought at the time that the deployment of NATO's nuclear warheads in Central Europe and the inevitable Russian response could be the trigger for Ukraine to reconsider the nuclear option. They criticized Western experts and politicians who "seem to have difficulty understanding that the main motivation behind Ukraine's decision to become a non-nuclear state and reject the Russian 'nuclear umbrella' was a strategic choice in favour of integration into the larger Europe and its structures, in particular the EU" (Manzhola and Galaka 1999, 115). Yet, being unable to integrate Ukraine into the EU and NATO, and being under existential pressure from the Russian armed forces, Ukrainian authorities could come to favor this extreme option in line with a global tendency, where nuclear armament has become a weapon of the "weak." This in fact was predicted by University of Chicago professor John Mearsheimer back in 1993.

---

[37]   "Leonid Kuchma 'vziav' Sevastopol," in *Den'*, No. 82, 1999 (electronic version).

He wrote that Ukraine would be justified in keeping Soviet nuclear arms since it "cannot defend itself against a nuclear-armed Russia with conventional weapons, and no state, including the United States, is going to extend to it a meaningful security guarantee" (Mearsheimer 1993, 50).

Within months of Crimea's annexation, a group of centrist parliamentarians proposed that Ukraine withdraw from the Treaty on Nonproliferation of Nuclear Weapons (NPT). In July 2014, a right-wing "Svoboda" faction of the Ukrainian parliament introduced a bill on the renewal of Ukraine's nuclear status. By the end of 2014, half of the Ukrainian population supported the renewal of Ukraine's nuclear status (49.3% up from the previous high of 33% in 1994) (Ukrayinska Pravda, 7 October 2014 http://www.pravda.com.ua/news/2014/10/7/7040018/.)

According to a feasibility study conducted by the National Space Agency of Ukraine (NSAU) back in 1993, developing an indigenous control and guidance system for the Ukrainian-built SS-24s, including a centrifuge enrichment facility, and building a warhead production facility would only be a matter of time (6-18 months) and resources (approx. $3bn) (Budjeryn 2017, 22). Mariana Budjerin who interviewed key 1990s decision makers on nuclear disarmament arrived at the conclusion that "Ukraine has a far greater indigenous technological capacity and nuclear starter package than other nuclear aspirants like India, Pakistan, or North Korea that doggedly pursued a nuclear option and, despite economic hardship and international opprobrium, succeeded." She concluded that only lack of "deterrence-thinking" precluded the Ukrainian leadership, including President Kravchuk, from opting for the nuclear deterrence option in defense (Budjeryn and Sinovets 2017, 30). In other words, the Ukrainian ruling elite has had both the rationale and the ability to opt for nuclear deterrence but until now *has not decided on such a course* due to its international commitments and cultural mindset. The latter might be at least partly explained by the experience of the Chernobyl nuclear accident creating aversion to nuclear technology in principle. The fact that the US government withdrew from the Intermediate-Range Nuclear Forces Treaty on 4 August

2019, while the Russian Federation deployed intermediate nuclear-capable missiles in Kaliningrad and likely in Crimea, rendered Ukraine's restrictive obligations under the now defunct INF treaty arguably void as well. This sentiment was expressed by Mykhailo Samus, a deputy chief of international issues at the Center for Army, Conversion and Disarmament Studies:

> So, amid the ongoing war with Russia, it would be better for us if no such treaty was in place so that we could safely begin the development and production of medium- and short-range missiles, which could become a tool to deter Russian aggression, and, therefore, create conditions under which the Russians would beware Ukraine. After all, now Moscow is convinced that there is no threat coming from Ukraine. And this unties Russia's hands, for example, in the actions we observed last November near the Kerch Strait. Europeans cannot ban Ukraine from moving in this direction. There are no mechanisms in place to allow Europe doing this.
> (Quoted in UNIAN: https://www.unian.info/world/10642002-termination-of-inf-treaty-implications-for-ukraine-and-beyond.html 6 Aug 2019)

As former US ambassador to Ukraine Steven Pifer (served in Kyiv from 1998 to 2000) explicitly pointed out: "if Kyiv decides to withdraw from the INF Treaty and consider building its own intermediate-range missiles, it should be able to do so without fearing or facing a negative reaction from the United States" (Pifer 2019).

The worst case scenario of a clash between nuclear-armed nationalist governments in both Russia and Ukraine is the best guide to what must be avoided and addressed on the international level between the EU-NATO Security Community and Kyiv, on the one hand, and Russia on the other. In the case of Ukraine, it is a matter of societal security concerns as both Ukrainian identity and the very right of the Ukrainian nation-state to exist have been clearly threatened.

Conclusions to Chapter 3

This chapter illustrated how a combination of international relations and sociological analysis of threats to a security community, operating from the systemic to the individual level, can illuminate the independence of society and state when it comes to identity (societal) security.

As the discussion in the chapter illustrated, horizontal competition within society for cultural domination as well as vertical competition manifested by polity-upgrading nationalism (like a Greater Albania or a Russian Super-ethnos/civilization), represent two major issues threatening societal security. This chapter also showed how the threatened societal security of Ukraine influences the foreign policies of Russia and Ukraine (sub-system level), and relations between Russia and Ukraine as a No War/No Peace Community, on the one hand, and the EU-NATO Security Community, on the other (system level). The Yugoslavization of Ukraine has already become a living nightmare for the Ukrainians in Donbas and has no plausible solution for Russia and the West unless they change strategy. On the national (sub-system) level, the state security of Ukraine is directly threatened by Russian hybrid warfare aggression, while Ukrainian identity is challenged by the opposing aspirations of a pro-Western majority and a still influential pro-Russian minority. This split is also vital at the level of competing political elites in Ukraine (bureaucratic level), where the balance is uncertain between the Russian-speaking oligarch minority elite oriented toward reintegration with Russia and the pro-Western expert majority elite, who do not believe in Russia's non-imperial future.

Looking back at NATO enlargement since 2004, we can see how expanding the EU-NATO security community to Russian borders in the Baltics propelled the "No War Community" between Russia and Ukraine first into an escalation of an inter-state security dilemma and then into armed Russian aggression in 2014. Despite the liberal nature of the Ukrainian nation-state and the initial disbelief that war with Russia was inevitable, the Ukrainian majority found it impossible to extend the theoretical right of secession/self-determination to the pro-Russian minority in Donbas. What Fearon considers to be a "commitment problem" is in fact a reflection of the inherent logic of any nation-building project as such. This logic reveals itself via analysis of societal security where the threat to the national identity of the majority, expressed through threatened national interests, does not allow political elites, however liberal, in a democratic society to ignore public consent regarding the territorial integrity of the nation-state. While in Crimea the ruling Ukrainian elite did not possess the confidence to launch a war against a "separatist" minority backed up by Russian troops, they would have lost all legitimacy to govern Ukraine if they had not done so in Donbas.

In a democracy, therefore, it is a matter of public perception when and whether to *consider* the threat to national interests to be of such significance that it is worth prosecuting a war against a separatist minority. Although, indeed, it is for the ruling elite to *decide* when to launch such a war or to use other means of coercion.

For instance, in the case of the two wars launched by the Kremlin in Chechnya, it is clear that the overwhelming support of the Russian public provided such a decision with democratic legitimacy. In other words, despite a relatively "satisfied" and, therefore, benign Russian nationalism under President Yeltsin, the Russian majority perceived a threat to its own national interests sufficient to give the ruling political elite, through public consent, the right to launch a war against a tiny minority. The fact that the decision to launch the war against a minority depends on the ruling elite supports the realist security dilemma arguments. However, the fact that it is a majority's perception of the threat to national interests and/or identity that provides public consent for the elites also makes the case for the idealist/constructivist argument.

Chapter 4 below, therefore, focuses on the analysis of empirical evidence as to how the elites in Russia and Ukraine as well as "groups of patriots" — Cossacks — develop their understanding of national interests as well as how they perceive threats to the national identity. The research presented in Chapter 4 shows that in Ukraine and Russia, as elsewhere, nationalist movements are always dependent on a wider political ideology chosen by the ruling elites of a given society. The chapter analyzes how the Cossack movements in Russia and Ukraine, albeit originally similar, took divergent and often opposed trajectories. The ruling Russian elites revived policies reflecting an ethno-geopolitical discourse and therefore reoriented their Cossack movement toward the creation of a distinct "ethnic" Cossack community ('Cossack sub-ethnos') in line with neo-Eurasian expansionist ideology, often perceived as "neo-imperialist," and geared toward the establishment of a "Supra-ethnos-state" or Russian civilization. Ukrainian nation-building ideology therefore developed as a counter to the expanding, "neo-imperialist" ethno-geopolitics of its Russian neighbor, and aimed at the creation of a civic Ukrainian nation-state, with a token reference to the historical Cossack origin of Ukrainians. Chapter 4 also shows how state-influenced policies of ethno-territorial or civic nationalism are reflected in real or rhetorical war preparations at the societal level—how, in other words, identity security or societal security depends on the ruling elites' nation-building projects and how the latter also depend on the socio-political history of the region.

4 From Soviet Ethno-Political Engineering to Ethno-Geopolitics: The Construction of a "Cossack" Nation in Ukraine, and the "Russian Civilization"

The seeming overproduction of theories of nationalism, as illustrated in previous chapters, suggests the need to relate the existing theoretical discourse on nations and nationalism to new data. According to the literature previously discussed, "Eastern" or "ethnic" nationalism accounts for most of the violent and negative expressions of this quite universal phenomenon. Prolonged "ethnic" battles in Eastern Europe, and attempts by European governments to find a remedy for violent forms of nationalism, provide an important focus for the study of nationalism and nationalism-related security issues.

This chapter examines how the nationality policy of the Soviet successor states of Russia and Ukraine influenced the ethno-political scene of these two largest countries of the FSU. It compares theoretical ethno-political discourses in the Russian and Ukrainian social sciences, as well as state policies toward nationalities, and specifically with respect to paramilitary Cossack revivals. The theoretical and political discourses of ethno-geopolitics in Russia, and to a lesser degree in Ukraine, were developed on the basis of the heritage of Soviet ethnic engineering. However, the two initially similar Cossack movements progressed toward different models of national and/or ethnic community, as a result of different state policies in Russia and Ukraine. This suggests that state policies can be a decisive factor in defining the "civic" or "ethnic" development of nation-building.

However, another important factor is the self-perception of the social actors or their self-identity constructs. In the Russian Federation, institutionalized "ethnic" federalism, together with the theoretical and political discourse on "ethno-geopolitics," became a decisive factor for the Russian Cossacks to "imagine," model and "re-invent" themselves as an "ethnic" community or an ethnos within the larger Russian super-ethnos also known as "Russian civilization" or the

"Russian World." The Ukrainian Cossacks developed their self-perception as a counter to Russian Cossack "ethnic" expansion, and their perception had to be re-created to be inclusive of other nationalities, to unite the "civically" defined Ukrainian nation against the "imperialist" threat. Both state policies and self-identity constructs resulted in two distinct nation-building projects and two different Cossack models of national community/nation: the Russian Cossack sub-ethnos as a part of the Russian Supra-Ethno-Nation, and the Civic Ukrainian Cossack nation.

4.1. The Heritage of Soviet Ethnography and the Revival of Ethno-Geopolitics in Russia

The literature on Soviet and post-Soviet Studies generally recognizes that "Soviet scholarship was long dominated by the need to legitimate the existing political divisions of the Soviet Union as natural ones'"(Aslund and Olcott 1999, 61). But has the situation changed radically? Valeriy Tishkov, who replaced Yulian Bromley as the Head of the Institute of Ethnography of the Academy of Science of the USSR (later the Institute of Ethnology and Anthropology of the Russian Academy), lamented that neither politicians nor, to a large extent, academics are prepared to admit that they were wrong in legitimizing the ethno-political hierarchy of the USSR. According to Tishkov, this "protective-conservative" approach on the part of academics is not simply an expression of "scholarly provincialism," since "the real problem is the tradition of servility and the distorted craft of social science scholarship throughout post-Soviet space. It shows itself in a lack of distance between politics and research" (Tishkov 1997, 295).

The dependence of scientific research on agendas set by political and interest groups is not only a problem for the FSU, however. There must be other reasons for the "'protective conservatism" of post-Soviet scholars. One possible reason is that the theoretical findings of Soviet Ethnography created a coherent framework for conceptualizing ethnic and national phenomena, one that successfully served the need of the USSR to delineate and legitimize internal borders among various republics and regions. As Ernest Gellner puts it, some concepts in Soviet Ethnography were "neat, complete and tight, but not, as far as I can see, vicious. This does not mean that the position is necessarily valid, but it is not inconsistent or incoherent" (Gellner 1995, 149).

Another possible reason is that, after many years of Soviet social engineering, post-Soviet societies have become quite different from those in the West and therefore need different theoretical approaches. This can be seen in how the Russian legal system institutionalizes the hierarchy of ethnoses, peoples and nationalities that resulted from Soviet ethno-nation state-building. After many years of repressive Soviet nationality policy, a hierarchical, ethnically defined federation of nations in Russia became a reality. It continues to influence both political and academic discourse. Although President Yeltsin introduced in official documents a definition of Russia as a "political nation," it did not change the reality on the ground dominated by ethnically-defined federal entities with local cultures being promoted within their administrative borders. Terminology itself cannot change the desire by federal parts of the country to pursue separate goals. Political confrontation with the center continued: "about 70 percent of the regional legislative acts passed since 1991 in the republics, *oblasts*, and *krais* contradict federal legislation" (Olcott and Tishkov 1999, 77). Under such conditions, Russian scholars and politicians faced a dilemma: either use old recipes to sort out constantly evolving and often ethnically-based conflicts or try to develop new policies. The latter would require developing a new theoretical framework of inter-ethnic/national relations, which was nonexistent immediately following the collapse of the Soviet Union. Since the political leadership was quick to proclaim their policy of building *Rossiia* as a country of *Rossiians,* inclusive of not only ethnic Russians (*Russkiie*), but also non-Russians, academic discourse followed.

Academic writing could be divided into two broad categories. The core of the old school at the Institute of Ethnology, tried to place Soviet Ethnography's heritage into the Western tradition in order to achieve the best synergy of both intellectual streams. Scholars like

Tishkov had not only already established academic links with Western institutions, but also could no longer accept theories from the alternative Soviet/Russian Eurasianist tradition. In fact, Tishkov concluded that "Gumilev's works are riddled with construed pseudo-scholarly terms and categories which could never be placed in any disciplinary discourse or tested seriously ... [T]hey nevertheless revive and strengthen the existing primordialist treatment of ethnicity" (Tishkov 1997, 2-3). Tishkov admits that he finds himself in the minority of Russian scholars because most of them "have remained strongly attached to a primordial vision of ethnicity. I have come to the conclusion that it is *not* a crisis. No, it is something more serious: a failure of a discipline to meet the challenges of today" (Tishkov 1997, 4-5).

Tishkov firmly locates himself in the "modernist" (constructivist) paradigm within the Western academic tradition. The latter, however, does not provide easy and effective recipes for solving inter-ethnic problems, simply stating that ethnicity is a constructed phenomenon, and that could be one of the reasons why the scholars from the Institute of Ethnology who followed Tishkov found themselves in the minority.

The second category of post-Soviet Russian scholars either could not integrate their concepts into "modernist" traditions or did not consider this necessary. Some tried to introduce pre-Soviet Russian writings into Soviet Ethnography or continued with Gumilev's theory of ethno-genesis. The Russian "primordialist" approach seemed to have wider appeal despite being rather eclectic.

Konstantin Ippolitov suggests considering the continuity of the Russian Empire, the Soviet Union and the Russian Federation as national expressions of Russian statehood, where the multitude of inhabiting peoples should be considered as a *mnogorodnaia natsiia* ("multi-origin nation") with a separate sense of nationalism which overcomes particularistic ethnicity. As an alternative to this (*mnogorodnaia natsiia*), he also suggests using Gumilev's term "super-ethnos" in its sense of "ethnic system." Ippolitov also refers to *mnogorodnaia natsiia* as a Russian civilization with the Russian Idea at its core. The essence of the Russian idea is as follows:

> Only Russian state patriotism, which acquired a character above the ethnic level and includes ethnic patriotism as its constituent part, can provide Russia with territorial integrity, unity of the people and the status of a Great Power. All that acquires Global meaning due to the value orientation of Russian, Eurasian civilization which is a result of many centuries of devoted suffering. (Ippolitov 1997, ch. 3)

The Center for Global Programs at the Gorbachev Foundation published a collective report under the title "National Interests and Problems of Security in Russia," supervised by the academic Shakhnazarov, whose authors claim that historical Russia was built by a Russian ethnos which includes *velikorosy* (Great Russians), *malorosy* (Little Russians — Ukrainians) and *belorusy* (White Russians — Belorussians). Although the authors did not use the term "superethnos," Gumilev's influence was quite clear; as in the Soviet sociospheric approach, each of these nationalities would be associated with different ethnoses while together forming "non-ethnic" or civic "Soviet people." The report tries to "explain" why the Russian Constitution does not and ought not envisage the right of other ethnic nations who inhabit the Russian federation to create their own states and exercise, in this way, the right to self-determination. The authors, led by Shakhnazarov, suggested that:

> Nation as the ethnic community of a people is not the highest and self-sufficient value, but only a stage in the historical development from the ethnic division of people to their integration into a civic, political nation that would be based on a heterogeneous ethnic basis. Therefore, the republics of the Russian Federation should not be "states of titular ethnoses" but states of residence, which would provide citizens with the sociocultural multiplicity of society.[38]

However, this last prospect would be reserved for the distant future. In the meantime, self-determination within the Russian polyethnic state, according to the authors, is to be achieved in two ways: through territorial entities and national-cultural autonomies. Here, the authors refer to the official Russian Concept of National Policy

---

[38]   Natsionalnyie interesy I problemy bezopasnosti Rossii. (1997) Natsionalnaiya elekronnaya biblioteka. Internet version: (www.nns.ru/analytdoc/dok97_4.html)

(*natsionalnaiia politika*), where, despite the preferred civic meaning of the Russian nation, its ethnic essence is considered primary.[39]

The Russian State Duma's Committee for Geopolitics also promoted scholarly discourse on *Etnogeopolitika* (ethno-geopolitics) in order to develop recommendations for solving contradictions among ethnoses, as opposed to political entities. The following definition of ethno-geopolitics was suggested by the advisor of the Committee, Sergei Smirnov:

> Ethno-geopolitics is a multitude of concepts, criteria, models and scientific methods, which allows an ethnic entity or several ethnic entities to enter the structure of World civilization and to solve its political tasks. Distinct from geopolitics, as its constituent part, ethno-geopolitics pays more attention to the behavior of ethnoses as opposed to nations, and studies of poly-ethnic spaces (*prostranstv*) and not inter-state relationships. In short, ethno-geopolitics is the sum total of techniques for an ethnic entity to conquer a decent place within the world community. (Smirnov 1998, 80)

This kind of ethnic approach to regional politics has inevitably created new "ethnic entities" and in some cases open violent conflict on the territory of the FSU. After only a few years of post-Soviet Cossack revival, the Russian state had to recognize the Cossacks as a "people," and therefore a separate ethnic entity, as formulated in President Yeltsin's decree *On the State Register of Cossack Communities in the Russian Federation* signed 10 August 1995. Considering the varied ethnic background of many Cossacks, Smirnov suggested that, *ethnically, Cossacks are a sub-ethnos of the Russian Supra-ethnos,* which should solve, in his opinion, the problem of whether Cossacks are a separate people or a social stratum. Smirnov's definition of sub-ethnos is highly eclectic, combining both socio-spherical and bio-spherical approaches of Soviet Ethnography, i.e., Cossacks are an "ethno-social system with distinct synergetic effect (self-organization)". Cossacks also have "dual ethnic self-identification (*ruskii-kazak, kalmyk-kazak,* etc.)." On the one hand, the author assumes the social nature of the ethnic system, yet, on the other, sug-

---

[39]   "The existential secret of the Russian state is the balanced combination of the objectively key role of the Russian ethnos, its language and culture, with recognition of the right of nations to self-determination and the equality of rights of citizens as '*Rossiian*'". Ibid. (www.nns.ru/analytdoc/dok97_4.html).

gests that the system is organized by energy, as if it were a natural construct, which is a clear reference to Gumilev's theory of ethnos as a biological organism.

Such eclectic application of Soviet concepts gradually developed in line with revived theories of Eurasianism (*yevraziistvo*). Kamuludin Gadzshiev, in *Introduction to Geopolitics*, remarks that *yevraziistvo* suggested a set of interesting observations; however, the ideology itself was developed in the 1920s and 1930s, and so became outdated. His main criticism of *yevraziistvo*, however, is that Russia could be unnecessarily isolated from the world community if it insisted on its own messianic stance. At the same time, Gadzshiev does use the concept of *passionarnost*, suggested by Gumilev, and quotes the ideas of Nikolay Trubeskoy, who was co-founder of the pre-Second World War *yevraziistvo* (Gadzshiev 1998, 71, 221). Gadzshiev also accepts the definition of geopolitics formulated by K. Pleshakov, where *geopolitika* is defined as the "objective dependence of a subject of International Relations on the sum of material factors [geographically defined] which allows this subject to control its space" (Gadzshiev 1998, 25). In other words, the essence of *geopolitika* is defined very much along the lines of the bio-spherical concepts of Soviet Ethnography as the eternal struggle of ethnoses for their own habitat.

We can conclude that post-Soviet Russian *Geopolitika* (geopolitics) as a theory absorbed that part of the Soviet Ethnography heritage which was most heavily inclined toward "primordialism." The strong influence of Gumilev's ethnology on post-Soviet scholars in Russia resulted in the creation of Ethno-geopolitics as a subdiscipline of Geopolitics, or rather a set of ideas and concepts where the main actors of geopolitics are considered to be sub-ethnoses, ethnoses and supra-ethnoses in their different interpretations. By the early 2000s ethno-geopolitics in Russia evolved as a coherent theoretical framework and ethno-geopolitical discourse was well-established within academic thinking and a political trend known as the "New Eurasianism."

Aleksandr Dugin became the most prominent Russian intellectual associated with the new Eurasianism and probably the most controversial one. His political activism led in 2014 to his expulsion from Moscow University, where he worked as a professor of sociology of international relations. Anders Aslund identified Dugin's Eurasianist ideology as neo-fascist and pointed out his influence on United Russia's ideological directorate as the Kremlin's ruling party:

> Mr. Dugin sees his Eurasian movement as a secret Order of Eurasia that existed for centuries, and included various German ultra-nationalists. While, at times, strongly distancing himself from Hitler's crimes, Mr. Dugin, throughout the 1990s, repeatedly expressed his admiration for certain aspects of the Nazi movement. For instance, he called the theory sector of the Waffen SS an "intellectual oasis" within the Third Reich, and admitted that National Socialism "was the fullest and the most total realization of the Third Way" that Mr. Dugin still advocates. In one of his numerous pro-fascist articles, Mr. Dugin gets excited about the prospect that, after the failures of Germany and Italy, there will, in Russia today, finally emerge truly "fascist fascism." (Aslund 2018, 2)

Dugin's ethno-geopolitics follows the same logic of Classical Eurasianism, assuming that Belorussians and Ukrainians are part of the same "Russian people," hence Dugin has advocated the Russian takeover of Ukraine since his 1997 "Foundation of Geopolitics." (A more detailed analysis of Dugin's contribution to Putin's Eurasianism is offered in sub-chapter 4.2.).

The inevitable implication of ethno-geopolitical discourse is its contradiction to the declared Russian state policy of building a political, civic nation.

This contradiction was reflected in the proposed law on a single Russian nation, "On the Unity of the Russian Nation and Management of Interethnic Relations," developed in 2017 and then watered down as the law "On the Fundamentals of State Nationality Policy." Academician Valery Tishkov led the working group drafting the law and, in an interview with to Kommersant newspaper, admitted that the initial proposal was rejected as "society is not ready to accept the idea of a single nation. It is calmer that way. It transpires that society is not very prepared to accept the concept of a single nation uniting all nationalities." Vladimir Zorin, former Minister for Nationality Affairs, confirmed that the new law aimed at "strengthening pan-Russian civic self-awareness and spiritual commonality of the multinational people of the Russian Federation (the Russian nation); the preservation and development of peoples' ethnic and cultural diversity; the harmonization of interethnic relations; and the adaptation and integration of immigrants." Kommersant concluded with a quote from another Russian scholar Magomed Omarov that the expert community "is not brave enough to talk about the real problems and is not prepared for a frank conversation on this subject with the regime and society" (Kommersant website, 7 March 2017).

The concept of a single Russian nation triggered a public debate that continues to this day and reflects the hopes and fears of various social groups in Russia. For instance, scholars from the various ethnic republics feared that the Russian nation would become a nation of Russians, while the indigenous populations would lose their ethnic identities. The Russian Orthodox Church was keen to promote its concept of the "Russian world," encompassing all Russians, including those living abroad as well as Orthodox Belorussians and Ukrainians. The Cossacks demanded that the new law enshrine the Russian people's "state-forming role," and that the status of ethnic Russians should be defined in legislation, suggesting a federal program to support ethnic Russians. According to a Kommersant source in the Presidential Council for Interethnic Relations, the Russian Orthodox church representative Vladimir Legoyda requested that the working group underline the unifying role of the Russian people, language, and culture in the "Russian world." In other words, the old Soviet dogma about the unifying role of Russians in the USSR evolved into a neo-Eurasian ideology blessed by the Russian Orthodox Church.

Scholars and politicians who share an ethno-geopolitical discourse tend to substitute the civic meaning of the term "political nation" with various interpretations of "political nation" as an ethnic system, supra-ethnos, ethnic civilization (Russian civilization, etc.). Although the Russian constitution states that the source of power in the Russian Federation comes from "*the peoples*," no single "*people*" is considered to have the right to leave the Russian Federation. Ethnogeopolitics in contemporary Russia, just like Soviet Ethnography in the Soviet Union, legitimized the principle of ethnic federalization where *Russian Supra-ethnos* or *Russian civilization* is considered to be an absolute value. On the other hand, ethno-geopolitics provides powerful justification for the expansionist policies of the Russian Federation. Not only are breakaway republics, like Chechnya, considered to be eligible to be forced back, but according to the same logic, so are those "unfortunate parts" of the "Russian supra-ethnos," or "ethnic system" that succeeded in legitimate self-determination, such as the Ukrainians and the Belorussians. According to ethno-geopolitical discourse, both nations are considered to be Russian sub-ethnoses and therefore are to be included in its "natural" ethno-social organism, which used to be called the "Soviet people," and is now advocated as the "Russian political nation" — Russian Supra-Ethnos — Russian Civilization — Russian World.

It took only one change of presidency in Russia for the political discourse to shift towards reintegration of ex-Soviet territory. Although initially Vladimir Putin announced the continuity of Yeltsin's nationality policy, it was clear from the assertive regional policies and the Second Chechen War that the Kremlin wanted to review its federal arrangements. Secretive, non-transparent negotiations between members of the federation and federal authorities evoked insecurity and suspicion among the ethnically diverse communities of the most independence-oriented subjects of the Russian Federation. For instance, the Tatar and Bashkir public movement "Tugan Tel" ("Native Tongue") held its *kurultay* (forum) on 10 March 2002 in the Ulyanovsk region and adopted an appeal to the Tatar people, condemning Moscow's ethnic policy aiming at undermining Tatar homogeneity and cohesiveness by dividing the Tatars into subgroups. The appeal says that:

> The Russian government is carrying out yet another inexplicable action as regards the Tatar people — it is trying to divide a single nation into Mishars, Kryashens [baptized Tatars], Tiptars, Nogaybeks, Astrakhan and Siberian Tatars. If some villages in Ulyanovsk Region are populated with Mishars, they call the whole area Misharstan. Following the same logic, Russians could then be divided into Old Believers; Molokans; Kulugurs; Kuban'; Orenburg; Baikal or Don Cossacks; Russians with almond eyes or bushy eyebrows; etc. But nothing of the kind is being done. For example, no papers or books in Saransk [capital of the Russian Autonomous Republic of Mordovia] are published in the Mordov dialects of Erzya or Moksha. And during the census they all will

be registered as Mordovs. The same is the case with the Chuvash people. "Let us be vigilant! We are Tatars and nothing but Tatars!" (Tatar-Inform news agency, Kazan, in Russian 0827 GMT 14 Mar 02: BBC Mon FS1 MCU 140302 kd/evg)

Similarly, Chechen rebel leaders accused Russian security services of plotting the revision of borders in the North Caucasus, so that the Chechen Republic would simply cease to exist. This time, the Kremlin was suspected of planning the unification of Chechnya and Ingushetia into a single Vaynakh Republic, reminiscent of the Chechen-Ingush ASSR of Soviet times:

> The plan to change the Russian map geopolitically — merge Chechnya and Ingushetia — was devised more than two years ago, at the beginning of the second war in Chechnya. It was subsequently resuscitated by Viktor Kazantsev, plenipotentiary representative of the president in the Southern Federal District, at the end of last year. He convinced Putin that by giving birth to the Vaynakh republic, the Russian Federation would wipe the name Chechnya off the map — raze it to the ground and dissolve it into Ingushetia. The capital of the Vaynakh republic should definitely not be ravaged Grozny, which is like a thorn in the flesh, especially to those who destroyed it, but Magas, the new, modern and clean Ingush capital, where it is not embarrassing to invite a European guest and demonstrate how well the Vaynakhs are doing — except for rebel mountain districts, where separatists have dug themselves in — and unobtrusively draw parallels with the Basque country and rebellious Mexican states. This is probably Kazantsev's main idea. (Chechen-press web site, Tbilisi, in Russian 22 Apr 02: BBC Mon TCU 220402 bk/ek)

In contrast to ethnic republics, Cossack organizations in Russia immediately expressed their support of Putin's policy in the Northern Caucasus, considering Putin as the "savior" of Russia. A congress of Cossack atamans in Moscow was held as early as 18 March 2000 to support Putin in presidential elections for his determination "to see through the antiterrorist operation in Chechnya." According to Russian media reports, nearly all atamans from all over Russia expressed their readiness to take part personally in military operations in the hope that President Putin "will let them restore order in their former homeland." Russian Public TV quoted a Supreme Ataman of the Union of Cossack hosts, Viktor Ratiyev, who expressed the general mood of the Cossack commanders:

> The Cossacks support Putin not because it is fashionable right now. They support Putin because their hearts tell them to support this man, because in him they see [the early sixteenth-century Russian freedom fighter] Minin and [Prince Dmitry] Pozharskiy, the savior of the Russian state. (Russian Public TV, Moscow, in Russian 1200 gmt-18-March-00, BBC Mon FS1 Fsu Pol)

Once Federal troops re-entered Chechnya, Cossacks collected nearly 50,000 signatures in favor of separating the northern Naursky and Shelkovsky Districts from Chechnya and (re-)integrating them into Stavropol territory (NTV International, Moscow, in Russian 0900 gmt 11 Feb 01, BBC Mon FS1 FsuPol). Although federal authorities denied such plans, ethno-geopolitics had clearly found its way into public discourse and contributed to the societal insecurity of the regions. President Putin's revival of ethno-geopolitics of political Eurasianism acquired a logic of its own and would lead to major armed conflicts with Georgia (2018) and Ukraine (2014-), so the next sub-chapter will look at Putin's Eurasianism as a semi-state ideology and a form of nationalism that calls for Russian culture to be at the core of the new Eurasian supra-state entity — "Russian civilization."

4.2. Ethno-Geopolitics of Putin's Eurasianism

Russian military affairs analyst Dmitry Trenin, Director of the Carnegie Moscow Center and a Member of the Council on Foreign and Defense Policy, concluded in 2018 that President Putin has chosen to rely on "the ideology of patriotism and Eurasianism. Putin sees his long presidency as a mission given by God" (Trenin 2018). The Russian president quoted a number of Eurasian thinkers in his public speeches, so the link to Eurasianism is well documented. "Who will take the lead and who will remain on the periphery and inevitably lose their independence will depend not only on the economic potential but primarily on the will of each nation, on its inner energy, which Lev Gumilev called *passionarnost*: the ability to move forward and embrace change." (President Vladimir Putin, December 2012: Quote from http://government.ru/docs/17248).

Western ability to understand the future projection of Russian power was challenged when Moscow invaded Georgia in 2008 and annexed Crimea in 2014. The Pentagon's Defense Intelligence Agency allegedly briefed the US Congress that Russian troop concentrations around Ukraine were a bluff only few weeks before the invasion in 2014. No mainstream Western politicians predicted that Russia would challenge the existing security framework in Europe despite the fact that Moscow warned about its "red lines" in Eastern Europe on numerous occasions, including such extreme actions as rehearsals of nuclear strikes against a major Central European capital. The only politicians who predicted the invasion of Crimea were such mavericks, well to the right of the mainstream center, as the Alaskan ex-governor Sarah Palin and Polish President Lech Kaczynski. Palin explicitly predicted the invasion of Crimea as a follow-up of Russia's war in Georgia (2008), thus showing a better insight into Moscow's intent than the US intelligence services with their formidable funding. Lech Kaczynski warned that the invasion of Georgia will be followed by the invasion of Ukraine and then Poland. Neither statement was taken seriously at the time and Putin's foreign policy is often characterized as unpredictable. Understanding Putin's Eurasianism, which has been semi-officially accepted by the Kremlin as a state ideology since 2011, could help make sense of what seems like unpredictable foreign policy and gain better future insight. As General Dmitry Trenin observed: "Ukraine occupied a key position in the Eurasian Union concept that became the foundation of the foreign policy section in Vladimir Putin's presidential program in 2011. The success of the entire Eurasian integration project, in essence, was dependent on Kyiv's economic and political orientation" (Trenin 2017).

4.2.1 What is Putin's Eurasianism?

The Kremlin's interpretation of various Eurasian ideas has come to be known as Putin's Eurasianism. It is often assumed that Putin's regime lacks any national ideology and some analysts even claim that corruption is the only modus operandi that binds modern Russian elites. Indeed, unlike Lenin, Stalin and other Soviet leaders, Putin produced a modest PhD thesis dedicated to the political economy of natural resources in Russia, with no grand designs for Russia or the world. Putin's public speeches are the only official source of his publicly declared views, but they are not necessarily the expression of his inner beliefs. Qualitative content (operational code) analysis of all Putin's public speeches available on the Kremlin's website (over one million words), performed by a group of American scholars, produced little insight, except that Vladimir Putin values personal and state control slightly more than the average international leader (Dyson 2017). However, who would expect a former KGB officer to tell the public what he really thinks as opposed to what he wants the public to believe? In this sense it might be just as important to understand what Putin does not say in public, but is likely to believe, as it can uncover his real intent more than a million words published online. This is not to say that there are no public pronouncements that express views shared by both President Putin and the Russian public. So what is it safe to believe and what is relevant to the outside world?

When Putin claimed in public that he is "the biggest nationalist in Russia," it could be interpreted on a number of levels. First, that the President of Russia is the ultimate national leader and nobody is allowed to position himself as a bigger patriot (nationalist). Second, that Putin is the right kind of nationalist, i.e., patriot, but not the kind of xenophobic thug denying the rights of minorities to be part of the Russian nation (*Rossiyskiy narod*). Third, that Putin is indeed the greatest Russian nationalist but publicly admits only the politically correct interpretation of the term. If we apply Gellner's definition of nationalism (Gellner 1983) as a political principle that one culture should coincide with its own state, then understanding Putin's nationalism would enlighten us as to his vision of where Russian state borders should end. In other words, establishing the geography of Putin's nationalism will inform us where he sees the ideal existential space for Putin's Russia vs. Europe and Asia, i.e., Putin's "Lebensraum," as mentioned by a leading Russian expert in Germany (and himself a Eurasianist), Alexander Rahr (Lau 2013). The key similarity between the discredited concept of Lebensraum and Eurasianism is that both share a common belief in the natural "biological habitat" for nations whether it be an Aryan race (German nation) or the Russian super-ethnos (people)/"Russian civilization."

4.2.2 Putin's Nationalism: Known Knowns

Newly elected, President Putin accepted in his Millennium message (2000) Yeltsin's term *Rossiiskiy Narod* (Russian people or nation) as opposed to *Russkiy narod* (the more narrow ethnic definition). He stated explicitly that Russia is a multi-ethnic nation while addressing the United Russia conference in 2011: "Let those who proclaim the slogans of social and ethnic intolerance, and are smuggling in all kinds of populist and provocative ideas that actually lead to national betrayal and ultimately to the break-up of our country, know that we are a single Russian nation, a united and indivisible Russia." In this context, Putin could be considered a "statist" (*gosudarstvennik*) as he is preoccupied first of all with survival of the Russian state, with its 20 million Muslims and over a hundred officially recognized ethnically defined nationalities. He disbanded (in 2001) Russia's first ministry for nationalities set up by academician Tishkov under president Yeltsin to deal with bilateral treaties demanded by Tatarstan and other national (ethnic) autonomies. Putin explained clearly that he would not tolerate any regional (ethnic) movements seeking greater autonomy or self-determination:

> As for the notorious concept of self-determination, a slogan used by all kinds of politicians who have fought for power and geopolitical dividends, from Vladimir Lenin to Woodrow Wilson, the Russian people made their choice long ago. The self-determination of the Russian people is to be a multi-ethnic civilization with Russian culture at its core. The Russian people have confirmed their choice time and again during their thousand-year history — with their blood, not through plebiscites or referendums.

Putin's article "Russia: The National Question" appeared in *Nezavisimaya gazeta* in January 2012 and two years later the Russian government criminalized any public pronouncements that could be considered as expressions of separatism. The above quote is important not only as a de facto warning against future attempts by federal autonomies to claim the right to self-determination but also as a clear rejection of Soviet (Leninist) nationality policies. Putin openly criticized Lenin in the past saying that the Soviet nationality policy, which accepted the right to self-determination of 15 Soviet republics, was a "time-bomb" laid under the foundations of the Soviet Union. By 2012, Putin openly disassociated himself from Lenin, whom he numbered among "all kinds of politicians," including a US president, who believed in the "notorious concept of self-determination," merely fighting for personal power dividends (Hill 2012). Putin's "national question" manifesto proclaims a clear departure from the Marxist-Leninist postulate about the inevitable evolution of nationally-divided oppressed peoples into a future classless and culturally homogenized (communist) society. Instead, Putin states his belief in "a multi-ethnic civilization with Russian culture at its core." This is effectively Putin's statement of his civic nationalism, i.e., a political principle presupposing that Russian culture should coincide with the borders of the multi-ethnic Russian state. Borders, in Putin's view, that could not be challenged from inside or outside, but which are not limited from expanding.

4.2.3 Putin's Nationalism: Known Unknowns

In August 2014, a left-wing activist, Darya Polyudova, was charged with the crime of inciting separatism and placed in pre-trial detention soon after she finished serving a prior two-week sentence for a rally demanding broader autonomy for the Krasnodar region (a North-Caucasian region associated with the historical Cossack Kuban). Grani.ru reported it was the first time that Russian authorities brought criminal charges under the new law taking effect that year criminalizing calls for separatism. The rally organizers' page on the social network VKontakte called for broader economic autonomy and self-governance rights for their region, but made no demands for secession. Grani.ru commented that at the same time that the Russian government calls for broader autonomy for eastern Ukraine (Donbas), it jails a domestic activist for advocating the same kind of federalization rights for a southern Russian region, accidentally populated historically by the Cossacks from the Don Region and Ukraine.

The irony, of course, is that while Russian borders cannot be challenged they can expand according to the Kremlin's design. NATO-sponsored research conducted by the GLOBSEC Policy Institute states that Russia launched an information warfare campaign targeting Crimea two years before the invasion and attempted illegal annexation. That coincides in time with Putin's above-mentioned nationalism manifesto proclaiming the reign of "Russian civilization." The GLOBSEC report, "Countering Information War: Lessons Learned from NATO and Partner Countries," explained that similar infowar tactics were applied to other Central and Eastern European countries: "Propaganda effects are similar to cooking a frog—heating up the water until it is too late to react ... Russia's influence in CEE [Central and Eastern Europe] works like a microwave—heating up water molecules inside the meat [these countries] that are home-grown for this purpose." It is clear that Putin's nationalism has two aspects: conservative inside the borders of the Russian Federation and expansionist outside. In fact, the Russian president staged a TV statement in 2016 saying that Russia's border "doesn't end anywhere," while addressing a televised awards ceremony for geography students.

In the past, Putin pledged to defend ethnic Russians wherever they live, so the "known unknown" is where Putin believes the Russian borders should naturally lie in order to coincide with the culturally "Russian civilization." Is his vision limited to the former USSR countries, the Warsaw Pact countries, or does it include "Russian Alaska"? Answering these questions could provide insight into the likely intent of what General Philip Breedlove called "the most amazing information blitzkrieg we have ever seen in the history of information warfare," waged by Russia (Pomerantsev 2014).

4.2.4 Revival of Political Eurasianism Ideology in Russia

Putin's departure from Soviet nationality policy and the use of Eurasianism terminology suggests more than a pure coincidence. Some scholars suggest that Putin embraced Eurasianism only reluctantly, after his hope for integrating Russia with the West during his first two presidential terms had failed. Unwanted (misunderstood) in Europe, Putin had to find a justification for his new course of reorientation (*povorot*) toward China and the "Eurasian" ideology suited best. However, the official launch of the Eurasian Economic Union in January 2015 suggests a much more profound approach toward the restructuring of the geopolitical space between the European Union and China. Eurasianism as an indigenous Russian political philosophy assumes an inner connection between the Slavic populations of Russia, Belorussia and most of Ukraine, with the Turkic-speaking peoples populating the historical space between the Great Wall of China in the east, the Carpathian mountains in the west and Central Asia in the south, and as such offers the ideal solution for a common unification ideology for what is essentially a Russian empire at its largest.

Historically, Eurasianism "was an emotional reaction" of the White emigré intellectuals to the Catastrophe, i.e., the Bolshevik revolution in Russia (in the words of philosopher Nikolay Berdyaev). Key figures like Prince Trubetskoy or Petr Savitskiy believed in a unique Russian, spiritual "otherness," in contrast to materialistic and decadent Europe, that originated in a Russian synergy with the Turkic people of Eurasian steppes. Nikolay Trubetskoy claimed that Russia is not a country but a separate civilization — the "Russian World," based on the superior Orthodox Christianity, and as clearly distinct from Europe as it was from Asia. Trubetskoy prophesied that Russia as a continental power would create a new Eurasian order, once Communism would expire, as the unnatural Western European ideology introduced by the Bolsheviks. Petr Savitskiy introduced the key idea of early Eurasianists about Mongol rule in Russia being a symbiotic process of Eurasian state formation and not the Tatar-Mongol Yoke widely accepted in Russian historiography previously. As Andreas Umland observed, early Eurasianists supported USSR ideology as long as it was "anti-Western, isolationist and imperialist." Some of early Eurasianist thinkers were openly anti-Semitic (Vasiliy Shulgin) and fascist (Ivan Illyin). The latter worked in Goebbels' Ministry of Propaganda (as head of the anti-Comintern department) until 1938 and advocated fascist ideology even after World War II. Some Eurasianists were supportive of multiculturalism and social inclusiveness as they could not envision the Russian empire being rebuilt on a mono-ethnic basis (i.e., "Russia for Russians" only).

Lev Gumilev developed Eurasian ideology after World War II in a way (just) acceptable to the Soviet authorities who would not permit any explicit Russian nationalism. Gumilev's theory of the Russian super-ethnos as a biological organism embedded in its geographical niche became a foundation for the new Eurasianist movement that flourished after the collapse of the USSR. Gumilev's theory of an ideal cohabitation of Slavs and Turkic-speaking peoples proved to be very popular in Tatarstan, and especially Kazakhstan, where President Nazarbayev was the first to adopt an anti-imperialist version of the Eurasian ideology, and even named a new national university after Gumilev. However, all of the poetic humanism of Gumilev's heritage was lost in the "new Eurasianists,"' who picked up mostly the White emigrés' imperialist tradition and, in the case of Aleksandr Dugin, an openly fascist ideology. Most worryingly, President Putin not only quoted the fascist Eurasianist Ivan Ilyin three times in his official speeches, but also personally took part in the televised repatriation and re-burial of Ivan Ilyin in a new Moscow shrine, organized by Patriarch Kirill in 2009 (Snyder 2016).

4.2.5 New Eurasianism: Implications and Contradictions

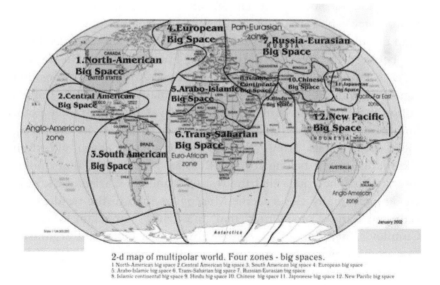

2-d map of multipolar world. Four zones - big spaces.
1. North-American big space 2.Central American big space 3. South American big space 4. European big space
5. Arabo-Islamic big space 6. Trans-Saharian big space 7. Russian-Eurasian big space
8. Islamic continental big space 9. Hindu big space 10. Chinese big space 11. Japoneese big space 12. New Pacific big space

Map: **Future vision of the multipolar world published by the International Eurasianism Movement http://med.org.ru/article/1886**

Adoption of Eurasianism as a semi-official Kremlin ideology has contradictory implications for Putin's Russia. On the one hand, Eurasianism does have the potential to unite a multi-ethnic society around the idea of a neo-imperial project with the Russian majority at its core, i.e., "making Russia great again.". This could be presented as a joint project with ethnic minorities who can share in civic Russian (*rossiyskiy*) patriotism. This would however, require ethnic Russians admitting an equal role for Turkic-speaking minorities in their empire-(nation)-building project, which could be difficult, considering the high level of xenophobia against the very Turkic speakers who come to the Russian capital often as feared labor migrants. Russian "ethnic" nationalists explicitly attack the new Eurasianists for attempts to promote "Turanian" minorities at the "expense" of ethnic Russians.

At the same time, 20 million Russian Muslims would find it difficult to share the ideology of the Orthodox Christian "Russian World," which is promoted along with Eurasianism by its founding fathers and Patriarch Kirill. The Muslims of Tatarstan are more likely to support Nazarbayev's anti-imperialist version of Eurasianism than Putin's. Different interpretations of Eurasianism could lead to a rift between the two key participating Eurasian states, Russia and Kazakhstan, if not to open confrontation. Additional opposition comes from the unexpectedly fierce Ukrainian opposition to Putin's notion that Ukrainians are the same people as Russians (a key point for all Eurasianists and a clear departure from the Soviet tradition). Most Eurasianists admit that predominantly Catholic Western Ukraine does not belong to the "Russian World" and that undermines their whole idea that the rest of Orthodox Christian Ukrainians are spiritually closer to the Muscovites than to the residents of Galician Lviv. Considering that most new Eurasianists accept Gumilev's thesis about the super-ethnos as a biological organism, compromise over what are considered the "biological parts" of the Russian super-ethnos is not really possible. A zero-sum game in inter-ethnic conflicts usually means a war of attrition and the physical destruction of the opposition. A messianic Christian mysticism with neo-fascist undertones underlying the "Russian World" in

Dugin's interpretation does not help either. All of these considerations explain Dugin's appeal in 2014 to stop any negotiations with the Ukrainian government and kill all Ukrainians resisting expansion of the Russian world: "Kill, kill, kill" (Quoted from the Chicago Tribune http://www.chicagotribune.com/news/nationworld/ct-d ugin-trump-putin-turkey-20170203-story.html).

4.2.6 Unknown Unknowns of Putin's Eurasianism

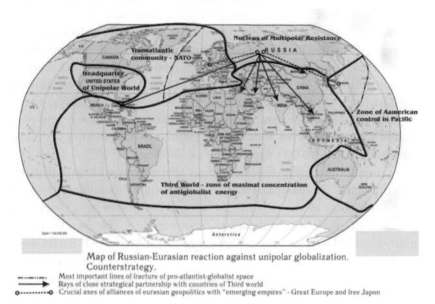

Map of Russian-Eurasian reaction against unipolar globalization. Counterstrategy.
- - - - - -   Most important lines of fracture of pro-atlantist-globalist space
————▶   Rays of close strategical partnership with countries of Third world
o------------o   Crucial axes of alliances of eurasian geopolitics with "emerging empires" - Great Europe and free Japon

Map: Dugin's counter strategy to create a multipolar world http://med.org.ru/article/1886

Although Alexander Dugin's links to the FSB, the GRU, the Russian General Staff, the Duma and the presidential administration are well documented (Basin 2017), it is not quite clear whether he is the product of or an inspiration for Putin's Eurasianism. He is often referred to as Putin's "favorite philosopher" or even "Putin's brain," although others consider him not influential in the Kremlin (Ratner 2016). Dugin certainly does not hide his fascination with the Russian leader: "There are no more opponents of Putin's course and, if there are, they are mentally ill and need to be sent off for clinical examination. Putin is everywhere, Putin is everything, Putin is absolute, and Putin is indispensable."

Taking into account the KGB's tradition of social engineering ("active measures"), it would be prudent to assume that the Eurasian movement is a test laboratory where one could safely play out ideas before implanting them in the wider Russian society and beyond. Not all ideas will take root, so experimenting might be essential in order to avoid negative political consequences, i.e., popular rejection of ideas associated with Russia's leadership. The *Novorossiya* project is a good example: the 'Young Eurasians' movement was sponsored by the Presidential administration in order to penetrate Eastern Ukraine and test this ideological construct from Kharkiv to Odesa. Once the *Novorossiya* project failed, the idea was quickly withdrawn from the state-controlled Russian media. Dugin's public appeal to kill Ukrainians resisting the Russian takeover caused a public outcry and cost him his professorship at the Moscow State University after 10,000 people signed a petition.

So, what are other relevant ideas that the new Eurasianists are playing with? Shaping Europe as a joint living (settlement) space with Germany, at the expense of Central European neighbors, is a persistent one. Some Eurasianists even entertain the idea that Germany could "buy into" the great bargain with Moscow if Berlin were "granted" East Prussia (Kaliningrad oblast') back. Could Putin's success in the "Schroderization" of Germany be a hint of more to come?

The formation of major Russia-Eurasian alliances with Tokyo and Tehran is another consistent theme, even though slightly corrected by Putin's (tactical?) reorientation toward China. Despite pursuing an aggressive policy of "land-grabbing" in the FSU area, the Kremlin seems to be quite liberal in settling territorial disputes with Japan dating from World War II. Could the formation of the Berlin-Moscow-Tokyo axis be on the mind of the Russian leader as portrayed on the geopolitical drawings of the new Eurasianists?

Isolation of Great Britain as the American "floating aircraft-carrier" in Europe is another prominent theme in opposing American "Atlanticism" and making sure that Russia controls the entire

Eurasian landmass and, therefore, in the Mackinder tradition, the whole world. How many of these ideas are shared by Vladimir Putin personally? The answer is unknown but might be irrelevant, in the same way that nobody really knows whether Hitler believed in theories of Aryan racial superiority or just used them to impose his will on the Germans and the outside world. What is clear is that more Eurasianist ideas could be tested unless the rest of the affected world offers credible deterrence against the confrontational agenda of Putin's Russia. As German foreign minister Sigmar Gabriel has warned, the world is facing a "new phase of nuclear rearmament," and is in the midst of "Cold War 2.0" (Quoted from Politico https://www.politico.eu/article/sigmar-gabriel-world-in-cold-war-2-0/).

The following sub-chapter 4.3 analyzes how Russian state policies influenced the Cossack movement from the early ethnographic societies to "sub-ethnos" and from armed settlers of the borderland to the army units and deniable mercenaries appearing in various armed conflicts around the world.

4.3. The Cossack Revival in Russia

The Russian Cossack revival can be traced back to the first organizations that studied the history and culture of Russian Cossacks, as was, for instance, the case with the Association of Cossacks in Moscow in 1990 (see also the endnote for a short overview of Cossack history[40]). During the popular wave of reviving everything pre-

---

[40] Cossacks—warriors of the steppe seemed to disappear from the historical scene after the Second World War. By that time, Red Army Cossacks seemed to represent more a simple form of cavalry than a social group. So, how did it happen that in the countries of the contemporary Commonwealth of Independent States (CIS) the Cossacks now claim millions in their ranks and effectively influence regional, and sometimes international, political scene? In most of the available English-language literature, the Cossack movement is rarely correctly distinguished in its varieties in countries of FSU. Usually the historical roots of the Cossack phenomenon are identified as spontaneous revolts against growing class and religious oppression in both the Russian and Polish Kingdoms at the end of the fifteenth and beginning of the sixteenth century. Those dissatisfied with increasing exploitation in the latter and the introduction of serfdom in the former had found a niche on the borderland between the two states and the un-

Soviet and having living descendants of Cossack origin, who often preserved not only family relics but also grief for past repression, such organizations successfully spread the Cossack movement so that the idea of cultural revival smoothly shifted to a political phase. Particularly active were the Don Cossacks, who protested against drastic damage to the environment and demanded local government. As more and more Cossacks publicly reclaimed their identity, the Communist Party sought to co-opt them into a docile "Union of Cossacks," launched in 1990, but within months this body spawned an anti-communist offshoot, the Union of Cossack Troops of Russia

---

conquered steppes, outside the influence of the Ottoman Empire. These armed settlers of the borderlands became hunters, fishers and farmers in addition to their main activity as warriors. With time, two major communities formed around two centres on the Don and Dnipro rivers. Consequently, two different collective names became distinguished as Don Cossacks and Zaporozhian Cossacks, the latter named after waterfalls on the river Dnipro. Apart from regular service to the Russian Tsar or Polish king, the two communities had many similar characteristics particularly with regard to 1) social origin and 2) economic activities. On the other hand there were quite substantial differences in organisation and ideology. Unlike their Russian colleagues who served the Russian tsars as settled farmers-warriors, the Ukrainian Cossacks quickly developed a social organisation which Karl Marx called the 'first Christian republic in Europe', i.e. a society of members equal in their rights and Christian in their worldview. A different evolution occurred within Russian Cossackdom. Early runaway people dispersed their settlements along the southern borders of the Moscow Kingdom and gathered together to hold Cossack assemblies where appropriate. Although the principles of democratic election were very much the same as those in the Zaporozhian Sich, their performance varied from host to host. Following the Russian colonisation of Siberia and parts of Central Asia, Cossack bands settled in different geographical areas and created various sub-cultures. Perhaps due to the lack of a single centre, Russian Cossacks did not manage to homogenise their organisation and consequently were more easily influenced by external political, economic and military factors. The Cossacks of Don and other hosts had to start regular farming from the seventeenth century onwards (it was previously not considered an 'honourable' activity). They also gradually became involved in state service, so that starting from the end of eighteenth century, they became largely settled farmers with certain privileges and military duties. The nineteenth century, in fact, is known as the "Golden Age" of Russian Cossacks because of the status and importance attached to their armies by the Tsarist government. As this type of militarised peasantry they entered the twentieth century and contributed to a worldwide stereotype of Cossacks as the most ferocious servants of the tsar and anti-revolutionary forces. On the one hand, the settlement of 'freedom fighters' on the lands granted by the tsar put an end to the idea of Cossacks as a group of people who knew no oppression and inequality. On the other hand, it allowed Russian Cossacks to adapt themselves to constant social change and survive longer than any other Cossack group. The revival of their culture, once undermined by Stalin's genocidal policy of persecution, began with Gorbachev's Perestroika in late 1980's.

and the Near Abroad, which backed Boris Yeltsin (The Cossacks 1996, 26). As Mark Galeotti pointed out, it was the decision by a Cossack ensemble to establish a Cossack State Service to support the Russian regime that brought to the fore the role of Cossacks in Russian politics (Galeotti 1993, 104-106). A mass civic movement from below in this way met the requirements of certain political groupings.

In February 1991, two *rayons* (districts) of the Karachay-Cherkesk Autonomous *Oblast* in the Northern Caucasus were declared a Cossack *okrug*. The Zelenchukskiy-Urup Okrug was proclaimed at a Congress of people's deputies of all levels from the Zelenchukskiy and Urup *rayons* (SWB SE/0988 I, 5 Feb 1991). The situation in the Northern Caucasus was worsening and the psychological, if not physical, threat to the Slavic population was one of the more obvious reasons why the first claim for Cossack rights for independence was voiced there.

An appeal to all people and residents of the Northern Caucasus region by the Great Council of Atamans of the Cossacks of Southern Russia, which was held in Novocherkassk on 17 November 1991, was another illustration of Cossack concern over the security of their communities in the Northern Caucasus. Participants called for inter-ethnic fights to cease, and for all matters causing inter-ethnic discord and conflict to be resolved. The Great Council was attended by Cossack representatives of Moscow, Siberia, the Far East and Sakhalin as well as representatives of Cossacks from Ukraine. Telegrams demanding the immediate issue of a decree on the formation and arming of a national Cossack guard on the territory of southern Russia were sent to the Presidents of the USSR and RSFSR. The Council of Atamans decided to form a Union of Cossack Republics of Southern Russia and Associated Cossacks. It was also decided that the Great Council of Atamans would be considered the supreme body of the Union, and Sergey Meshcheryakov, Ataman of the Don Cossacks, would be elected to be Ataman of the Union of Cossack Republics of Southern Russia and Associated Cossacks. The scale of Cossack ambitions was reflected in a resolution of the Council to open a Cossack mission, a single Cossack bank and a commodity exchange in Moscow.

At this stage the Cossacks of different hosts in Southern Russia tried to establish an independent policy toward the center and various multinational peripheries of the Russian Federation. Terek Cossacks warned Chechen President Dzhokhar Dudayev that they were ready to take arms if their interests were harmed. In December 1991, Kuban' and Don Cossacks formed the Association of Cossacks, which lost little time in claiming the "Cossack" lands transferred from the Stavropol *kraiy* to Chechen-Ingush ASSR in the 1950s. In early March 1992, the mayor of the Cossack-dominated town of Nadtereknaya on the Terek river began to hand out weapons in order to resist Dudayev (SWB, SU / 1233, 19/11/ 91, B/3).

Some circles within the Cossack leadership at that time hoped to form a Cossack Republic of Southern Russia in order to create a counter-balance to the Caucasian Federation, which was formed in November 1991, and to establish more independence from Moscow. Cossacks wanted to re-establish their traditional model of collective village land ownership. The Russian government's policy of privatizing land, however limited, was highly displeasing to the Cossacks. Thus there was scope for many shady alliances: Caucasian leaders were trying to take advantage of Cossack-Moscow antagonism to persuade the Cossacks to join the Caucasian Federation; Terek Cossacks, while forging stronger ties with the Kuban' and Don Cossacks, were looking for allies in North Ossetia, who in turn were embroiled with the Ingush people and were hence in need of Cossack assistance.

In October 1991, the Dniestr Cossack Host appealed for assistance in its fight for Dniestr independence from Moldova. This resulted in the arrival of armed units of volunteers.[41] Similar groups of volunteers were fighting alongside the Armenians during the war over Nagorno-Karabakh and with the Abkhazians in Georgia some time later.

---

[41]   Komsomolskaya Pravda, 21 March 1992.

In this situation, Moscow could not afford to lose time and started to respond to the appeal of the Cossacks for recognition. Several individual Russian leaders such as Vice President Alexander Rutskoi and Marshal Yevgeniy Shaposhnikov were extolling the virtues of Cossack life, and let it be known to the Cossacks that demands for the reinstatement of a Cossack army were being considered. In February 1992, the head of the Terek Cossacks, Ataman Vasiliy Konyakhin, had detailed talks in Vladikavkaz to discuss the setting up of regular Cossack military units there (The Cossacks 1992, 4).

At the end of April 1992, the former head of the state legal directorate, Sergei Shakhrai (a Cossack by birth from the Stavropol Territory) held, in Moscow, the first session of the "Commission on the rehabilitation of the Cossacks," which was established in accordance with an instruction from Boris Yeltsin. Land, military service and Cossack self-government were the first questions on the agenda. On 15 June of the same year, the Russian President signed a decree in which he instructed his government to draft a program for the economic and cultural revival of the Cossacks. He also asked the defense ministry to draft proposals on service by Cossacks in the armed forces (SWB SU/1408, 16 June 1992). Two weeks later another presidential decree, "On measures to implement the Russian Federation law 'On the rehabilitation of repressed people' in relation to the Cossacks," outlined the duties and rights of Cossacks, with an emphasis on rights to traditional forms of self-government, agriculture and military service. The Russian parliament accordingly adopted a resolution on the rehabilitation of the Cossacks, which had been prepared by the parliament and government representatives. The Ministry of Defense did not wait long either, and in November 1992 Colonel-General Valery Tretyakov, commander of the Transbaykal Military District, issued an order to create the first Cossack sub-unit as a part of the Port-Arthur motor-rifle regiment (SWB SU/1534 C1/2, 10 November 1992). A similar decision was taken for the Russian divisions on the southern borders. As Russian TV reported in February 1993, one thousand servicemen arrived at the airborne assault brigade base in Stavropol from the North Caucasus to serve in a Cossack regiment ("Russia" TV Channel, 21 February 1993). Servicemen were supposed to study Cossack history as well as undergo traditional training.

This was also a time of increased Cossack demands for self-government. At a rally held in Rostov-na-Donu, Don Cossacks demanded that Rostov *oblast'* be declared a Cossack territory and put forward economic demands, such as exemption from tax, transferring ownership in order to open shops, as well as land and hunting-grounds. The local authorities had hoped in vain to delay answering these demands. Therefore the Don Cossacks, in accordance with their own understanding of the presidential decree of 15 March 15 1994, "On Reforming Military Structures of the Frontier and Internal Troops on the Territory of the North-Caucasian Region of the Russian Federation and State Support for the Cossacks," proclaimed the Don Republic on 24 March 1994. This was the first such attempt since 1918 (i.e., the start of the Russian civil war). This time local authorities laughed off the announcement and assured foreign journalists that they were in control of the situation. And the next day Vladimir Naumov, leader of the Union of Cossacks, an umbrella group of Cossacks in Russia, criticized the decision of the Don Cossack meeting in Rostov-na-Donu as illegitimate. In fact, the Don Cossack Army in this way declared its independent position from both the main All-Russian Cossack organizations: the Union of Cossacks and the Union of Cossack Troops in Russia and the Near Abroad. In other words, the Grand Council of the Don Cossacks created a precedent in an attempt to make the territory of the Don Army Host a subject of the Russian Federation. The Prosecutor General of Rostov *oblast'* had instructed the Security Ministry directorate to investigate whether such a claim violated the Russian constitution. Criminal proceedings were instigated against the Ataman of Rostov district, G. Tsykin, who signed an order to occupy administration buildings and set up court martials. Russian police issued an official warning to V. Zhdanov, Ataman of the Rodionovo-Nesvetskiy settlement, who, together with five atamans of the neighboring village, arrived in the *rayon* police department and announced that ataman government had been introduced in the *oblast*, that all Soviets had been discarded and that the Cossacks had taken power.

This precedent caused wide debates in Russian society. The parliament repealed Yeltsin's decree on state support for the Cossacks, not only because of its timing but also because of the consequences of its potential implementation. The representative of the parliamentary commission on human rights, O. Orlov, argued, for instance, that:

> There is a tendency in restoring the Cossacks as a class, and the presidential decrees create all the necessary prerequisites for consolidating class privileges. They envision giving the Cossacks land in exchange for a commitment to serve the state. Thus the ownership and use of land among the Cossacks may differ sharply from the forms of land use for other citizens of Russia. It follows from the decrees that traditional forms of self-government can be instituted on the territory where Cossacks live. But Cossack administration was based completely on class principles, and is incompatible with the standards of a law-governed state and lays the foundation for discrimination against the non-Cossack minority. (Orlov 1993, 11)

The author also argued that according to the Soviet laws that were still valid in Russia, militarized organizations must be banned. He accused the Cossacks of trafficking weapons from the "trouble spots" of the former USSR, as well as Yugoslavia, into Russia as well as of participating in armed conflicts there. Yet in a way it was already too late for such criticism, for as Moscow News Military analyst V. Dudnik pointed out: "The Cossacks are part and parcel of Russia's spiritual revival. It is important who will add them to the armed forces: if the ruling power, then Cossacks will be its ally, if the opposition, then the Cossacks will be the source of a new discord" (Dudnik 1993, 11).

Another reason for state support of the Cossack movement could be that, in 1992, the Russian army was under-manned by 50 percent. Among the least staffed was the North Caucasian military district, and the government could possibly change the situation by calling up the Cossack units. The Russian Cossacks were ready to ensure a 100 percent spring call-up to the Cossack units and detachments of the Russian Armed forces in 1993, Vladimir Naumov, the field ataman of the Union of Cossacks, told Interfax, the Moscow-based agency on the 17 March 1993 (SWB SU/1642 C3/2, 20 MAR 93). In reality, by the end of 1994 Cossacks provided only 8,000 draftees from all over the country (Dubnov 1994, 18). The Russian Armed Forces benefited from Cossack volunteers only when professional units were introduced later in the 1990s, on a full-time pay basis. By July 2000, already 20,000 out of 220,000 Cossack volunteers had managed to gain employment in the Russian Armed Forces, paramilitary formations or law-enforcement agencies (*Agenstvo Voyennykh Novostey*, 2000, July).

A presidential decree of 15 March1993 established the procedure for serving in Cossack units of the Russian Federation Armed Forces. It was incumbent upon the Defense Ministry of Internal Affairs to confirm the list of Cossack combined units, submit proposals on their traditional designations and set up structures for Cossack affairs within the departments of these ministries.

This decree also enabled the Russian government to elaborate a statute on land relations with the Cossacks engaged in military service, along with a special regime for land use in the Cossack communities. An interdepartmental commission for Cossack affairs under the Russian Federation Council of Ministers had been set up in line with the decree ("Pravda," 17 Mar 1993).

The Russian Vice Prime-minister Sergey Shakhray openly believed that unless the Cossack movement and its interests were recognized, none of the North Caucasian problems could be solved. He said that the Cossack problem could not be ignored; Cossacks had set up their own power structures before the decree was issued; and in addition to the Cossacks, other national movements in the Caucasus had their own militias, suggesting that it was not the decree that brought about the problem. "The qualities displayed by Cossacks, such as patriotism, readiness to serve the country, discipline, and efficient use of land must be put to the service of Russia," Shakhray said, in an interview with Interfax news agency on 2 April 1993 (SWB SU/1659 C3/8 9 April 1993). In return, the council of atamans of the Russian Union of Cossacks, held in Moscow on 10-11 April 1993, assured "its unanimous support for the institutions of presidential power" (SWB SU/1666 B1 19 April 1993).

The presidential policy expressed by Shakhray turned out to be effective at least in the short term. At the end of April 1993, the Confederation of Peoples of the Caucasus signed an agreement with the Organization of Cossacks of Southern Russia after difficult negotiations that took place in Stavropol. The agreement, "On the principles of co-operation and mutual assistance between the Confederation of the Peoples of the Caucasus and Cossacks of Southern Russia," gained the full backing of the delegations of Chechnya, North Ossetia, Kabarda-Balkaria and Dagestan, as well as that of South Ossetia and Karachay-Cherkessia. It stipulated that all problems should be settled by exclusively peaceful means, that it is impermissible for any of the participants to be used as a force in opposition to another, and should there be a threat of destabilization, talks will immediately start to work out effective measures (SWB SU/1676 B/3, 30 Apr 1993). Later on, this agreement was overstepped by all sides, but it was still positive as a stabilizing formal accord.

The agreement of the Cossacks of Southern Russia with the Confederation meant also a new period of Cossack self-exhibition, on a wider, international scale. The leader of another Cossack organization, "The Cossack League," ataman Vladimir Naumov, for the first time officially recognized that some Cossack volunteers participated in the Yugoslavia war (on the Serbian side). He admitted casualties and said that the number of Cossacks in Serbia was permanently changing as many went there for a short term (a month or two). In an interview with the Russian news agency RIA on 12 May 1993 he said, "At present, we do not approve of the Cossack volunteer service in Serbia. There are about 150 Cossacks there now. But if the situation changes and America joins the Serb suppression effort, we shan't stay aloof, and the number of volunteers will grow" (SWB SU/1691 A1/1, 18 May 93).

On 17 July 1993, the Council of atamans of the main Cossack organizations took a decision at an assembly held in Moscow to establish the Union of Cossack Forces of Russia. However, the attempt to consolidate the Cossack movement was hardly successful. One month later, the Terek Cossacks, at their extraordinary general meeting in Mineralnye Vody, called for the creation of a Cossack Republic, and supported the action carried out by the forces of the Pyatigorsk Cossack district to block roads in protest against the repression of the Slav population in the North Caucasus republics and the failure to fulfill the president's decree on the rehabilitation of the Cossacks, as reported by "Izvestiya" on 12 August 1993 (SWB SU/1769, 17 Aug 93). After a few days of blockade, the Cossacks decided, by a small majority and with objections from the elders, to send a delegation to Moscow for talks with Deputy Premier Vladimir Shumeiyko. The package of recommendations included renewed demands for autonomy, and a call to establish order in the North Caucasus where Slavs were persecuted, as well as new and more radical demands, including the demand for the return of Kizlyarskiy rayon from Dagestan, Mozdokskiy rayon from North Ossetia, Prokhladnenskiy rayon from Kabarda-Balkaria, and of the Cossack villages along the Terek in Chechnya, as well as the recognition of the state and the legal status of the Terek Cossacks as subjects of the federation. This latter demand had previously been conditional upon the stipulation: "unless the position of the governments in neighboring republics changes." This was the first time it had been stated categorically, albeit without unanimous backing (SWB SU/1769 B/8 [31], 17 Aug 1993).

A new boost to the Cossacks' demands took place in September, when the Constitutional Court of the Russian Federation recognized Yeltsin's decree on the Cossacks, dated 15 March 1993, as being constitutional. The official verdict, announced on 15 September by the Constitutional Court's press service, noted that the court had not agreed with the view of the Supreme Soviet, which had submitted the claim to verify the decree. The Supreme Soviet believed that the decree established a special regime of military service for the Cossacks and that this did not correspond to the constitution in terms of the division of competence between legislative and executive power. The constitutional court drew the conclusion that the "essence of the decree does not establish any special regime of service for the Cossacks and does not create any new military formations or units" (Interfax News Agency, Moscow, in English 1706 GMT 15 September 93 [editorial report]).

In return, the most numerous and organized of the Cossacks, those of the Don, declared their satisfaction and demonstrated their support for the new draft of the Russian constitution, which provided the Russian president with additional powers, powers that were criticized by the opposition and most of all by Russian Communists. The Union of Cossack Forces of Russia and Abroad (an anti-communist organization) announced at a press conference in Novocherkassk on 3 December 1993 that a decision supporting the draft constitution had been taken at a session of the Council of Atamans. The leaders of the Union used this opportunity to declare once again that they would oppose elections to the Russian Federal Council of all four Rostov *oblast'* candidates, whose stance contradicted their interests.[42]

The defense ministry acknowledged the Cossacks' support and issued another directive in which the Cossacks were promised that they would serve in combined-arms units, airborne Cossack formations and Cossack *spetsnaz*. Accordingly, the directive implied the elaboration of a legal status defining the status of Cossack servicemen (SWB SU/1871 S1/1, 14 December 1993 [4]).

By early 1994, the acknowledgment by Cossacks of their participation in the conflict between the parties in Bosnia found its confirmation in media reports from the former Yugoslavia. The Tanjug agency from Belgrade reported in January 1994 that a delegation of the Republic of Serbian Krajina (RSK), led by RSK Minister of Foreign Affairs Slobodan Jarcevic, was planning to pay a visit to the supreme command of the joint Cossack troops of Russia and the Near Abroad (SWB EE/1890 C/5 08 January 1994 [13]). After the visit, the Croatian Defense Ministry issued a statement in which the

---

[42]   The fact that one of the candidates, namely oblast Soviet Chairman A.Popov, formally joined the Cossack ranks did not change the mind of the Cossack leaders. In the view of the atamans, representatives of the Democratic Party of Russia met their requirements best of all. As they informed the 'Kommersant-Daily', the Don Cossacks intended to back the Rostov candidate for the State Duma, Col-Gen. Yuriy Rodionov, the former commander of the Transcaucasus Military District, because he 'favours a stronger political influence for the Cossacks' ('Kommersant-Deyli', 4 December 1993, 4). It was the same general who had ordered Soviet army soldiers in Tbilisi to use force against civilians at a peaceful demonstration in 1988, which set a 'precedent' to be repeated under 'Perestroika'.

RSK Foreign Minister, Slobodan Jarcevic, who had led the delegation, stated after his return that the Cossacks ignored the sanctions against Yugoslavia and stressed their readiness to provide not only humanitarian help to local Serb authorities, but also in "all other fields." "Representatives of the Serb terrorists from the occupied Croatian territories also signed some kind of an agreement on scientific, cultural, educational and technical cooperation with the Cossacks," reported Croatian Radio in Zagreb (SWB EE/1900 C/2, 20 January 1994).

A few months later, the Ukrainian Ministry of Internal Affairs expressed concern when a considerable number of Russian Cossacks arrived in Crimea: "The Crimeans do not support and do not understand the appearance of the Russian Cossacks since the local police are capable of ensuring the reliable defense of public order with its own forces" (UNIAR News Agency, SWB SU/2013 D/2, 03 June 1994). According to the Russian news agency ITAR-TASS on 15 June, "Russia's Don Cossacks and the Crimea have signed an agreement of friendship and co-operation." In fact, the agreement was signed by the Russian Cossack leader Viktor Ratiyev and the Crimean president Yuri Meshkov, who stressed the "historic closeness and indivisibility of the history of Russian Cossacks and the people of the republic of Crimea and the irreversibility of the ongoing processes." The Crimean authorities planned to establish an embassy in the town of Novocherkassk, capital of the Don Cossacks, while the union of Russian Cossacks was supposed to open an embassy in Simferopol, the capital of Crimea (SWB SU/2025 D/9, 18 June 94 [8]).

Further international recognition came to the Cossacks from officials in Alma-Ata. State authorities in Kazakhstan gave the regional Cossack organization official status, although they stressed that Cossacks in Kazakhstan should form a cultural rather than quasi-military association. At this point, Kazakh statesmen assumed that it would be possible to win the favor of the Cossack movement and direct it into a multi-ethnic civic organization including ethnic Kalmykians and Ossetians. The Kazakh State Counsellor Kairbek Stileyinenov even said that it might be possible for Cossack troops to serve on the borders with China, Iran and the Caspian Sea, and that a Cossack platoon might be raised for Kazakhstan's Republican Guards (SWB SU/2045 G/8, 12 July 94 [6]).

> Quite soon, however, it appeared that this would not be the case. Kazakh-stan's Justice Minister had to warn the Cossack organization that its activities could be suspended if it continued to break the law. From the Kazakh authori-ties' point of view, the newly formed "Society for Assistance to the Semirechye Cossacks" was registered as a public association, but acted as a military organ-ization pursuing political and commercial aims. In fact, the very next day the organization held a conference, a sanctioned meeting and a funeral service, that caused the Kazakh Justice minister to make a statement on national TV that the "actions of this association's members run counter to their rules and our laws, our constitution, our law on public associations, our law on the ad-ministrative territorial division of the country, and our law on universal mili-tary service' (Kazakh TV on 22 July 1994, SWB SU/2056 G/2, 25 July 1994).

In Russia, the status of the Cossacks was enhanced when Presi-dent Yeltsin signed the decree, "On the Council for Cossack Affairs under the Russian Federation president'" on 5 July 1994. The decree stated: "The Council is a consultative body under the President of the Russian Federation, created for the purpose of informing the President of the Russian Federation on questions of the Rebirth of the Brotherhood of Russian Cossacks and the unification of Cossack societies, as well as for developing proposals on determining state policy in regard to the Russian Cossacks."[43] The Russian Ministry of Defense renamed the 21st Brigade of the Russian Paratroopers as the 21st Separate Stavropol Cossack Paratroop Brigade following "the repeatedly voiced wish to revive traditions of military service by *ethnic* Cossacks," reported ITAR-TASS (SWB SU/2066 S1/2 05 Aug 1994).

On 24 August 1994, following a few local conflicts between the Cossacks and various armed groups in the North Caucasus, the Great Don Host signed an agreement with the Chechen authorities that provoked the dissatisfaction of both other Cossack hosts and the Rostov *oblast'* local government. The statement by the Rostov re-gional administration and legislative assembly, issued on 1 Septem-ber 1994, claimed that "the agreement on friendship and co-

---

43   Rossiyskaya Gazeta, "Statute on the Council on Cossack Affairs under the Presi-dent of the Russian Federation," 7 December 1994, 4.

operation" represents a gross violation of the Russian constitution and carries a threat of destabilization of "the situation in the North Caucasus and the Rostov region." The authorities warned that any attempt by the signatories to implement the agreement's provisions and to arbitrarily assume governing functions and powers "might in a certain situation warrant a decision to suspend further activities of the Cossack Union of the Great Don Army or even to dissolve it." The Agreement, signed with the Chechen Republic (Ichkeria), on behalf of all the Terek and Kuban' Cossacks, was also blasted by a number of Don Atamans as "a stab in the back," because it had been signed without knowledge of the former group.

The threat to suspend the activities of Cossack organizations for the violation of the law materialized quite soon in Kazakhstan. In December 1994, Kazakh Justice Minister Nagashybay Shaykenov issued a ruling suspending the activities of the Alma-Ata region Cossack "society of mutual support." Semirechye Cossacks were accused of alleged military contacts with Russian-based Cossack formations. Registered as a public association, "the society, however, promoted itself into the ranks of the Russian Cossacks' military forces as an armed unit, in violation of Article 55 of the Kazakh constitution," the Kazakh news agency Kaztag reported, quoting the Justice Ministry ruling. However, on 5 December, Russia's former Vice President, Aleksandr Rutskoy, accused Kazakhstan of victimizing its ethnic Russian population, which did not help in defusing the confrontation (SWB SU/2173 G/1, 8 December 1994). Detained Cossack activists Nikolay Gunkin and Viktor Achkasov, identified by Kazakh authorities as military commanders, received prison sentences. An appeal by the Russian Foreign Ministry official, to start an immediate dialogue with Kazakhstan in order to normalize the situation around the Cossacks, "taking into account their legitimate interests and help consolidation of friendship and cooperation between the Russian and Kazakh peoples," also did not help, especially since it was accompanied by a statement that Russia was ready to protect the interests of Kazakh Cossacks (SWB SU/2174 B/14, 9 December 1994 [53]). In fact, the authorities in Kazakhstan continued to follow their laws and the Cossack leaders, released after a temporary detainment, were re-arrested a year later. Confrontation between Cossack organizations and Kazakh authorities continued throughout the 1990s into the new century, as the Ural'sk Cossack Host insisted on recognition of Cossacks as a separate ethnic community with a corresponding ethnic homeland on the territory of Kazakhstan, something clearly unacceptable for the Kazakh government. Kazakh authorities preferred to consider Cossacks as a part of the Russian minority and resisted the division of rural areas of Kazakhstan into Cossack *stanitsas*. The leader of Ural (Yaitsk) Cossack Host, A. Avilov, was summoned to the prosecutor's office in July 2001 and informed that the activity of his organization violated provisions of the Kazakh law, reported Kazakhstan Today News Agency in Almaty on 3 July 2001 (BBC Mon CAU 040701).

The relationship of the Cossacks with the peoples of the North Caucasus was developing no less dramatically. The agreement of the Great Don Host with the Chechen Republic, which drew so much criticism in Russia, was honored by the Chechen side concerning the release of Cossacks captured after the First Russian-Chechen War (1994-95). Chechen authorities handed over Cossack prisoners of war, who fought in unit No. 11879 of the Russian Federal troops, to the Don Army representatives. The POWs were handed over after Don Army ataman Kononov had sent Dzhokhar Dudayev a letter referring to an agreement on mutual assistance signed between the two leaderships (SWB SU/2220 B/9, 6 Feb 95).

In February 1995 the Central Cossack Force of Russia was set up in a grand ceremony at its headquarters in Moscow. It was announced that a new body brought together some 18,000 Cossacks from 18 regions in the European part of Russia. The newly elected chieftain of the Central Cossack Force, Boris Ignatyev, outlined several major tasks of the new organization: "We aim at providing the market with foodstuffs to capacity and reviving the agricultural sector," he emphasized. "The other task, of no less significance, is to revive Russia's ideals, the Orthodox Church, and to bring up the young in the vein of loving one's fatherland, because Cossacks as such are unthinkable without them" (SWB, 21 February 1995).

The Federation's Council Chairman Vladimir Shumeyko soon said that "it appears there is no military more professional than the Cossacks'," referring to the military potential of the Cossack movement, while an organizing committee for a draft law on Russian Cossacks opened the discussion of the law on Cossacks in the parliamentary center. On 30 April 30, President Yeltsin sent a welcome message to the emergency congress of Russian Cossack military commanders, saying that they faced "a noble and responsible task: to unite Russian Cossacks and renew their best traditions" (SWB SU/2291 B/3, 1 May 1995). Indeed, Cossack atamans from 59 regions of Russia agreed to do away with all differences existing between various Cossack formations "for the sake of consolidation, to serve the people and fatherland." The agreement was reflected in the treaty, "On unity and accord of the Cossack community of Russia," adopted by Russian atamans' council in Moscow on 1 May 1995 (SWB SU/2292 B/2, 2 May 1995).

These developments illustrated the tendency of the Russian authorities to unify the Cossack movement early on in order to take better control of it; but, at the same time, they show that the movement itself had matured enough to make an attempt to overcome regional fragmentation and create a united Cossack organization. Although this unity was not achieved in practical terms at this council, the consolidation attempt stimulated the Cossacks to emphasize their interests in reforming Russian agriculture and electing Cossack MPs.[44]

Land has become of crucial importance not only economically, but also as a political card. Local authorities in Russia realized that they could trade vast and often unused territories for political gain. So, for instance, the head of the Maritime Territory administration, Yevgeniy Nazdratenko, transferred to Cossack ownership an area of land destined for China under a 1991 Soviet-Chinese agreement. The local Ussuri Cossacks were glad to set up a joint-stock company to

---

[44]   The head of the Duma's fraction of the Agrarian party, Mikhail Lapshin, even made a joint statement with the head of the Union of Russian Cossacks, Aleksandr Martynov, pledging to join forces to field their candidates for scheduled parliamentary elections. (SWB SU/2303 B/1, 15 May 95).

develop land where they planned to establish Cossack settlements, protecting the state border and farming. Nazdratenko's move to oppose official Russian foreign policy immediately triggered a statement by the Russian Security Council, chaired by President Yeltsin, aiming to "overcome negative tendencies that have been noted in the Cossack movement." The Security Council outlined measures to develop and implement a unified policy toward the Cossack movement (SWB SU/2306, 18 May 1995, SU/2312, 25 May 1995). On 9 August 1995, President Yeltsin issued a decree, "On the state register of Cossack communities in the Russian Federation," thereby putting the Ministry for the Affairs of Nationalities and Regional Policy[45] in charge of the Cossack communities.

However, the continuing First Chechen War and the deterioration of the security situation in the North Caucasus became the most pressing concern for the Cossack organizations. According to the ataman of Pyatigorsk district, Yuriy Churekov, Ter Cossacks put on alert 5,000 men when information spread that in June 1995 an armed gang of more than 200 hundred men, Chechens, Ingush, Kabardins, Karachays and mujahideen from Turkey and Iran, appeared on the border with Karachay-Cherkesiya. In an interview with the radio station *Ekho Moskvy*, Churekov said that the Cossacks blocked the roads through villages within a 200 km radius of Mineralnye Vody in the Caucasus (SWB SU/2335 B/13 21 June 1995). Leaders of the Cossacks in the Stavropol Territory had demanded the creation of an independent North Caucasian republic, after Chechen fighters took several thousand people hostage at the hospital of Budennovsk town in June 1995, which resulted in bloodshed and an appalling loss of human life that distressed not only the Russian public but affected all countries of the FSU that had not experienced terrorist attacks on such a scale before.

---

[45] Under the presidential decree, the federal bodies of executive power must ensure the necessary conditions for drawing those members of the Cossack communities included in the state register to perform state service in the established order, and to grant them economic and other privileges in keeping with federal legislation (SWB SU/2379 B/1, 11 August 1995).

The Cossacks Union of Georgia was established in July 1995 in order to "achieve real stability in Georgia and promote further closeness among newly-established democratic states." A few days later, Georgian radio broadcast a special statement, in which the Cossacks announced that they defined themselves as a part of the Republic's population and regarded Georgia as their homeland. It also said that they were ready to protect the territorial integrity of the Georgian state and stressed the historical ties between the Cossacks of Russia and Georgia, only to promote good-neighborly relations between the two countries. A delegation of the Union of Cossack hosts of Russia and the Near Abroad, led by Vadim Boyko, offered its support in combating terrorism to the Georgian prime minister Otar Patsatsia when they met in September 1996. The supreme ataman of the Union of Cossack Hosts of Russia and the Near Abroad, Viktor Ratijev, suggested that if the Cossacks would serve on the Abkhaz part of the Russian-Georgian border jointly with Georgian border troops, the problem of Abkhazia could be resolved (SWB SU/2398 F/2, 2 September 1995). The irony is that it was the Russian Cossacks, with the unofficial support of the Russian Federal Army, who had contributed to the civil war in Georgia, resulting in the separation of Abkhazia from Georgia a few years earlier. At a time when the Georgian state was weak, and there was a relatively weakened Russian border service, Cossacks really became an option to consider. By that time, the Russian media reported that around 20 Cossack units were in the process of forming in the Russian army, including 12 in the Russian Federal border guard service (SWB SU/2385 S1/1, 18 August 1995). Ataman Martynov told a press conference in Moscow that the Russian Union of Cossacks were forming 29 units which would serve in the armed forces and 31 units for service in the Border Troops. Martynov also said that the Cossack regiments had taken part in combat operations, including operations to "restore the constitutional order" in Chechnya, for which four regiments were awarded the Cross for Faith, Freedom and Fatherland. Martynov claimed that unions of Cossack troops and organizations represented more than 10 million Russian Cossacks, who constitute a people in their own right, not a social layer. In his opinion, 11 alternative Cossack unions had been established by "certain forces" on the basis of the "divide-and-rule principle," implying state interference (SWB SU/2445 S1/2 29 September 1995).

The status of the Cossacks as a separate people was directly recognized in the President's decree issued on 10 August 1995. The decree, "On the state register of Cossack communities in the Russian Federation," directed the Ministry for the Affairs of Nationalities and Regional Policy to deal with the Cossack claims to autonomy in the same way that it dealt with similar claims from other ethnic-territorial entities such as Tatarstan. This was a new development, since the Cossacks were recognized as a separate ethnic or national entity with the prospect of a new status and, therefore, rights. As N. Yegorov, chairman of the Council for Cossack Affairs, explained later, the state was desperate to avoid the militarization of the Cossack communities. Hence, all Cossack military units from the start would be placed under the federal law. Recognition of Cossack status seemed to work and diverted Cossacks' energy from internal to external challenges. Ataman of the All-Kuban' Cossack Troop V. Gromov called for the creation of an Orthodox Christian league of Slavonic states, "in connection with the developments in Bosnia and the need for rendering assistance to Serbs," against whom "all the might of the West has been turned" (SWB SU/2409 B/12, 15 September 1995). From now on, Russian Cossack communities would gradually become the breeding ground for mercenaries and contract soldiers for both the Federal Army as well as private military companies helping to achieve the foreign policy objectives of the Russian state.

The new status of Cossacks as a people gave a new impulse to the Russian Foreign Ministry and Ministry for the Nationalities and Regional Policy to put new pressure on Kazakh authorities to free Cossack leaders in Kazakhstan and provide Kazakh Cossacks with greater civic rights as an "ethnic minority." Cossacks themselves threatened to take hostage Kazakh ministers arriving in Moscow for negotiations unless ataman N. Gunkin was released. The Kazakh minister for foreign affairs called such demands a "violation of international legal standards" and the Russian request "an artificial problem." From the Kazakh point of view, Cossacks' behavior in Kazakhstan ran against the legislation prohibiting the possession of arms and the annexation of lands belonging to the Kazakh state.[46] President Nazarbayev has also criticized the Russian media for its coverage of Kazakhstan, in particular reports about the detention of the leader of the Semirechye Cossacks in Southern Kazakhstan. He linked the campaign in the Russian media around the "Cossack question" to the parliamentary elections in Russia, when some Russian politicians were prepared "to use every means possible, however dirty, to achieve success in the campaign" (SWB SU/2461 G/1, 15 November 1995).

The Cossack Union of Georgia was a notable exception in the FSU countries in the sense that it supported Tbilisi and criticized Moscow after the failure of so-called Abkhaz-Georgian talks in December 1995. The Cossacks of Georgia condemned the placid stance taken by Russia in respect to the Abkhaz separatists who were acting in accordance with the Chechnya scenario. The failure of the Abkhaz-Georgian talks in Moscow, according to the Cossacks of Georgia, clearly demonstrated the lack of seriousness in Russia's attitude toward settling the conflict. On behalf of all ethnic Russians residing in Georgia, the Cossack Union of Georgia called on the Russian president, Boris Yeltsin, to take decisive measures to secure the return of refugees to Abkhazia and the restoration of Georgia's territorial integrity (SWB SU/2482 F/2, 9 December 1995). That appeal was repeated in vain again in September 1996. Two years later the Cossacks elected President Shevardnadze as their leader and volunteered to serve for the Georgian State Department for Border Protection, reported the Prime News Agency in Tbilisi on 17 March 2000 (BBC Mon FS1 FsuPol).

Meanwhile, President Yeltsin skillfully played the Cossack card in his re-election campaign when he signed a decree creating the

---

[46]   According to the official version of the deputy police chief of Alma-Ata, Vladimir Kurbanov, N.Gunkin was detained on 28 October for 'repeated violation of the procedure for organising and holding assemblies, rallies and demonstrations'. The activity of the Society for Promotion of Semirechiye Cossacks was suspended due to its re-registration as the Union of Semirechye Cossacks (SWB SU/2461 G/1 15 Nov 95).

Main department for Cossack Troops under presidential administration in January 1996, in order to "achieve better coordination of state institutions and the Cossack hosts." *Rosiyskiye Vesti* commented that, not surprisingly, Boris Yeltsin received the backing of the Cossack organizations in the election campaign. Leaders of the Volga Cossack Host, the Terek Cossack Host, the Kalmyk Cossack Host and a number of other local atamans signed a joint statement issued by the Presidential Cossack Affairs Council with an appeal to all Cossacks to vote for President Yeltsin as the "only candidate to guarantee that there would be no Communist revenge" (Volodina 1996, 1).

Speaking to residents of the Russian border town of Budenovsk in April 1996, where in the previous summer Chechen fighters had taken hostage more than a thousand hospital patients, President Yeltsin stressed that "the legal provision for the revival of the Cossacks continues to be strengthened." Yeltsin meant, among others, his two new decrees, "On the procedure for recruitment of members of Cossack communities to state and other services," and another on economic benefits for the Cossacks who undertake duties for the state. A weakened Russian state could not provide guarantees of security for its border regions in the North Caucasus, and the Cossack initiative to support Federal troops was mutually beneficial. Russia's Defense Minister, Pavel Grachev, expressed his support for the creation of Cossack units predominantly in the North Caucasus Military district and explained the inability to win the war when "fighters are acting in small subversive groups using ambushes and organising terrorist acts" (SWB SU/2590 S1/3, 19 April 1996). Later, the coordinating council for the struggle against terrorism and other serious crimes in Stavropol Territory supported the Stavropol Cossacks' intention to create armed self-defense units in the area of the territory that bordered Chechnya (SWB SU/2728 B/9, 27 September 1996). The Cossack population in Chechnya and elsewhere in the North Caucasus was also becoming a legitimizing factor for the Federal army to protect "Russian interests" in those areas. As A. Voloshyn, atamanof the Terek Cossack District, said in an interview for the Russian television network NTV, Cossacks had come to fight in Chechnya not only to show the government that they were able to serve the state, but also to "resolve once and for all" the question of land in the North Caucasus (SWB SU/2588 B/8, 17 April 1996). Yeltsin's promises of free frontier lands in return for service were echoed in an optimistic Cossack response.

Despite such optimism, neither Cossacks themselves nor the Federal troops could overcome the resistance of the Chechen army and the First Chechen "campaign" ended on terms favorable to the Chechen separatists. In these circumstances, Cossack claims to the Naurskiy and Shelkovskiy districts in Northern Chechnya became a real threat to Russia's security after General Lebed mastered a peace deal. The Russian State Duma held a closed session on 19 December 1996, to discuss the conflict between the Terek Cossacks and the Chechen authorities. Some Russian deputies, including a few leading figures, were inclined to arm Cossacks in Northern Chechnya. The State Duma Deputy Chairman Mikhail Yureyev, for instance, supported the Cossacks' claims. In his view, since the leaders of the Chechen Republic of Ichkeria had disassociated themselves from the heritage of the Chechen-Ingush Autonomous Soviet Socialist Republic, the three districts transferred after World War II to the Chechen-Ingush ASSR did not belong, in fact, to the present Chechen state. As the Russian human rights activist S. Kovalyov put it boldly at that time: "These demands mean war" (SWB SU/2819 B/3, 17 January 1997). Therefore, it was unsurprising that the Russian Security Council's Deputy Secretary, L. Mayorov, made a statement for ITAR-TASS claiming that demands to return some areas on the left bank of the River Terek to Stavropol Territory were unrealistic (SWB SU/2817 B/4, 15 January 1997). The Russian Federal Security Service public relations center denied "rumors" that Russian special services were planning to provoke Chechens and Cossacks into armed clashes. This followed a statement from the Chechen side that some Russian institutions were trying to provoke conflict.

Although the pro-presidential council of Atamans of Russia's Cossack troops had decided to "refrain from any actions deemed capable of destabilizing the situation in the North Caucasus," its leaders asked the Constitutional Court to examine the constitutionality of the decree by the Presidium of the Russian Federation Supreme Soviet, "On the restoration of the Chechen-Ingush ASSR and the abolition of the Grozny Region," dated 9 January 1957, regarding the inclusion of the Naurskiy and Shelkovskiy Districts in Chechen-Ingushetia (SWB SU/2817 B/4, 15 January 1997). The meeting of Cossacks in Chechnya issued a more extreme resolution, not only making territorial claims but also declaring the right to arm for self-protection. The Cossack leaders called on the Russian government to take measures to ensure the protection of the Russian population in Chechnya or they would make efforts to have Chechnya's Naurskiy and Shelkovskiy districts reintegrated into Stavropol Territory (SWB SU/2818 B/10, 16 January 1997). The Council of Cossack Atamans of Southern Russia (Stavropol Territory) supported territorial claims in Chechnya and the right to arm Cossack units in Chechnya, with open support of the Russian Security Council Deputy Secretary Boris Berezovskiy, who attended the meeting on 17 January.[47] On his return to Moscow, Berezovskiy said that he agreed completely with the Cossacks' right to arm themselves in Chechnya and would resign if the opinion of the Security Council differed on that matter.

Chechens reacted immediately with a statement from the head of the Confederation of the Peoples of the Caucasus and Chechen presidential candidate Yusup Soslambekov, who described the decision of the Cossack Council as "a crude provocation directed at undermining the situation in the region." He denied claims that Russians were discriminated against in Chechnya and urged the federal authorities "immediately to make an assessment of the [Cossack] council decisions that actually call for the beginning of a new Caucasian war." Soslambekov also said that Council decisions did not reflect the sentiments of all Cossacks and there may be a joint session of the confederation leadership and Cossack representatives: "I am convinced that nobody will manage to set Cossacks and the moun-

---

[47]   Addressing Cossacks at the meeting, Berezovskiy said: "My position is that all interests, all interests of Russians should be defended without exception in Chechnya. And when you today say: 'Give us weapons since the other side has them!' I can tell you that I personally support you one hundred per cent on that. I state quite clearly that, as far as my own personal position is concerned. If the position of executive power differs from the position I am expressing now, I personally will not work in that executive power" (SWB SU/2819 B/3, 17 January 1997).

tain people against each other" (SWB SU/2820 B/3, 18 January 1997).

The Russian authorities appeared to be divided on that issue. The Russian State Duma instructed its law committee to work out additions to the law on weapons that would allow Cossack organizations to arm. The Russian Minister of Internal Affairs, A. Kulikov, said that to arm the Russian population in Chechnya would mean war with the Chechens and that, in the absence of Russian troops and police in the region, this would simply lead to the genocide of ethnic Russians in Chechnya. Therefore, the only way to improve the situation, in the view of the Minister, was to use all forms of pressure on Chechen authorities to ensure the safety of all the population on its territory even if that meant rendering the assistance to the Chechen side (SWB SU/2820 B/4, 18 January 1997). The same day, 17 January 1997, a high-ranking official from the Russian Security Council expressed his categorical opposition to the proposal for the creation of armed units among Cossacks in Chechnya. He said that Cossacks could wear bladed weapons as a part of their costumes and could serve with arms in army units. The arming of the Cossack population would lead, in his opinion, to war. A few days later the Security and Defense Committee of Russian Federation Council initiated a statement, "On the situation in the North Caucasus," approved by an absolute majority of the upper house of the Russian Parliament, which condemned the actions of Boris Berezovskiy, the deputy secretary of the Security Council, for "his inflammatory and provocative appeals to arm the Cossacks and the readiness which he has expressed to achieve this by using his official position." The members of the Federation Council therefore expressed no confidence in Berezovskiy and recommended that the Russian president immediately release him from his post. The statement, adopted by the Federation Council on 23 January 1996, expressed the hope that "reason and law will finally get the upper hand over emotions" (SWB SU/2825 B/8 24 January 1997).

The Russian Communist opposition in the Duma, however, supported the idea of arming Cossacks, but under strict state control and with simultaneous negotiations with the Chechen government.

Russian public opinion was divided as well, with almost half of the Russian population supporting the idea of arming the Cossacks (Moscow News, Mnenie, 17-19 January 1996). Stavropol Cossacks themselves, after all, decided to "act with restraint regarding developments in Chechnya." The Stavropol Cossack Council issued a statement with careful wording about the right to arms. After elections took place in Chechnya on 27 January 1997, the council of military commanders of Cossack troops in Southern Russia, along with representatives of the Kuban', Terek, Stavropol, Astrakhan and Kalmyk Cossack troops, appealed to President Yeltsin saying elections in Chechnya "confirmed the Cossacks' chief concern: that terrorists will not relinquish their weapons." The draft resolution, passed by the council, envisaged a set of Cossack security arrangements, like a permanent headquarters in Stavropol, but no claim to arms was issued (SWB SU/2870 B/5, 18 March 1997). This was one of the most dramatic moments in the Cossack saga since the Cossack revival had started a decade earlier. On 20 February 1997 the State Duma passed a law, "On Cossacks," stressing that the admittance of Cossack units to state military service did not further any political goals. The law described Cossacks as "a community of people formed in the process of historical development who have their own traditions, areas of residence, culture, economic system and a special attitude to army service and to their relationship with the state" (SWB SU/2850 B/2 22 February 1997).

The situation changed when hostilities between Chechen fighters and Russian Federal troops renewed on the territory of Dagestan in 1999. What started as rebel incursions into Dagestan areas turned into a full-scale war, with Russian Federal Troops entering the Chechen Republic with the aim of "crushing terrorists." The Second Chechen War, however, for all its cynical pre-election flavor, had not become a war of Cossack glory. In fact, Russian Federal troops based their military tactics mostly on airborne troops actions and "firewall" artillery. However, Cossacks were also used, first as professional soldiers in military units, and then more often as paramilitary "mercenaries" in the second echelon troops. By early 2000, military

analysts noticed a new Russian tactic of ethnic cleansing that had not
been used in the First Chechen war:

> Tough interrogation of all Chechen males in the age group 10-60, which re-
> quires concentration camps and actually means ethnic cleansing. On the oper-
> ational level, the key 'winning' idea might be to turn the stretch of land be-
> tween the River Terek and the mountains into 'burned land' ... Certainly
> large-scale expulsion and relocation of population would be necessary, but the
> methods are familiar and in fact half of this work is already done. (Bayev
> 2000)

As described in Chapter 3, most of the ethnic cleansing in the
"New Wars" is carried out by paramilitaries of nationalist orientation. Cossacks, with their extensive experience of "New Wars" from
Abkhazia to Bosnia, were certainly prime candidates for such a role,
and indeed, Chechen sources accused at least some of the Cossack
troops of war crimes:

> Mercenaries from so-called Cossack formations are committing excesses in
> Naurskiy and Shelkovskiy Districts of the Chechen Republic of Ichkeria.
> Gangs of drunken marauders on armored vehicles break into the houses of lo-
> cal inhabitants, robbing and killing those who resist. In the village of Borozdi-
> novka, a gang of marauders from the so-called Cossacks tortured local inhab-
> itants for several hours, demanding vodka and money (Kavkaz-Tsentr web
> site, in Russian, 0546 GMT 06 May 00).

Although there are no verified independent reports on war
crimes possibly committed by the Cossacks or indeed Russian soldiers in Chechnya, the Chechen leadership clarified that most of the
alleged crimes were committed not by local Terek Cossacks, but by
the Don or Kuban' Cossacks. This would fit the pattern of crimes in
Bosnia and Kosovo, where atrocities were often committed by
"weekend fighters" or "visiting" paramilitaries. It would be logical
to assume that in this case these were carried out by Chechen Cossacks from Naurskaya and Shelkovskiy Districts, as other Chechen
civilians would be more preoccupied with personal survival under
conditions of war. There is evidence that Russian federal authorities
encouraged Cossacks to move into northern Chechen districts in
order to establish a "friendly population" presence for the Federal
troops, who otherwise applied a policy of "scorched earth." General

Viktor Kazantzev explained to *Rossiyskaya Gazeta* why Russian authorities needed Cossacks in the Northern Caucasus:

> First, Cossack forces should take an active part in protecting Russia's borders as well as on the border between Chechnya and Stavropol Territory. Extremists from Dagestan, Karachayevo-Cherkessia and Adygea also present a danger. In these conditions the Cossacks must play a consolidating role with the local population. Second, there is the idea of the Cossacks supplying the enforcement structures with food. The Rostov region's budget for 2000 allocates R24m to support Cossack farmers, so there should be some return there. (*Rossiyskaya Gazeta*, Moscow, in Russian, 31 October 2000, BBC Mon FS1 FsuPol gar).

Rossiyskaya Gazeta concluded that the authorized presidential representative believed that the recruitment of that particular section of the population into state service could constitute the next phase in "maintaining interethnic accord" in Russia's southern regions. Accordingly, the Union of Cossack Formations was registered that year also in Ingushetia. The ataman of the Ingush branch of the Russian-wide union of Cossack Formations, Magomed Batyrov, explained in the interview to the Russian newspaper *Severnyy Kavkaz* that it was "proved" to the Ingush government that the Ingush people "needed" Cossacks and so they have to be officially registered. Almost immediately, newly registered organizations obtained two seats in the public chamber of the Ingush parliament "under the council of Russia and Belarus," which suggests direct support from Moscow (Severnyy Kavkaz, Moscow/Nalchik, in Russian, 16 May 2000, P.4. BC Mon TCU 240500).

The Chechen rebel leadership commented that Russian policy to resettle Cossacks in Chechnya and the North Caucuses generally aims to compensate for the necessary reduction of federal troops promised by the Russian General Staff. The Chechen web site Kavkaz-Tsentr accused the Russian authorities of masterminding the division of Chechnya into lowlands and highlands, so as to declare the former as "ethnically Cossack" and therefore separated from the Chechen Republic of Ichkeriya:

> As for the "Cossack companies," everything is completely clear here as well. The Kremlin is clinging to its last chance to stir up an interethnic conflict in the Caucasus in order to ideologically prop up their disintegrating military ad-

venture in Chechnya. They have started to make use of the thesis about "returning native Cossack lands" to Stavropol Territory, "restoring Cossack villages," "the claims of the Cossacks" to Sunzhenskiy and Terskiy areas, about dividing Chechnya into the lowlands and highlands and other rubbish prepared in the depths of the Federal Security Service. (Kavkaz-Tsentr web site, in Russian, 7 February 2001, BBC Mon TCU 070201)

Russian television reported that the Terek Cossacks had started to demand the integration of two Chechen districts into Stavropol Territory, referring to the tense situation as well as the incipient exodus of Russian refugees from the Chechen territory. NTV International stated that the Cossacks had collected 50,000 signatures in support of the separation of Naurskiy and Shelkovskiy Districts from Chechnya and plans to send two battalions of Cossacks there to take part in "counter-terrorist operations" (NTV International, Moscow, in Russian 0900 gmt, 11 February 2001, BBC Mon FS1 FsuPol).

The idea of redrawing borders in the North Caucasus became so vivid that the Russian presidential aide Sergey Yastrzshembskiy had to deny reports about proposals to attach the three Chechen districts to Stavropol Territory, allegedly made by the presidential commissioner in the Southern federal District, Viktor Kazantsev. Yastrzshembskiy described the federal authorities' goal: "achieving maximum stability and resolving festering ethnic conflicts and preservation of the stable administrative borders was one of the main aspects of this policy." The same day, Kazantsev's press secretary categorically denied media reports of plans to establish Stavropol Territory's "temporary control" of Chechen lowland areas, dismissing them as pure provocation and an attempt to destabilize the situation in the region (Interfax, Moscow, in English 1001 gmt, 15 February 2001, BBC Mon FS1 FsuPol).

Even if Russian plans to divide Chechnya and merge it with other federal republics were postponed or indeed canceled, the Chechen rebel leadership suspected that such plans would be revived in view of the presidential elections in Russia in 2004. The "election war" in Chechnya helped Vladimir Putin to win his first presidential campaign, but it could become a liability for the second campaign, taking into account that Russian federal troops were losing a soldier a day on average in "counter-terrorist" operations. The Chechen press news agency warned about plans to "wipe Chechnya off the Russian map" by merging the Chechen Republic with Ingushetia in a new "Vaynakh Republic" and accused Cossacks of acting as mediators in talks with Ingush authorities:

> The plan to change the Russian map geopolitically — merge Chechnya and Ingushetia — was devised more than two years ago, at the beginning of the second war in Chechnya. It was suggested at that time that Ruslan Aushev head of Chechen-Ingushetia should take account of the exodus of refugees, but he flatly refused. And the plan was put on the back burner. It was subsequently resuscitated by Viktor Kazantsev, plenipotentiary representative of the president in the Southern Federal District, at the end of last year [...] "Cossacks sent here" are holding bad conversations among the Ingush these days: Do you want Chechen land? For example, Sunzhenskiy District? Or something else? (Chechenpress web site, Tbilisi, in Russian, 22 April 2002, BBC Mon TCU 220402).

Both Chechen wars crystallized a clear tendency in the Russian Cossack movement to evolve in two different directions. The first path is that of the revival of the Cossack culture and way of life, Cossack identity and history. This is a grassroots movement arising out of the history of the Cossacks as a people repressed under Communism and, in this respect, puts Cossacks on the same side as Chechens, Crimean Tatars, and other communities that suffered under the totalitarian regime. This cultural movement does not necessarily claim that Cossacks are a separate "ethnic community" and often sees Cossack culture as part of a wider Russian culture as such. It is this movement that is encouraged by the Russian government *inside* the ethnically Russian *oblast'* of the Russian federation (e.g., Krasnodar *kraiy*). The other path is represented by the "ethnicitization" of Cossack history and claims that the Cossacks are a separate "ethnic group," a sub-ethnos or "ethnos" with its own history and "ethnic territory," often disputed with other peoples and "ethnicities." It is this second movement that is supported by the Russian federal authorities *outside* of the ethnic Russian *oblast'*. The Russian federal government played the "Cossack card" in Tatarstan, Chechnya, Ingushetia, Transdniestria, Kazakhstan and Ukraine, to exert pressure on the governments of either federal republics of the Russian Federation, or the FSU countries, in order to gain "ethnic" leverage, politicizing the Cossacks as "an oppressed minority." Cossack "rights" to the land that they might have historically conquered for the Tsars were now being used to claim that Cossacks are an ethnic minority that needs protection or else that they could be "reintegrated" into the Russian Federation along with "their ethnic lands." This pattern would be replayed again in the so-called Novorosiya scenario and the armed conflict in Eastern Ukraine that started with the illegal annexation of Crimea in 2014.

Russian Cossack organizations in Ukraine were considered as a Russian fifth column since the 1990s and, indeed, there is extensive evidence that they were used to infiltrate Ukraine before the open invasion of Crimea. Russian weekly *Tribun* (Yekaterinburg) described how Russian military officer Roman Shadrin joined the so-called Cossacks' organizations in 2012 and was elected a member of the Yekaterinburg city council as a candidate of the United Russia party in 2013. Unexpectedly, he became the head of the Luhansk People's Republic's counterintelligence service in 2014 only to return to Russia in 2015, journalist Andriy Ponomarenko reported. The former deputy minister of state security of the self-proclaimed Luhansk People's Republic (LPR), Roman Shadrin, after ending his "tenure" in Donbas, got a job as director of the municipal park in Yekaterinburg (Russia), the *Tribun* weekly said, citing Russian blogger Pavel Pryanikov's account on Facebook (*Tribun* weekly newspaper website, 28 December 2018).

Russian authorities encouraged Cossacks to train for fighting in Ukraine, to fundraise and to cross the border freely once the conflict was started by the former GRU officer Girkin (Strelkov) in Sloviansk (2014). Cossacks (real and masquerading) played the role of local Ukrainian "self-defense units" while Russian military officers were actually in charge of armed hostilities represented as a Ukrainian "civil war" (Valery Dzutsati, "Terek Cossacks Reveal Their Extensive Participation in the Annexation of Crimea," *Eurasia Daily Monitor*, 6 December 2016: https://bit.ly/2SV1P1c.)

Aleksandr Mozhayev told *Time* that Russian border-guards had an open-door policy for Cossacks from his "Wolves' Hundred" detachment: "They never even stamped my passport" when crossing into Ukraine. Mozhayev explained the Cossack motives to fight in Eastern Ukraine as being in line with President Putin's repeated claim that Russians and Ukrainians are "one people" and Ukraine is an artificial construct: "We decided to go reconquer some more historically Russian lands [...] There is no such thing as Ukraine. ... There are only the Russian borderlands, and the fact they became known as Ukraine after the [Bolshevik] Revolution, well, we intend to correct that mistake" (Simon Shuster, "Meet the Cossack 'Wolves' Doing Russia's Dirty Work in Ukraine," Time, 12 May 2014: https://bit.ly/1lvscnj.)

Don and Kuban' Russian Cossacks formed entire military battalions in Eastern Ukraine, such as the "Almighty Don Host" from Novocherkask that was based in Stahanov town, Luhansk region. Not all genuinely Ukrainian "separatists" welcomed so many Russian paramilitaries coming to reclaim "their land." The ataman of the "Almighty Don Host" Pavel Driomov was assassinated, most likely by local Luhansk paramilitary rivals, in December 2015. His replacement Mykola Kozitsyn was quick to learn the lesson and pledged that his Cossacks will vote for the acting head of the self-proclaimed LPR Leonid Pasichnyk (Pasechnik), the local *Realnaya Gazeta* reported in 2018 (*Realnaya Gazeta* website, 23 October 2018). Cossacks in the LPR are "banally adjusting themselves to the new boss in the LPR" that is, Leonid Pasichnyk, journalist Ihor Plotnyy said on the *Ostrovok* website. However, "it is not a secret that Pasichnyk is not very popular among Cossacks, to say the least, or, at most, is even disrespected and disregarded as somebody who now has to be put up with because our Russian brothers have decided so," the journalist noted. A local journalist concludes that "there is no movement of free Cossacks in the LPR, capable of openly saying their firm 'no,' but there are small groups of people who have just told themselves and everybody else that they are Cossacks," the website concluded (*Ostrovok* website, 7 November 2018). What the "Russian brothers" wanted was clear from statements by the influential Russian MP and Cossack general Viktor Vodolatsky, who instructed Russian Cossacks in Luhansk to be subordinated to Plotnitsky and continue their fight against the "fascist Poroshenko regime" (Quoted from Novoross.info http://www.novoross.info/ politiks/48902-so-svoroy-poroshenko-druzhit-nevozmozhno-kazach iy-lider.html).

Supporting local authorities also paid off for Russian Cossacks in Crimea. The HQ of the newly created "Black Sea Cossack Host" in Sevastopol registered 5,000 Cossacks, claimed Ataman Shagun in an interview with the Primechaniya website. Shagun said that some 11 million roubles from the Sevastopol city budget was spent on financing the Sevastopol Cossacks in 2018, which is 30 per cent more than in 2017. "The Cossackization of Sevastopol goes on," the website said (*Primechaniya* website, primechaniya.ru, 1016 gmt, 3 December 18).

So, why sponsor Cossacks in Sevastopol, allegedly the city of "Russian naval glory," if Crimea is one of the most militarized regions in Europe already? The radical pro-Russian newspaper *Krymskoye Ekho* hinted at the answer, when it reported a small rally in Simferopol devoted to the 365th anniversary of unification between Zaporozhian Sich and the Muscovite kingdom. Local officials and leaders of the self-proclaimed LPR and the self-proclaimed Donetsk People's Republic (DPR) took part in the event. The newspaper reported the main point of the rally: "Donbas and the whole of Ukraine would reunite with Russia very soon." The rally's resolution said that war in Eastern Ukraine was provoked by the West; the "mainland" Ukrainians were urged to "come to their senses." After the rally the speaker of the Crimean parliament, Vladimir Konstantinov, the head of the DPR's people's council, Volodymyr Bidevka, and the head of the LPR's people's council, Denys Myroshnichenko, signed a cooperation agreement (*Krymskoye Ekho*, Simferopol, 1546 gmt 18 January 2019). Vladimir Konstantinov said at the rally: "I am absolutely convinced that our Orthodoxy will win, that the Russian world will win. We will reunite with Ukraine, it will happen in one form or another and this is only a question of time," *Novoross*, a site controlled by ultra-right Cossacks, reported. "I honestly think that *the predominant majority of Ukraine's residents are our Russian compatriots.* And, undoubtedly, we should help them resist the Nazi invasion and the split of our Orthodox faith," the Russian MP from Crimea,

Andrey Kozenko, said. (*Novoross* website, novoross.info, 1441 gmt 18 January 2019). In other words, the Cossacks became the militant vehicle to realize the idea of the "Russian world" that denies Ukraine's right to exist as an independent nation-state, promoting the "liberation" of Ukraine from the Western-backed "Nazi regime," and reunification with Russian compatriots as "one people." As Kuzio explains: "Hybrid wars require imitation of local support that disguises foreign power invasion." There were not enough Russian Cossacks in Ukrainian towns such as Zaporizhya, as Putin's advisor Glazyev lamented in 2014, so Operation Novorosiya 2014 became limited to Donbas (Kuzio 2018, 371). Having combined Russian Cossack forces in Crimea, the DPR and the LPR would make more people available at short notice and their "Cossack" intention to "liberate" Ukraine is not disguised either.

The history of the Cossack revival in Ukraine, described in sub-chapter 4.5, illustrates that this was not the unavoidable course of history. It was the policy of the Russian Federal government that became one of the decisive factors gradually transforming the Cossacks into mercenaries for Russian neo-imperial expansion. As Krasnodar Territory Governor Veniamin Kondratyev reflected on the Kuban' Cossacks' war games conducted on local military ranges: "Cossackhood is now back in its place, and resumes its historical mission of being the country's reliable military backbone." (Kuban' 24 TV "Fakty" news, Krasnodar, 1630 gmt 23 August 2019). The Kuban' press speculated that Krasnodar Territory deputy governor Nikolai Doluda and Cossack chieftain (ataman) of the Kuban' Cossack Host would be appointed by President Putin to lead the All-Russian Cossack Society, set up in 2018 in order to take control over all Cossack hosts in Russia (*Novaya Gazeta Kubani* newspaper, Krasnodar, 23 August 2019). Ukrainian human rights NGO KrymSOS associated Doludov with groups of Russian Cossacks involved in kidnapping and torturing Crimean Tatar and pro-Ukrainian activists in Crimea during the 2014 invasion of "little green men" (Quoted from https://focus.ua/politics/368961). Ataman Doludov was decorated by the Crimea administration in March 2015 for his role in the illegal annexation (official act https://rk.gov.ru/rus/file/pub

/pub_242085.pdf), so placing him in charge of the entire Cossack movement of Russia would be notoriously symbolic. After 30 years of controversial revival, with the advent of the All-Russian Cossack Society Russian Cossacks finally achieved full state recognition, a singular register and substantial funding, but at the price of becoming Putin's paramilitary, deniable "hybrid" gendarmerie:

> Not surprisingly, the Putin regime has chosen Stalin's model for its pseudo-Cossacks, confident that few will challenge what Moscow is doing: creating a group of armed thugs who can be deployed against demonstrators in ways that will offer the Kremlin yet another possibility for shifting the blame, thereby denying its own culpability, and moving to deny all others who claim to be Cossacks their right to do so. (Goble 2019)

4.4. The Heritage of Soviet Ethnography and Ethno-Geopolitical Discourse in Ukraine

Independent since 1991, Ukraine, unlike the Russian Federation, is a unitary state. Thus, it proclaimed a similar policy of building a "political nation," something reflected in official terminology and political discourse. After gaining independence in August 1991, Ukraine issued a "Declaration of Nationalities' Rights," which offers the first definition of the Ukrainian nation. The term "people of Ukraine" was used to include over one hundred ethnically defined nationalities, together with the "'Ukrainian *narod* (ethnic Ukrainian people)." Initially, the term "Ukrainian people" was understood as the Ukrainian nation or Ukrainian "titular" ethno-nation, while the term "people of Ukraine" referred to a multi-ethnic political nation.

This formulation evoked protests from Ukrainian nationalists, who saw the term "people of Ukraine" as diminishing the status of Ukrainians in the newly established state to merely one of many "ethnic groups" among the "people of Ukraine." However, a new Ukrainian constitution, approved by the Ukrainian parliament in 1996 on behalf of "the Ukrainian people," explained that the term referred to "citizens of Ukraine of all nationalities."

While the difference between the two terms might seem insignificant, it reflects a change toward a more ambiguous Ukrainian nationalities policy, one which persisted throughout the late 1990s and into the new century. An example of this ambiguity is the reference in the constitution to the choice of self-determination made by the "Ukrainian nation," which was followed by "the Ukrainian people," i.e., specifying in this way that "the Ukrainian people" are a political nation as opposed to "the Ukrainian nation" in the ethnic sense. President Leonid Kuchma mostly used the term "the Ukrainian people" (e.g., Kuchma 1999, 345-346). He considered the creation of a political, i.e. a civic, nation, as along with liberal democracy and civil society as one of the greatest achievements of Ukraine since independence (Kuchma 1999, 3).

The heritage of Soviet Ethnography and Soviet nationality policy is directly reflected in several articles of the Ukrainian constitution, which deal with the rights of national minorities and indigenous peoples. Article 11 proclaims that "the State promotes the consolidation and development of the Ukrainian nation, of its historical identity, traditions and culture, and also the development of ethnic, cultural, linguistic and religious identity of all indigenous peoples and national minorities of Ukraine."[48] Neither the constitution nor other laws of Ukraine provide sufficient explanation as to which people in Ukraine are considered to be indigenous, apart from the Ukrainians when considered in an ethnic sense, i.e., the Ukrainian nation as in Article 11. Ukrainian scholars did not clarify this issue either and the "Short Encyclopedia of Ethno-State-Science" referred only to Ukrainians as an "indigenous" nationality in Ukraine. Other nationalities are usually referred to by scholars, as well as by Ukrainian law, as national minorities. The only exception is the reference to the Crimean Tatars as indigenous people of Crimea, made by Verkovna Rada in 2014, inadvertently accepting that ethnic Russians were newcomers to the peninsula (since 1789) (Quote from https://www.radiosvoboda.org/a/29426321.html).

National identity was generally understood by post-Soviet Ukrainian scholars in a cultural context defining, first of all, norms of "ethnosocial behavior." It was assumed that "national" meant

---

[48]   Constitution of Ukraine /Official translation/ (1996) Ministry of Justice of Ukraine (Ukrainian legal foundation 'Pravo' Kyiv 1996), 9-10.

"ethnic" in a wider sense, as it did within the framework of Soviet Ethnography. According to the "Short Encyclopedia" national identity assumes that "a group of people share a feeling of a common past, present and future, as well as having a certain consensus as to the principal issues of economic, political, cultural and social life, current development of the state and its policy" (Oliynyk 1996, 98). Articles on national self-consciousness (e.g., Pustotin 1996, 103) and on different levels of national self-consciousness (e.g., Rymarenko 1996, 103-104) illustrate that, generally, Ukrainian scholars continued to use the "socio-spherical" concept of Soviet Ethnography.[49] Western theories on nations and national identity were gradually introduced in the academic discourse throughout the 1990s (e.g., Ischenko 1994; Hrytsak 1996; Hryb 1998).

Despite the critical attitude of the majority of Soviet scholars toward Gumilev's original theory, post-Soviet scholars in Ukraine, as in Russia, initially used it. The whole set of ideas relevant to the creation of ethno-geopolitics as a theory was available in the Ukrainian scholarly tradition throughout the 1990s, only to be discredited by the rise of political New Eurasianism in Russia starting from the 2000s.

The constitution of Ukraine proclaims that "the people" (not "the peoples" as in Russia) are the source of power and sovereignty in Ukraine. "The people" is to be understood as the "Ukrainian people" or the Ukrainian political nation. The Ukrainian ethnic nation is also referred to in the Constitution as the "titular nation," which is another term from the Soviet past. In other words, Ukrainian law is rather ambiguous as to who is, and how these people are, included in the Ukrainian "political nation." It still emphasizes individuals who are included in the category of the Ukrainian people, regardless of their nationality, and does not state explicitly what is the difference in rights between those of titular Ukrainian nationality and those of the national minorities. The only explicit "privileges" to be discerned for the titular nation are those of the Ukrainian language

---

[49]   All articles by the authors mentioned are from the "Short Encyclopedia of Ethno-State-Science," ed. U. Rymarenko (NAN Ukrainy. — K.: Dovira — Geneza, 1996).

being the official language and of Ukrainian state symbols such as the national anthem and the Coat of Arms.

The ambiguity of Ukrainian law points to the contradiction between the heritage of Soviet Ethnography, which was oriented toward the institutionalization of ethnicity and dominates the perception of political actors and academics, and the proclaimed political discourse on the civic understanding of a political nation. This lack of consistent policy implementation reflected the more general hesitation of the ruling elite to accept the principle, "One (Ukrainian) state, one (Ukrainian) culture," where "Ukrainian" is referred to as the "titular" ethnically defined nationality. Substantially dominated by Russian-speaking post-Soviet *nomenklatura* from Central and Eastern Ukraine, the Ukrainian ruling elites were very slow, if at all able, to accept the Ukrainian language, remaining under the influence of the Russian mass culture that was freely streaming from radio and TV. The policy of building the "Ukrainian people" as a political nation resulted from conditions where neither the ruling elite nor the majority of the population were prepared to accept the idea of the "Ukrainian people" based exclusively on the culture and language of ethnic Ukrainians. The Cossack movement in Ukraine illustrates, on the one hand, an attempt to promote such a unified culture, and on the other hand, underlines the ruling elite's choice of a non-ethnic policy for Ukrainian nation-building.

The Cossack revival evoked much less discussion in Ukrainian society than in Russia. Having aggressive Russian Cossack organizations in Eastern and Southern Ukraine, the Ukrainian political elite chose without hesitation a non-ethnic definition of Cossackhood, despite the fact that the Ukrainian Cossacks were initially promoted by the conservative center-right organizations like *Narodny Rukh* and the Republican Party. The demands of the Russian Cossack organizations for autonomy in Ukraine's South and East or, even, unification with the historical Russian land of the Don Host (*Zemlia Voyska Donskoho*) were dismissed by the state on the grounds that the Don Cossacks in Ukraine represented solely civic organizations, and were not an ethnic minority separate from the Russian one. A Russian Cossack organization with separatist ideology in Odesa *oblast'* was disbanded in 1992 and was allowed to re-register only under the code of an All-Ukrainian civic organization *Ukrains'ke Kozatstvo* (Hryb 1999). This strategy proved to be successful, at least in the short term, since it placed both Russian and Ukrainian Cossack movements within a neutral civic framework and in this way undermined the right to ethnically oriented separatist claims. In the long term, such a compromise did not satisfy either side. Ukrainian multi-ethnic/national society was neither ready to fully accept the language and the culture of the titular Ukrainian nation as the common "currency" nor willing to accept the dominance of the Russian language as happened in the Republic of Belarus. This was one of the major reasons why ethno-geopolitics, despite being part of persistent the Soviet Ethnography heritage, could not become a viable option for the Ukrainian ruling elites. Civic peace in Ukraine much better reflected the national interests of the titular nation, which as a nation-state lacked the confidence to start building a Ukrainian Super-ethnos or a "Ukrainian civilization" like in Russia. Although the Ukrainian state anthem claims a Cossack origin for- the Ukrainians, the Ukrainian Cossack revival, unlike its Russian sibling, largely stayed out of ethno-geopolitics and could hardly claim any politically independent role at all. Instead, as the empirical findings illustrate, the Ukrainian Cossack movement, with the exception of Russian Cossacks in Ukraine, remained within the parameters of a public organization with substantial regional differences and with a moderate nationalist non-ethnic ideology aimed at protecting existing nation-state borders and interests.

4.5. The Cossack Revival in Ukraine

Historically, the Zaporizhian Cossacks played a key role in protecting the settled Slavic population of Ukraine from regular raids by nomadic and hostile Crimean Tatars who were practicing the slave trade with the wider Ottoman Empire between the fifteenth and eighteenth centuries. Once the Russian empire expanded into the Southern Ukraine and Crimea in the 1780s, Zaporizhyian Cossacks were either recruited into the Russian imperial cavalry and partly resettled to the North Caucasus or dispersed creating an independent new *Sich* on the Danube River. After the demolition of the Cossack *Sich* in 1776 by Catherine II, the Cossacks slowly disintegrated as a distinct social group on the territory of present-day Ukraine (see details on the history of Ukrainian Cossacks in the endnote[50]). The

---

[50]   In the nineteenth century historians wrote that life in the Zaporozhian Sich was so poor and simplistic that if it were not for constant warfare, it could be compared with a monastic order. The Sich was a remote and fortified settlement with an exclusively male population of up to a few thousand Cossacks. Due to its extreme conditions the way of life there was distinct from any other kind of settlement elsewhere in the country at that time. Historically, Cossacks who agreed to serve the Polish king (so-called registered Cossacks) maintained connections with the Sich but lived in towns or on their farms. The Sich also had distinct rules of self-organisation and self-government that were based on equality of every member and the rotation of a collectively elected leadership. It is this principle of free self-governance that made the Sich a source of idealisation among the exploited and oppressed masses mainly, though not solely, of the Ukrainian population. The Cossacks became a popular ideal of free armed men ruled by the principles of justice and equality. Of course, social differentiation in terms of wealth quickly appeared among Cossacks and some of them, particularly those lucky in war and investment, became rich and didn't need the Sich anymore. Later they formed the Cossack nobility and were the first to collaborate with the legitimate powers of the existing states. However, the unique, remote location of the Sich and regular warfare allowed it to preserve its character for centuries and to create an ideal type of what may be called an independent and institutionalised social (Cossack) movement. When external conditions no longer permitted the maintenance of this ideal and Russian State authorities demolished the Sich in 1776, this movement slowly but surely vanished. Ukrainian Cossacks as independent social and military strata are not mentioned after 1869. The remaining Cossacks from the Sich either moved under the Ottoman protection and created a new Sich on the river Danube or joined different Russian Cossack armies. After the Russian-Turkish war in 1827-28 the Danube Cossacks joined the Tsar's army as well, but none of the Ukrainian Cossack Hosts survived the Russian military reforms of 1868. For the last 40 years of its existence, Novorosiyskoe Kazachestvo, as it was officially called, was a military unit of conscripts, and as a result differed significantly from the voluntary Cossack communities. At this point the ethnic composition of the Cossack units was, as ever, complex. Local Gypsies, Romanians, Bulgarians, Slavs from the Balkans and even Jews were conscripted along with Ukrainians. Historical records suggest a fair degree of solidarity among the oppressed ordinary Cossacks of various ethnic background, dominated by mostly ethnic Russian officers (Bachynskyi 1995: 46-54). Following, the 1868 reforms, all Cossacks and their officers received land and settled as farmers and/or landowners. Cossack military formations in Ukraine are no longer mentioned, but as documents of the Odessian military district in 1871 indicated, the Ukrainians preserved their memories of 'free Cossacks'. On the one hand, Ukrainian Cossacks did not survive as a distinct military and social organisation. On the other hand, they avoided association with brutal policing that became typical for the Russian Cossacks. (For information about the Cossack image in the perception of minorities, and primarily Jews in Ukraine see Pelenski 1988). However, once the Russian imperial institutions

main objective of this subchapter is to illustrate that the revival of the Ukrainian Cossack movement at the end of the twentieth century was an attempt by the moderate nationalist elite, or using a Ukrainian term, the "national-democratic forces,"[51] to establish a new model of the *national* armed forces in Ukraine based on the Cossack ethos and to establish simultaneously an ideology of Ukrainian cultural homogenization for the newly created *national* state in the early 1990s.

---

collapsed on the territory of Ukraine at the end of the First World War, the Ukrainians created self-defence units to protect their villages and towns with a collective name as *'Vilne Kozatstvo'* or 'Free Cossacks'. The positive image of Cossacks in Ukraine or, as some prefer, 'the Cossack Myth', was widely shared by the Ukrainian intelligentsia, peasantry and nobility, which shows a certain consensus on the issue. The first Ukrainian government *Tsentralna Rada*, declared Ukrainian independence in February 2017 by publishing its first decrees called *Universaly*, clearly referring to the state tradition of the Cossack *Hetmanshchyna* of the seventeenth and eighteenth centuries. Soon after, the Russian general of Ukrainian Cossack heritage Pavlo Scoropadsky, was elected as 'honorary Hetman' of *Vilne Kozatstvo* in the old Cossack capital Chyhyryn. 'Hetman' was the title of the Highest Cossack Ruler used at the time of Ukrainian Cossack Autonomy in the seventeenth and eighteenth centuries (Reshetar 1952: 143-209). Hetman Skoropadsky created two corps of the Ukrainian regular army called Cossack divisions, which in fact were two units of the Tsarist army whose conscripts were largely Ukrainian and did not want to participate in the Russian-German war anymore. Scoropadsky took the office from the *Tsentralna Rada* in April 1918 with the full support of the German army on his side, but his regime did not last long and fell with Germans' retreat. 'The Hetman of all Ukraine' evacuated to Germany where he died in 1945. *Vilne Kozatstvo* existed until the early 1920s, briefly even under the Bolshevik regime ('the Red Cossacks'). However, it was always associated with a brief outburst of Ukrainian revolution and considered in Soviet Ukraine as a nationalist formation. The most prominent representative associated with Free Cossacks was the anarchist leader Nestor Mahno, who created effectively a republic in Central Ukraine and resisted the rule of German troops, Hetmanites, representatives of the Tsentralna Rada, the White Army and Bolsheviks. His guerrilla-type army changed allies and occasionally surrenered the capital Huliay Pole, but was never defeated in battle. Only after years of Bolsheviks' 'Red Terror' Nestor Mahno and the remains of his government emmigrated to Romania in 1924. The time of the 'free Cossacks' rule in Ukraine was over but their memory lived on. It took another six decades for the Ukrainian Cossacks to re-emerge as an organisation again, this time as a part of a national revival allowed by Gorbachev's Perestroika.

[51]   The term in Ukrainian—'*natzionalno-demokratychni syly*'—is used to include a wide spectrum of pro-Ukrainian-independence political and civic organisations that appeared during and after Perestoika and to exclude those extreme leftist organisations opposing an independent Ukraine or extreme right Ukrainian nationalist organisations.

Although the Ukrainian Cossacks failed to create their own military units, the movement showed a good potential to generate an ideology capable of uniting a large part of the Ukrainian population on a non-ethnic platform. In the last months of the existence of the Soviet Union, the Ukrainian leadership had been considering different possibilities: either to create new, or to nationalize the existing, armed forces on Ukrainian territory. The latter was achieved with remarkable success when Soviet troops gradually took the oath of allegiance to the Ukrainian state. Yet the national state of Ukraine was born in 1991 more out of the failure of the Communist coup in Russia than as a result of national revolution. The post-Soviet leaders in Ukraine were either too bound up with the old Communist *nomenklatura*, or too weak to take political power on behalf of the democratic forces. This caused a situation in which the revival of national traditions within the Armed Forces was practically delayed to 2014, and the Ukrainian Cossack movement became largely a public "revivalist" folklore organization.

The first to come up with the idea of reviving Cossackhood in the Ukraine of the 1980s was the organization of moderate nationalists (national-democrats) — *Rukh* — and the slightly more radical Republican Party. They made popular appeals to the Cossack ethos in order to promote "national awakening" in the Eastern regions of Ukraine, historically associated with Cossackhood, but had been highly Russified over the previous two centuries and had become resistant to any kind of nationalist Ukrainian mobilization. *Rukh*'s celebration of the 500th anniversary of Zaporozhian Cossacks[52] was highly successful and led to the renewal of contemporary Ukrainian Cossack organizations.

In September 1990, the Great Cossack Council (*Rada*) proclaimed the creation of the first All-Ukrainian Cossack organization — *Ukrains'ke Kozatstvo* (officially registered as a public organisa-

---

[52]   500 years of the Zaporozhian Cossacks was a symbolic date suggested by the leaders of the Cossack movement, which refers to the first historical records that mentions Cossacks. But the problem of chronology and certainly the time of the creation of Zaporozhian Cossacks remains unresolved. For the debates among Ukrainian historians concerning Cossack chronology see 'Zaporozke Kozatstvo v ukrainskiy istorii, kulturi ta natsionalniy samosvidomosti' (Kyiv 1997).

tion on 17 March 1992). *Ukrains'ke Kozatstvo* defined itself as a "voluntary, independent, charitable, All-Ukrainian, national-patriotic, sport and defense, civic organization of Cossacks in Ukraine" that includes "Cossacks and their heirs, *citizens of Ukraine* and Ukrainians from other countries, who share the idea of Ukrainian Cossackhood."[53] At first, Cossack organizations in the regions were created as parallel structures to pro-independence associations, and were primarily associated with *Rukh*. The Organization of Free Cossacks (*Vilne Kozatstvo*) was set up in 1988 to support and protect most of the actions and gatherings initiated by the new democratic organizations during the late 1980s and early 1990s.

In time, both the Ukrainian opposition and the old political elite in Ukraine realized that they needed armed forces other than those controlled by Moscow. As early as 1990, Ukrainian national-democrats started to promote the idea of creating the Republican National Guard. At the same time, city councils in the western provinces, dominated by national-democrats, organized a municipal police force. By analogy to the national revolution of 1917, the first Congress of the Ukrainian officers took place on 27 July 1991. Nationalistically-minded officers called on the Ukrainian Supreme Soviet to establish the Armed Forces of Ukraine. But it was only after the Moscow coup and the declaration of Ukrainian independence on 24 August 1991, that the Ukrainian parliament *Verkhovna Rada* issued the decree, 'On the military formations of Ukraine." A few days later recruitment to the National Guards began, and by 29 August 1991 the Soviet MVD Internal troops based on the territory of Ukraine had been nationalized to create the basis for the new National Guard units.[54] The same day Lieutenant-General Kostiantyn Morozov was appointed the minister for the newly created Ministry of Defense. *Verkhovna Rada* approved a resolution on the National Defense Concept and the creation of the National Armed Forces on 11 October 1991.

---

[53]   Code of Ukrainian Cossacks, in *Ukrainske Slovo*, 5 September 1996, 3.
[54]   National guards effectively became a special security force under the control of President Kravchuk, but fell out of favour with President Kuchma and was abolished in 2000, only to be re-established in 2014.

By the beginning of 1992, most of the nearly million strong Soviet army on the territory of Ukraine was nationalized and, despite objections from Moscow, were persuaded to take a new oath to the independent Ukraine. In terms of immediate military and political security, it was an obvious success; however, in terms of long-term defense prospects and societal security it was highly problematic. Ninety percent of senior officers and seventy percent of the rank-and-file officers were non-Ukrainians, and most of them were ethnic Russians who simply reflected the ethnic composition of the Soviet Army. An unofficial survey at that time confirmed that the majority of the officers would not fight in a conflict if the enemy were Russia (Baev 1996, 10). Nationalistically-minded politicians were highly suspicious of the reliability of the armed forces due to the assumption that, indeed, Russia was the biggest threat to national security.

In 1992, attempts were made to create a more "national" character for the national Armed forces. At first, Minister of Defense Kostiantyn Morozov took a hard line, making membership of the radicalized Union of Ukrainian Officers (*Spilka oficeriv Ukrainy*) a precondition for any promotion. At the same time, Viacheslav Chornovil, as a Hetman of Ukrainian Cossacks, called on Defense Minister Morozov to create a Cossack military lyceum out of the Sumy High officers' artillery school, while Chief Otaman of *Ukrains'ke Kozatstvo* Yevhen Petrenko called on President Kravchuk to adopt a parliamentary decree creating Cossack units within the National guard, Armed Forces, SBU (the transformed KGB in Ukraine), the Border Guards and the Internal Troops.

Both Viacheslav Chornovil and Yevhen Petrenko were elected to their positions by the Grand Cossack Council on 14 October 1991. In July 1992, Hetman Chornovil called on the Ministry of Defense to introduce Cossack cavalry units into the structure of the Armed Forces (a regiment in Kyiv and squadrons in the cities, where Military district HQs were based). Similar proposals were sent to the Chief of National Guards, General Major Kuharetz', as well as to the Central Committee of the Association for Ukrainian Defense (*Tovarystvo spryiannia oboroni Ukrainy*). Chief Otaman Petrenko prepared special suggestions for the Head of the Socio-psychological Service

of the Ministry of Defense, Colonel Volodymyr Muliava, suggesting
the creation 1) of joint military Cossack formations to "defend
riverbanks and sea coasts where armed actions are possible, to prevent mass disorder during natural disasters; 2) of special Cossack
units fighting the Cossack formations of other states; and 3) of special Cossack units to operate on the territory of the enemy." To ensure the safety of Ukrainian borders and customs, the organization
of Cossack settlements along the borders was proposed. The Cossacks were particularly concerned with Russian Cossack formations
organized in Odesa *oblast'*. Hetman Chornovil reported to the Head
of the Ukrainian Security Service that a Russian Cossack organization had been set up in Bilhorod-Dnistrovsky in the Odesa region.
One of the commanders of a Ukrainian military regiment was elected an ataman of the Cossack formation and took an oath to the Don
Army. The ataman of the Russian Cossack Union, Martynov, was
present at that ceremony. Disbanded the same year, this pro-Russian
Cossack formation was set up in 1994, as again reported by the
alarmed Ukrainian Cossacks.

Pro-Russian Cossack leaders in Southern Ukraine merely
claimed that they represented civic organizations reflecting the traditions of historical *Novorosiyskoye Kazachestvo*, which had historically
served the Russian Tsars in Ukraine, and referred to the Pereyaslav
accords between the Ukrainian Cossacks and Moscow agreed in
1654. *Ukrains'ke Kozatstvo* therefore took the symbolical action of
repudiating their historical oath of allegiance to the Russian Tsar in
the town Pereyaslav-Khmelnyts'kyi on 21 June 1992, an idea proposed by *Rukh* and the Ukrainian National Assembly. It attracted
nearly 200 representatives from Cossack associations all over
Ukraine. The event had historical and symbolical meaning, since it
was held in the town where a Ukrainian Cossack Grand Council
under Hetman Hmelnytskyi voted for the Treaty with Moscovy and
pledged an oath to the Russian Tsar in 1654. The Deputy Head of the
Ukrainian parliament was present, which underlined its political
significance (SWB SU/1419 B/17, 29 June 1992). Soon after that,
Chornovil resigned from the Hetman position due to his commit-
ments in Parliament and the Grand Council of Ukrainian Cossacks

elected a new Hetman, General Volodymyr Muliava, on 13 October 1992 (SWB SU/1512 B/5, 15 October 1992). Muliava was also originally a *Rukh* activist and a former philosophy lecturer at a military academy. He joined the Ukrainian Ministry of Defense when it was created and was one of the main ideologists of the new Ukrainian Armed Forces, and the head of the newly created Socio-psychological service of the Ukrainian Ministry of Defense. General Muliava believed that it would be possible to "Ukrainize" the inherited Soviet officers' corps gradually and his election as the Hetman of the Ukrainian Cossacks could have been a symbolic step in this direction. Transforming the Soviet mentality of Russian-speaking officers using Ukrainian Cossack folklore did not prove successful, and the service was transformed after Muliava's dismissal in May 1994 following the election of President Kuchma, who played a pro-Russian card (*Rossiya*, No. 17, 4-10 May 1994). An opportunity to create a loyal and reliable Ukrainian Armed Forces (UAF) right at the beginning was lost. Twenty years later, seventy percent of the Ukrainian army and up to ninety percent of the security forces in Crimea would defect to Russia. The election of President Kuchma, ex-Party *aparatchik* from Dnipropetrovsk, who considered himself an ethnic Russian before he entered politics, put an end to attempts to Ukrainize the UAF using a Ukrainian Cossack ethos. *Ukrainske Kozatstvo*, the main Ukrainian Cossack organization, would remain an NGO with no direct support from the Ukrainian state, relying mostly on public donations.

It is important to distinguish between the two different *modern* Cossack movements in Ukraine—much more than the case of the historical pre-modern, pre-nation-state Cossack phenomenon. First of all, the mainstream national Ukrainian Cossack organizations that were united under the name *Ukrains'ke Kozatstvo*; and then the marginal, regional Russian Cossack organizations in Ukraine, which were the offspring of a much better developed Cossack movement in Russia.

The Ukrainian government, dominated by ex-Communist *nomenklatura* and newly emerging oligarchs, paid little attention to both the Russian and the Ukrainian Cossack organizations. The otaman of the Luhansk Cossacks, Vladimir Fedichev, complained to Russian TV that "the Ukrainian leadership ignored the problem of the Cossacks in Ukraine" (SWB SU/1589 B/2, 18 January 1993). An attempt by the Russian Cossack ataman in Donetsk (I. Bielomiesov) to introduce the rule of the Don Army in Proletarskiy *rayon* of the city at the end of 1991 seemed not to have been seriously considered even by the Don Cossack Army, namely, by Ataman Meshcheriakov, who received a special letter with such an appeal. Both Meshcheriakov and the ataman of the Kuban' Cossacks Viktor Gromov also received appeals for cooperation from the first Grand Council of the Ukrainian Cossacks held in Kyiv. Gromov replied to Hetman Chornovil on 13 November 1991 that Kuban' Cossacks do not have territorial claims to Ukraine and condemned the idea of creating a Cossack Republic of the South. President Yeltsin's administration struggled with its own regional separatism at the time and creating trouble in Ukraine was not on the agenda yet.

However, on 14 May 1992 the Luhansk Council of Atamans of Don Cossack associations called on the *Verkhovna Rada* to introduce dual citizenship in Luhansk Oblast', make Russian an official language, and put the symbols of the Don Army next to the Ukrainian ones. *Luhanskaya Pravda* also claimed that the Council of Atamans requested the abolition of customs on the border with the Don Army *Oblast* and the banning of all Ukrainian Army units on their territory. The Luhansk *Rukh* organization condemned this statement of the Council of Atamans and set up an alternative Ukrainian Cossack organization (30 May 1992) that would be part of the loyal *Ukrains'ke Kozatstvo*.

The tension between Ukrainian and Russian Cossacks in Ukraine had never disappeared completely, but tensions eased, since none of the Russian Cossack organizations received significant support in Ukrainian society. The presence of Russian paramilitary and sometimes armed formations in Ukraine did attract the attention, however, of the newly established Ukrainian Security Forces. A National Guards colonel, Anatoliy Shmilo, wrote in his article "The National Guard of Ukraine and Its Enemies":

> Analysis of the situation shows that destabilizing conditions could arise in the near future either in individual regions (Crimea, Donbas, etc.), or in several regions simultaneously. Were this to happen, reconnaissance-sabotage groups would infiltrate these regions, possibly in the guise of "Cossacks," as happened in Transdniestra or in the present conflict in Abkhazia. Who will then defend Ukraine against these forces? (Shmilo 1993, 5)

The answer for Colonel Shmilo was, of course, not *Ukrains'ke Kozatstvo* or even the regular Ukrainian Armed Forces, but the National Guard that by then had successfully protected the Ukrainian border with the pro-Russian breakaway Transdniestra Republic. The Russian Cossacks, among other mercenaries, took part in the armed conflict between this breakaway republic and Moldovan Armed Forces, but the fighting did not spread to the Ukrainian Odesa *oblast'*.

Despite the fact that Ukrainian Cossacks considered themselves to be part of the Armed Forces and were rhetorically supported by Ukrainian politicians, *Ukrains'ke Kozatstvo* never became a meaningful paramilitary force. Even after the Border Guard Service in Ukraine signed an agreement with *Ukrains'ke Kozatstvo*, in August 1993, to form special units to defend national borders, nothing happened. According to this agreement, regional Cossack atamans were supposed to form Cossack detachments of up to 40,000 Border Troops to help protect state borders (SWB SU/1782 C1/2, 1 September 1993). No funds were allocated for Cossacks and therefore, officially, no such detachments existed, despite the fact that *Ukrains'ke Kozatstvo* claimed to be between 15,000 and 150,000 strong.

Lack of state funding was not the only weakness of the *Ukrains'ke Kozatstvo*. Membership of this organization was not formalized until 1993 when Otaman Yevhen Petrenko issued an order to register members of the organization and to provide them with relevant documents. Petrenko ordered local Cossack organizations to prepare lists of conscripts for the Armed Forces and to arrange, with the relevant military conscription centers, to send Cossack conscripts into army units separately. This, as well as another appeal to local Cossack organizations, to provide the *Otaman* with lists of young conscript-volunteers, never received a sound response. *Ukrains'ke Kozatstvo* had not yet become a force of its own, unlike its

Russian equivalent in Crimea, where the newly elected pro-Russian President Yuriy Meshkov issued a decree on 16 May 1994 pledging support to the local pro-Russian Cossacks.

On 28 May 1994, an extended Cossack assembly opened in Simferopol. It was organized by the Union of Cossack Armies in Russia and Abroad in support of the Crimean president. President Meshkov was proclaimed a "Cossack president" and elected to the Cossack Council of the Union of Cossack Armies in Russia and Abroad. Representatives of the Don, Kuban' and Siberian Cossacks supported the idea of "reviving" the Russian Cossacks in Crimea (Pavliv 1994). Cases of arms smuggling from the Don Cossacks into Crimea were not unheard-of at that time (Kuzio 1994, 125). So, the Ukrainian Ministry for Internal Affairs issued a statement on 31 May 1994 about the "complicated criminal situation" in Crimea after a considerable number of Russian Cossacks arrived on the peninsula. The ministry claimed that "Crimeans do not support and do not understand the appearance of the Russian Cossacks since the local police are capable of ensuring the reliable defense of public order with its own forces" (SWB SU/2013, 31 May 1994).

The Crimean leadership disagreed with Kyiv. The leader of the Don Cossacks, Viktor Ratiyev, and the Crimean President Meshkov signed a friendship and cooperation agreement on 15 June 1994. Meshkov stressed the historic closeness and indivisibility of the Russian Cossacks and "the people of the republic of Crimea." To facilitate the establishment of a "common economic space," the two sides committed themselves to open a Crimean embassy in Novocherkassk and a Don Cossack embassy in Simferopol (SWB SU/2025, 18 June 1994).

The presence of *Ukrains'ke Kozatstvo* in Crimea was ignored. The Crimean Organization of *Ukrains'ke Kozatstvo* (*Ukrains'ke Zaporizko-Tavriyske Kozatstvo*) at the end of 1994 condemned the aggression of the "Russian imperialist forces against the Chechen people" and criticized the Crimean parliament for its intention to split the Black Sea Navy[55] in the local newspaper. Two weeks later the same

---

[55]   "Chto vozmushchaet i bespokoit ukrainskoye kazachestvo," in *Yuzhnaya Stolica*, 30 December 1994, No. 52.

newspaper published a statement by the (Russian) Crimean Cossack Union denying the very existence of any Cossacks in Crimea other than themselves. The Russian Cossacks in Crimea lamented that they did not publish anything concerning the Russian-Chechen war.[56] Finally, the newspaper published a statement by the Crimean otaman of the *Ukrainske Kozatstvo*, Tambovcev-Lysenko, who explained that a Crimean organization of the *Ukrainske Kozatstvo* had existed since the summer of 1992 and included local organizations from 14 *rayons* of Crimea. The irony in the newspaper's headlines was that two Cossack organizations existed in two parallel dimensions of the same administrative space and had never met.[57]

On 4 January 1995, the newly elected Ukrainian President Leonid Kuchma signed a decree, "The revival of historical, cultural and economic traditions of the Ukrainian Cossacks." The decree recommended that local authorities support the activities of the Cossack organizations; it suggested that the Ministry of Education and the Ministry of Youth Affairs and Sport organize Cossack festivals and sport competitions; it also required the Ministry of Defense and the State Committee of Border Guards to resolve the issue of conscripting Cossacks to special military units. The decree had little impact on the military. By that time, Ukraine had its first civilian Minister of Defense, Valeriy Shmarov, who ended a brief and half-hearted campaign to Ukrainize the Army and tried to base his staff policy purely on a "professional basis" without taking the loyalty of officers into account. He not only successfully marginalized the Ukrainian Union of Officers, but also ordered the removal of the portraits of the "glorious Ukrainian Hetmans" from the walls of the General Staff, which was also quite symptomatic of the situation under the Kuchma presidency (Bayev and Bukkvoll 1996, 9). The rift between *Ukrains'ke Kozatstvo* and the post-Soviet Ukrainian political elite deepened as all attempts to provide national armed forces with loyal staff started to fail. The old *nomenklatura* was busy privatizing state assets and creating the new class of ruling oligarchs and showed little interest

---

[56]   "Kazak kazaka vidit izdaleka," in *Yuzshnaya Stolica*, 13 January 1995, No. 2.
[57]   "Kazaki pishut," in *Yuzshnaya Stolica*, 27 January 1995, No. 4.

in any ideology, despite the increasingly low morale of the Ukrainian armed forces (Kuzio 1995, 305).

Unsatisfied with this situation, the Ukrainian Cossacks made an attempt to change the leadership and to dismiss Hetman Muliava, who had struggled to unite different Cossack movements and promote Cossack interests in the Armed Forces. Some regional Cossack organizations decided to break away from the *Ukrainske Kozatstvo*. The separation of the Zaporozshian Cossacks under the name *Viysko Zaporozhz'ke Nyzove* in November 1994 from *Ukrainske Kozatstvo's* official body *Zaporozhz'ka Sich* was the first serious blow. The leader of the "separatists, Oleksandr Panchenko, was excluded from the *Ukrains'ke Kozatstvo* by Hetman Muliava who himself was to face a coup at the next Grand Council of the *Ukrains'ke Kozatstvo* in October 1995. Disgruntled Cossacks declared *Chorna Rada*, an alternative Cossack council, electing an alternative Hetman and seizing the archive and official stamps of the *Ukrains'ke Kozatstvo*. Hetman Muliava banned these Cossacks from the *Ukrains'ke Kozatstvo* and they later created an independent *Zvychayeve Kozatstv'* ("Cossacks of custom law") as well as other organizations.

Struggling for legitimacy, the Cossack leadership registered *Ukrains'ke Kozatstvo* as an international public organization in August 1996. Apart from the aim of attracting wealthier Ukrainian Diaspora from abroad, the new status reflected a legal attempt to claim that this new Union of All-Ukrainian Cossacks was "a legal successor to the All-Ukrainian public organizations of Ukrainian Cossacks." The new enhanced status of the Ukrainian Cossacks was formally supported by registering their partnership with the Ministry of Defense, the Command of the National Guard, the Border Troops, the Civil Defense, and other ministries and departments in Ukraine (Muliava 1996, 3-4).

On 22 December 1996, the Ministry of Defense, under the new leadership of Oleksandr Kuzmuk (previously commander of the National Guards), mentioned the Cossack organization in its Directive No. D-41, "On the development of relations between the military command and public organizations." The directive suggested that military commanders of various districts and departments should collaborate with public organizations for the patriotic, cultural and linguistic education of the staff and, particularly, for preconscript education. At the same time, however, the Directive, signed by the Minister of Defense, required the commanders to comply with Ukrainian military doctrine, the law on the Armed Forces and article No. 37 of the Ukrainian Constitution, which prohibits the activities of political parties and movements in the Armed Forces. Thus the military leadership in Ukraine, unlike its counterpart in Russia, effectively resisted collaboration with the Cossacks despite declarations that did not help to consolidate the movement.

The unity of Cossack organizations turned out to be difficult to achieve. One of the largest and most successful organizations with a national status was the Association of Cossacks in Ukraine (*Spilka kozakiv Ukrainy*), which had supporters primarily in Central and Eastern Ukraine and was led by the General Otaman of the Zaporizshia Host, Oleksandr Panchenko. Panchenko claimed there were around 20,000 members in his organization, rivaling the *Ukrains'ke Kozatstvo*, but the two organizations were ideologically similar.[58] The Cossack organization *Viys'ko Zaporiz'ke Nyzove* (Lower Zaporizshia Host) was also registered as a national Cossack organization. Among the regional organizations were *Vilne Kozatstvo* (Free Cossacks) and *Zvychayeve Kozatstvo* (Cossacks of custom law). Yet, only *Ukrains'ke Kozatstvo* was seen as the legitimate All-Ukrainian national organization, and its leader Hetman Bilas chaired the Presidential "Coordination Council for the Development of the Ukrainian Cossacks."

Despite all the organizational divisions, the popular image of Cossacks as a distinct part of Ukrainian culture was widely accepted in society. Usage of the Cossack image became common in television shows and in all sorts of festivals and mass entertainment, as well as in cigarette and alcohol branding. In 1996, the Institute of History at the National Academy of Science, with the support of *Ukrains'ke Kozatstvo*, founded the Research Institute of Cossacks, which aimed at conducting research on the history of Cossacks as well as "form-

---

58   V. Puzshaychereda, "Cossack movement is a reaction to life conditions," in *Den'*, No. 92, 30 May 1997, 4.

ing a nationally conscious Ukrainian elite."[59] On 5 July 1995, this Institute, together with Kyiv State University and the Main Directorate for Education of the Ministry of Defense, organized a conference entitled "Contemporary Cossack Pedagogy" to develop a program for Ukrainian youth, educating them about Cossack traditions in order to prepare for their future service as conscripts in the Ukrainian Armed Forces.

Notwithstanding the popular appeal of the Cossack image in Ukrainian society, Hetman Muliava admitted in 1997 that, despite the Presidential decree of 4 January 1995 requesting the Ministry of Defense to consider conscripting Ukrainian Cossacks into separate army units, no formal regulations were issued.[60] Moreover, the law on Cossacks, prepared by Hetman Muliava and submitted to the Ukrainian Government, was rejected in August 1998 by the Ministry of Justice, the Interior Ministry, the Customs Committee and the National Academy of Science.

It was not surprising, therefore, that the Kyiv Regional Cossack organization of the *Ukrains'ke Kozatstvo* expressed its mistrust of Muliava before the next election of a new Hetman. In an open letter dated 30 September 1998, Cossacks blamed the Hetman for violating Cossack traditional law, for failing to ensure free and fair elections, and for economic failure and financial mismanagement. Disaffected Cossacks accused Muliava of undermining the Cossack organization and called on him to resign.[61] An attempt to postpone the new Hetman election did not help the retired general, who also lost his seat in the Ukrainian parliament.

On 31 October 1998, the Grand Council of the *Ukrains'ke Kozatstvo* elected a new Hetman, a Major-General of the National Guards and an MP, Ivan Bilas. Bilas was also Head of the Union of Ukrainian Officers and an active member of All-Ukrainian Brotherhood of UPA Veterans (World War II Ukrainian Resurgence Army).

---

[59]   "The Institute of History of Ukrainian Cossacks," in *Vecherniy Kyiv*, 12 December 1997, 2-3.

[60]   O. Shapovalenko, "Slavnyh Velykyh Pravnuky," in *Vecherniy Kyiv*, 12 December 1997, 3.

[61]   See: Kozacka Rada, September 1998, No5. P.1- 4

In other words, the newly elected Cossack Hetman belonged to all the nationalist patriotic organizations which had fallen out of favor with the Ukrainian political establishment during the administration of President Kuchma (1995-2005). This did not assist his cause.

The *Ukrains'ke Kozatstvo* attracted, nevertheless, thousands of active members, established organizational structures, defined its status in society and proved its own viability. By the late 1990s, the Kyiv Regional organization of the *Ukrains'ke Kozatstvo* had already suggested creating a Cossack political party. The Cossack name later would appear in dozens of political projects and organizations but none would achieve significant electoral success. The problem seemed to be that *Ukrains'ke Kozatstvo* could not mobilize a distinct social base of supporters in Eastern Ukraine, even as other patriotic organizations dominated Western Ukraine. Having established extensive and relatively reliable security forces, the executive powers did not really need Cossack units, nor did they have sufficient funds to maintain numerous regular Armed Forces, let alone paramilitary formations. The Armed Forces were constantly demoralized by under-funding and were increasingly turning into "an army of theoreticians," so there was no motivation to spend its modest funds on establishing Cossack training for future conscripts, as was the case in the Russian Federation.

Lacking mass support, the Cossacks in Ukraine looked to private donor funding. Members of the new Cossacks General executive body included at various times, among others, Serhiy Arzshevitin, Head of the association of commercial banks in Ukraine, who was awarded the rank of Cossack Lieutenant-General. On 10 January 1999, Hetman Bilas organized a ceremony at which the Head of the National Bank of Ukraine, Viktor Yushchenko, and a few other business representatives and bankers were accepted into the Cossack ranks. Ivan Bilas himself also decided to enter the presidential race as a candidate for the Congress of Ukrainian Nationalists as well as *Ukrains'ke Kozatstvo*, although later he withdrew in support of the acting President Kuchma. In this way, Bilas became the second Ukrainian Cossack Hetman to be considered for the post of Ukrainian President. Despite Bilas's bleak chances as a presidential candidate, the attempt demonstrated that the Cossack movement was institutionalized enough to have a clear political discourse.

During the parliamentary elections of 2002, *Ukrainske Kozatstvo,* led by Hetman Bilas, dramatically changed its course from supporting the national-democrats' coalition of Viktor Yuschenko, *Nasha Ukraina,* to joining a coalition of powerful oligarchs and ex-government officials. This reflects not so much the ideological reorientation of *Ukrains'ke Kozatstvo,* as an attempt to "privatize" the Cossacks by various shadowy political and business forces. Regional differences in the Cossack movement were highlighted when the Zaporizshia Cossack Host granted Russia's ambassador in Ukraine, Viktor Chernomyrdin, the rank of Cossack general and awarded him the Order of Cossack Glory for his "substantial efforts in reviving the Cossacks not only in Ukraine and Russia, but also around the world" (Interfax, in Russian, 12.02 gmt, 22 November 2001). The fact that the Zaporizhian Cossacks awarded their first Order of Cossack Glory to the head of the Ukrainian Orthodox Church of the Moscow Patriarchy, Mytropolyt Vladimir, as opposed to the Ukrainian Autocephalous Church, showed that some of the regional Cossack organizations had geopolitical orientations different from the mainstream *Ukrains'ke Kozatstvo.*

The drift of *Ukrains'ke Kozatstvo* from the national-democratic opposition to the pro-government organization by the end of the 1990s did not change the Cossacks' fortunes. President Kuchma appreciated Bilas's support for his re-election, and instructed the Minister of Defense, Oleksandr Kuzmuk, to "study the possibility of creating Cossack Units within the Armed Forces." However, because of Kuzmuk's personal objections, the idea was "shelved," once again. Only after Kuzmuk's sudden resignation (due to an unrelated incident) did President Kuchma approve the "National Program for the Revival and Development of Ukrainian Cossackhood in the years 2002-2005" in November 2001, instructing the Ministry of Defense and the Ministry of the Interior this time to "consider" the possibility of "Cossack public formations serving to protect state borders and support rescue operations." Unlike in Russia, the Cossacks in Ukraine did not receive any financial support from the state until 2002, and even then, it was not significant enough to make a difference and counter separatist tendencies latent in the Crimean and Donbas Cossack movement. Former VDV Colonel and Hetman of *Ukrains'ke Kozatstvo*, Mykola Pantelyuk (elected in 2005), ran his own security agency (*Sluzhba Bezpeky Ukrains'ke Kozatstvo*) and lived in Donetsk region when the Russian infiltration in Donbas led to the creation of separatist republics. He later recalled that in the absence of state support Ukrainian Cossacks lost 7 colleagues in fighting with the "separatists" and had to evacuate to government-controlled areas:

> We guarded 17 administrative centers in Donetsk region when this tragedy unfolded in 2014. Unfortunately, the central authorities did not send us any orders and the local authorities "sold out" to the separatist sentiments. We know who was president at the time. All local officials from the village level to heads of *rayon* state administrations, with few exceptions, were pro-Russian. The local population used to obey the authorities. We were betrayed and lost 7 Cossacks in hostilities. When the Russians moved in their soldiers undercover, we wanted to avoid casualties and the majority of us had to leave. The hetman of *Ukrains'ke Kozatsvo* was sentenced by the local [separatist] authorities to death ...Today, 5,000 Cossacks fight on the frontline in the Armed Forces of Ukraine and the National Guard.
> Mykola Pantelyuk "Kozak tse ukrayinets, a ukrayinets tse kozak,i" In *Misto*, 18 Jan 2017 http://misto.vn.ua/news/item/id/10028.

Hetman Pantelyuk expressed satisfaction that the Armed Forces of Ukraine planned to create separate Cossack units for his 300,000 strong Cossack membership. However, the reality was rather different. The Ukrainian government, indeed, decided to capitalize on the Cossack warrior ethos and mythology but named *existing regular military formations after historical Cossack ones*. For instance, 72 Mechanized Brigade of the UAF (formerly 72 Soviet Army mechanized infantry division) received the name of the Black Zaporozhians to reflect the ethos of a historical regiment that existed in 1918-20. Despite adopting some elements of a Cossack insignia, it remained a regular armed formation relying on both conscription and professional contract personnel, where Cossack sentiment is not necessarily a selection criterion.

The idea of Cossackhood reflected in Ukrainian literature and art, and in thousands of Ukrainian songs is at the core of Ukrainian historical identity and its appeal is therefore likely to exist as long as the identity itself. As noted by Serhiy Plokhiy, the Cossack myth in independent Ukraine was revived to oppose Russian imperial ideology and territorial claims, and therefore had to develop initially as a counter-myth:

> In view of the current Russian-Ukrainian dispute over Crimea the traditionally anti-Tatar character of Cossack mythology has dramatically changed. In order to foster cooperation between the Ukrainian and Tatar national movements episodes of such cooperation in the past have been revived, thus transforming traditional Cossack mythology into the realm of counter-myths (Plokhiy 1993, 14).

By the end of the 1990s, the Cossack myth had turned into a nationalizing ideology of a non-ethnic nature, not only in the case of the interpretation of Ukrainian history, but also when it came to the definition of Ukrainian society or, accordingly, the Cossack Nation. With civic as opposed to ethnic membership criteria, the Cossack myth accepted a civic definition of the Ukrainian Cossack nation as such. This is not to say that the Cossack ideology is inherently a peaceful one because it is "non-ethnic." In fact, with strong traditions of militancy at the core of Cossack identity, and easy justification of territorial claims to neighboring Russia (e.g., Kuban) and Moldova (Transdniestria), the Cossack movement contains a substantial conflict potential. Ethnically-minded, the Russian Cossacks in Ukraine formed their own military detachments to fight alongside the Russian-led "separatists" in Donbas. The Ukrainian Cossacks opted to join either voluntary battalions formed on a territorial basis or the regular UAF. Of more than 40 voluntary battalions, no Ukrainian Cossack military units were set up in order to defend Donbas in 2014-2015. Ukrainian authorities announced five waves of mobilizations, so any Cossacks willing to defend the country had an opportunity to sign up for regular military service. The unwillingness of the Ukrainian ruling elites to exploit the Ukrainian Cossack movement beyond its mythology of a common Cossack ancestry became a crucial factor in the civic, culturally "revivalist" nature of the Cossack movement in Ukraine, in contrast to its militant, expansionist and "ethno-geopolitical" Russian counterpart.

Conclusions to Chapter 4

As we can see from the discussion in this chapter, post-Soviet Russian and Ukrainian scholars and policy-makers initially heavily relied on the heritage of Soviet Ethnography with its "primordialist" tradition emphasizing the ethnic origin of nations. A similar approach was chosen also by Russian policy-makers and academics who legitimize corresponding state policies. Consequently, the attempt at nation-building through a form of renegotiated ethnic federalism in the Russian Federation had the opposite effect to the proclaimed goal of developing a political nation.

The Kremlin's policy, both within the Russian Federation and toward the FSU countries, is a clear attempt to build a Russian super-ethnos/civilization by means of Eurasian ethno-geopolitics, with the Cossacks being merely one of many platforms of hybrid coercion. At the same time, representatives of federal autonomies are not prepared to abandon their ethnically-defined nationalities and adopt the *Rossiyane* identity in its exclusively civic meaning to reflect a single political nation of Russians. Likewise, ethnic Russians are not willing to abandon their *ethnonym Russkie* and use only the civic *Rossiyanie*. The debates around the law on the Russian nation show that ethnic minorities are weary of ethnic Russian assimilation and feel that their culture and identity are threatened.

The contradiction between the desirable, i.e., the political Russian nation and the real, i.e., ethnic federalism in the context of institutionalized ethnonationalist discourse in Russian academia and politics, will continue to exist in the near future. The academic and political tradition in Russia, as well as wide popular support for this tradition, legitimizes policies based on what can be broadly defined as ethno-geopolitics. The latter is based methodologically on the revived concepts of political *yevraziystvo*, mainly from Gumilev's theory of ethnogenesis, and partly on contemporary, newly-developed Russian geopolitical theories.

Ethno-geopolitics as a policy finds its formal justification in the reality of institutionalized federative ethnic entities that are the result of both Soviet Ethnography and Soviet nationality policy. The longing for the superpower status once enjoyed by the Soviet people provides Russian intellectuals with a powerful drive to restore that status, at least through theories of the Russian Supra-Ethnos or "Russian civilization," which are developed within a framework of a proclaimed Russian political nationhood. In fact, such theories substitute the civic meaning of the term "political nation" with a supra-ethnic one under the "Eurasian," but in fact Russian, ethno-nationalist ideology.

It is the lack of public support, as well as the will of the ruling elite in Ukraine, that explains why ethno-geopolitics in Ukraine never evolved beyond the realm of academia. Another important factor is that the newly-created post-Soviet Ukrainian state lacked a strong tradition of ethno-nationalism, and thus far has not shown a real intention to rely on it. The law in Ukraine, however, still reflects the ambiguities of Soviet ethnic engineering, so the Ukrainian nation, in its ethnic meaning, is granted a "titular" status among other nationalities that all together constitute the "Ukrainian people." Despite this status, ethnic Ukrainians do not have many real privileges, since the emphasis in Ukrainian law is on the rights of individuals, rather than on any kind of ethnic groups. After 5 years of war for independence from the "Russian World," the majority of Ukrainians elected a president, Volodymyr Zelensky, who proclaimed libertarianism as the predominant ideology of his administration. (Ukraine also briefly became the only nation in the world, apart of Israel, in which both the president and the prime minister identified themselves as Jewish.)

Despite the fact that some academics and parts of the Ukrainian political elite share an ethno-geopolitical discourse similar to that found in Russia, Ukraine simply lacks the democratic consensus to implement ethno-geopolitics as a policy. In other words, the Ukrainian majority does not provide the ruling elites with the public consent necessary in a democratic state to implement policies that discriminate against other minorities.

In the wider regional context of the FSU, however, ethno-geopolitics will retain its negative implications for as long as Russia accompanies every political campaign to boost domestic public support with accusations of suppression of Russian minorities by its neighbors and, indeed, attempts to redraw ethnopolitical boundaries within or outside of the Russian Federation.

The rhetorical ethno-geopolitics of the late 1990s eventually led to both Russian-Georgian and Russian-Ukrainian armed conflicts in 2008 and 2014-. Putin's war on Ukraine was crucial to his Eurasian ethno-geopolitics, as it was the key country needed to make "Russian civilization" complete. In response to these ethno-geopolitical tactics of the Russian political elite, the Ukrainian government has pursued the policy of building the political nation of the Ukrainian people. The Cossack narrative of common origin was successfully employed in Ukraine for this purpose, initially as a counter-myth and later as a "nationalizing" non-ethnic ideology. The Cossack ideology was meant to emphasize the civic aspect of nation-building in Ukraine, as opposed to the ethnic one. According to a survey by the Donetsk-based NGO Kalmius Group, 53-63 percent of respondents in Donbas believed that Ukrainian Cossack history and Ukrainian pop-songs were the two key factors that continued to unite them with the rest of Ukraine despite 4 years of continuing armed conflict (*Novosti Donbasa* website, 1249 gmt 6 September 2018).

However, whether and for how long Ukraine will continue on its course to build a civic political nation under conditions of ongoing armed conflict remains to be seen. The crucial difference between Russia and Ukraine until 2014 was that the Kyiv authorities had been successful in avoiding both federalization by ethnicity and civil war. Russian military aggression against Ukraine and attempts to manufacture a "civil war" had limited success, and in fact led to even deeper consolidation of the Ukrainian people behind the idea of liberal democracy, with a strong civil society receiving a boost from a widespread civic volunteer movement. Ukrainian voters showed consistent support for centrist parties and the second-lowest support for right-wing populist parties in Central and Eastern Europe between 1990 and 2010 as reflected in the table below (Polyakova 2013).

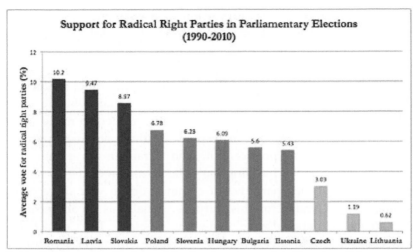

Table: Polyakova, A., "Let's stop blaming the economy". in Eurozine, 30 January 2013. Internet version https://www.eurozine.com/lets-stop-blaming-the-economy/

This was reflected in the shaping of two distinctive Cossack movements in Ukraine that developed -opposing narratives. The Ukrainian Cossack movement evolved into civic organizations of patriots with a progressive "revivalist" agenda focusing on local community, ecology and history. The Russian Cossack movement in Ukraine resembled its brethren in the Russian Federation with its ethno-geopolitical revanchist agenda and tendency to militarize conflicts as required by the Kremlin.

The analysis above suggests that similarities between the Cossack revival in Russia and Ukraine and the subsequent introduction of two distinct Cossack movements lie more in the dimension of genesis than in the nature of organizations. In other words, a similar origin and socio-historical composition, similar economic orientations toward state service and/or agriculture are the features which define both phenomena as similar social movements with a "revivalist" community agenda. On the other hand, there are crucial differences that indicate two separate paths of development.

The Cossack revival of the 1990s had a clear and successful start in Russia when the Cossack movement was recognized by the state with a clear legal status defining Cossacks in Russia as an "ethnic community." A clear tendency within the Russian Cossack movement of the early 1990s toward separatism in the form of different Cossack republics gradually evolved, by the end of the 1990s, into a struggle for the right to self-government within the Russian state borders. Crucially, however, since President Putin consolidated his regime, the Cossack movement was directed by the Russian state toward policing internal dissent and supporting the expansion of the Russian super-ethnos. The Russian Cossacks therefore evolved as "revivalist" patriotic organizations domestically, and as successful paramilitary formations actively used by the Russian state, both within the Russian Federation ethnic autonomies and abroad. In Crimea and Donbas, the Cossacks are being used as a tool of hybrid warfare in order to achieve foreign policy objectives in a deniable form.

The Ukrainian Cossacks evolved as public organizations and did not develop any ideology other than a moderate Ukrainian "civic" nationalism. The mainstream Cossack movement aimed to "improve" the fortunes of Ukrainians generally, providing an example of the classical "revivalist" discourse of Groch's "groups of patriots" observed in Central Europe since the nineteenth century. Despite the Cossack myth of origin being clearly a distinct part of Ukrainian national identity, Cossack organizations have not gained more public support than any other "revivalist" patriotic movements, and they certainly failed in paramilitary mobilization for the war effort.

Unlike their Russian counterparts in the North Caucasus, the Ukrainian Cossacks did not experience the extreme conditions of civil war on their territory until 2014, and therefore did not feel that their lives were directly threatened. Once the Russian military invasion was underway, the Ukrainian Cossacks joined either the regular Ukrainian Armed Forces or volunteer battalions later integrated into the Ukrainian Ministry of the Interior's regular formations.

The Russian Cossacks in Chechnya, Ingushetia, or other hot spots of the 1990s had little choice but to protect themselves with arms in conditions where the state could not provide for their safety or uphold the rule of law. The latter explains how the Russian Cossack organizations evolved first as paramilitary self-defense units

and then into fully militarized formations serving as military con-
tractors/mercenaries abroad.

The Cossack organizations in Russia developed a distinct out-
ward aspiration to "protect" ethnic Russians and/or Slavs generally
abroad. They participate in armed conflicts as mercenaries or professional soldiers of governmental units and de-facto act as ideologists
of Russian expansionism from Crimea to Syria and even as far as
Venezuela. The Ukrainian Cossacks were involved mostly in cultural activities and are not known as active participants of armed conflicts in neighboring countries for ideological motives. Nevertheless,
they have been successful in blocking the Russian Cossacks' neo-
imperial narrative of Ukraine (i.e., of Russians and Ukrainians being
"one people") — arguably their single and most important achievement.

Finally, war preparation always was and still is an important
part of Cossack ideology in Ukraine, on the rhetorical level, for both
movements. The Russian Cossacks found a political role from the
start and were actively involved on behalf of different political forces
in the Russian Federation and abroad. They are also often used by
the Russian state authorities as "a Cossack card" when there is a
need for hidden diplomacy toward other communities or governments. The Ukrainian Cossacks have not found a clearly defined role
in politics and seem to be more interested in state (army or civilian)
service. The Ukrainian Cossacks did take part in fighting for their
country in Donbas, as individuals, but their motive was to defend
the territorial integrity of Ukraine in what they consider to be a war
of national liberation from Russian neo-imperialism.

The comparative study of the two distinct Cossack movements
also provides important implications for theoretical findings. Ethno-
geopolitics, as a theoretical discourse on relations and struggles
among ethnoses as opposed to nation-states, highlights the importance of studying violent expressions of nationalism by con-
trasting the relationship within a security community both as opposed and in addition to a political community.

As discussed in Chapter 3, a security community is defined by
a sense of widespread communal commitment to resolve conflicts of

interests by peaceful means, when war among members of the community is unimaginable and no war preparations are made. Such a sense of commitment to peaceful conflict resolution implies the strong homogeneous identity of such a community. It appears that a security community could weaken when this sense and/or identity is undermined: the process well-described by the concept of societal (identity) security as an independent level of security analysis. The second part of Appendix 1 focuses on a case study of two opposing Cossack communities of the Odesa region, in order to identify those markers of their ethno-national group identity that make war preparations inevitable. It does so, however, in the context of different levels of analysis conducted in sub-chapter 3.3, starting from the system level of security community represented by the New European Order, the sub-system level represented by no-war communities formed by the newly-established nation-states of Ukraine and the Russian Federation in the 1990s, moving to the bureaucracy level of governmental policies, and then to the unit/individual level of Cossack formations and Cossack individuals. The empirical findings suggest that when the *state security of Ukraine in respect of Cossack movement was ensured* by the non-recognition of the Russian Cossacks as a separate people (nationality or ethnos) and their formal integration under the umbrella of a Ukrainian National civic Cossack organization/movement, *societal security remained threatened* by competing Cossack nationalisms. On the individual and unit levels of analysis, threats to the identity of Ukrainian "groups of patriots," who aim at national agitation and mobilization, are manifested by opposition to the counter-movement of the Russian Cossacks inspired by the Russian Supra-State project. Perceptual factors (i.e., divergent beliefs and historical grievances) further inhibited the quite low interaction and integration capacities of the two Cossack movements, making war preparations rhetorically and/or practically inevitable.

Chapter 5 summarizes the empirical findings gained from the different levels of analysis and correlates them with existing as well as proposed theoretical notions in order to show how the development of nationalist movements, even within a democratic framework of nation-building, depends on societal security, i.e., on the perceived threats to national identity.

5   The Insecurity of National Identity in Ukraine and Russia: Towards a Normative Theory of Nationalism

This final chapter of the monograph discusses how the empirical findings presented in the previous chapter improve our understanding of existing theories of nations, national identity and nationalism in general, and their relations to Ukraine and Russia specifically. They show how identity constructs as well as threats to national interests influence what conflict resolution strategies are available to democratic states engaged in nation building. The findings also establish the usefulness of the concepts of "security community" and "societal security" for analyzing the war-causing potential of nationalism, and the inherent insecurity of nationalism as a consequence of competition among alternative nation-building projects. In brief, the insecurity of nationalism is a result of its own success in making the right to self-determination a universal principle and, as a result, turning the world of peoples into a world of potentially warring nations.

Before proceeding to a summary of the monograph and a discussion of its findings, however, the next sections focus on normative aspects of nationalism that are the basis of both its success and its conflict potential.

5.1. Nationalism as a Modern Belief System

It is understandable why the general literature on nationalism should be so critical of it, and why nationalism, generally, gets such bad press. The horrors of nationalist violence in the last century and the nationalist violence that continues to erupt throughout the world today have made it likely that damning judgements will be made of anything that sounds like nationalism. This was not always so, as Judith Lichtenberg (1999) reminds us. In the nineteenth century nationalism was associated with freedom and liberalism. It was:

> An expansive, cosmopolitanizing force. In colonial territories, nationalists fought foreign domination; nationalism meant freedom and self-determination. (Lichtenberg 1999, 167).

So, morally justified nationalism is possible not only in the case of anti-colonial struggles, but also in the case of struggles for the internationally enshrined right to self-determination. In this sense, nationalism is justified as a universal principle, not merely accepted but approved. Ernest Gellner speaks, for instance, of Masaryk's "highly moral nationalism," based on the premise that "the overall tendency of history towards freedom and democracy . . . vindicated Czech nationalism and independence as one of its instruments. It was not wilful, inward-looking nationalism. Quite the contrary" (Gellner 1997, 99).

Other authors argue that nationalism is morally neutral, and can align itself either with good or evil. Lea Brilmayer explores the nature of the two existing justifications of nationalism: first, that national rights are universal and apply to all nations; and second, that national rights should be granted for the suffering caused by the nationalism of others. She argues that:

> … the overwhelming relevant normative feature of today's nationalism is the justice (or lack of justice) of the claims nationalists advance on behalf of their nation. The single most important normative feature—indeed, perhaps, the only important normative feature—is the right of the nation to the thing that nationalists assert on its behalf, and this right is not itself a consequence of nationalism but a consequence of other underlying moral claims. (Brilmayer 1995, 7).

There is no simple answer as to which moral claims justify nationalist discourse and which do not. Gellner illustrates his argument against the principle of the right to self-determination by pointing to the dilemma of Kosovo, where both sides believed that they had moral justification for possessing that territory. The Serbs believe that Kosovo was the ground of their biggest national disaster at the hands of the Turks in the fourteenth century, and therefore they claim a moral right to hold on to their historical heartland where they are presently an absolute minority. The Albanians believe their suffering under the nationalist regime in Belgrade morally justifies their right to self-determination on the territory where they claim a ninety percent majority. World opinion on this matter was divided. Critics feared that the Kosovo Albanians' claim to self-determination would provoke a revision of other European borders. Thus, the early military actions of Albanian separatists in Kosovo in the mid-1990s were condemned as brutal Balkan nationalism deserving suppression. By the end of 1998, however, this perception had been transformed into almost its opposite. These drastic changes were recorded in Philip Hammond and Edward Herman's analysis of world media coverage before, during, and after the Kosovo campaign by NATO countries in 1999. Hammond and Herman recall that:

> As late as February 1998, US special envoy Robert Gelbard described the KLA [Kosovo Liberation Army] as a 'terrorist organisation', saying of it on 22 February: 'it is the strong and firm policy of the US to fully oppose all terrorist actions and all terrorist organisations'. But once Nato had decided to occupy Kosovo and teach Serbia a lesson, word usage and frames shifted drastically, and the KLA became 'freedom fighters', whose interest in provoking the Serbs in order to expedite the desired NATO attacks was barely noticed. (Hammond and Herman 2000, 202)

Kosovo's independence certainly came back to haunt Europe when the Russian Federation used armed force to alter the borders in Georgia (2008) and Ukraine (2014) with a clear reference from the Kremlin to the Western precedent in the Balkans. Putin presented the attempted annexation of Crimea as a morally justified "homecoming" and laid claims to the wider Ukrainian territory that he referred to as the "New Russia." Kyiv responded with both legal and moral arguments about the inviolability of its territorial sovereignty, and received support from the international community, e.g., the UN resolutions on human rights making clear reference to Russia as an occupying power in Crimea.

Such ambiguity with respect to what is moral and what is not led Yael Tamir to the conclusion that scholars need to develop a normative theory of nationalism in order to be able to place different nationalist claims in a more general moral framework. Unlike Rogers Brubaker, who does not believe that a theory of nationalism is necessary, even if possible (because the expression of nationalism varies and is context dependant), Tamir argues that a theory of nationalism must structure itself independently of all contingencies and around universally applicable values; that it must take into account general facts concerning the existence of nations, the role they play in human history, and their importance for their members irrespective of the status, size, wealth and power of each particular nation. All these issues, Tamir argues, cannot be resolved on the basis of particular case studies, but only on the basis of abstract principles (Tamir 1999, 77-87).

So, what are the essential components of a normative theory of nationalism? The analysis of the previous chapters suggests that such a theory should define nationalism as a modern belief system that evolved gradually within Europe and the rest of the world, assuming the right for every people to have a separate political roof and preferably a state of its own, so that its culture would be able to flourish.

Some of the assumptions on which a normative theory of nationalism might be based might be drawn from the following conclusions.

First, nationalism is profoundly influenced by, and indeed might be caused by, the development of modernity as understood in social, economic and cultural terms; thus, nationalism is no more "natural" or "accidental" than any other form of human development at a certain "civilizational stage": it is, in other words, neither God-given nor artificially invented by an "evil force," and might outlive its usefulness as a political principle of self-organization of human society.

Second, although distinctions of nationalism as cultural or political, civic or ethnic, liberal or conservative, Eastern or Western, etc., reflect different historical and ideological aspects as variations of the same phenomenon, they are not all-encompassing on their own and do not constitute real alternatives to each other. From a moral point of view, neither of these forms is better or worse, as either could lead to aggressive, violent outcomes within a certain *political* context.

This leads to a *third* conclusion: that *nationalism is not necessarily an independent political ideology, but a political principle founded upon various ideologies.* Nationalism can be liberal, conservative, aristocratic, democratic, and so on, depending on the forces that are promoting the idea of the modernization of a given society according to their own political agenda.

Fourth, the compatibility of nationalism as an organizing social and political principle with liberal democracy in those Western countries that were first to pass the stage of early industrialization, and did not need to appeal to ethnic markers for the mass mobilization of society, proves that at least this mature version of post-industrial society can comfortably accommodate both the liberal values of individual freedom and collective nationalistic sentiments and ideals. On the other hand, as long as we live in the age of nations and nationalism, there is no guarantee that even within liberal democratic societies some groups would not exploit ethnic or other cultural markers in order to advance their argument that "their culture" should have a political roof of some sort. As long as nationalism can exploit the principle of self-determination, any attempt to limit the number of social groups claiming the right to self-determination would be arbitrary and, most likely, self-defeating. Nationalism as an organizing political principle will last as long as people believe in its ability to provide them with a sense of positive self-identity as members of a successful social group or community. At the moment, the most universal image of such a successful community in the globalized world is the nation-state. Even the EU, successful as it is, can only hope to compete with such leading nation-states as China and the USA.

This leads to a *fifth* conclusion: nationalism is embedded in the national identity of every nation (people) as a belief system, sometimes called, though arguably, a myth, namely, that humanity is naturally divided into nations, which are framed into nation-states as the most suitable form of political organization for the cultural as well as economic development of the human community. National identity in itself is considered in this sense to be a *complex* belief system that consists of a set of other beliefs, of a rational and irrational-emotional nature. The latter, irrational beliefs include myths and stereotypes that could be of a highly emotive nature for the individual. The highly emotive nature of the components of national identity explains why national sentiments can be so explosive when some minor intrusion or challenge, not necessarily important from a rational point of view, triggers an outburst of individual and group anger, for which nationalism is commonly blamed.

Sixth, for good or ill, moderate nationalism fulfills within liberal democratic nation-states the same function that patriotism fulfilled in the age before nations and nationalism. Democracies need their peoples to be cohesive and their citizens to be ready to sacrifice themselves in defense of their democratic states. Nationalism is more effective than any other political principle in bringing about the homogeneity of national society based on a single national culture that was so essential for the socio-economic as well as military success of most developed Western liberal democracies.

Seventh, although the world of nation-states has never been stronger, the development of the European Union, and potentially of the Eurasian Economic Union, suggests the possibility of a new stage of social organization in Europe and wider Eurasia. It is not clear yet whether the new European Union will develop into a supra-nation-state in its own right, of the same breed as other nation-states, or whether it will create a new post-national political principle of social organization that will have, for instance, a civilization as its socio-economic and cultural unit of humanity. Theoretically, it is possible to imagine that as soon as the idea of civilizational unity overcomes the previously held belief of the national unit as an absolute value, European civilization will be able to progress to the civilization of the Northern hemisphere, along with Russian civilization east of the river Volga, and North America across the Atlantic as its sub-civilizational siblings. The next logical step would be the United Civilizations of the World. However, this abstract theorizing, so appealing to a cosmopolitan, has to end abruptly, as there is little evidence as yet that the world of nation-states is fading away. However, the useful side of the exercise is to show that nations are not necessarily here for good. Nations were invented by human social evolution, so they could be merged into larger units if, and when, they become more adequate for the postmodern world and a more worldly human identity. This leads us to the next problem of nationalism, namely, how to restrict this political principle to work within the framework of liberal democracy as the most aspirational ideology of the new global order.

5.2. Nationalism, Federalism and Civil Society

The arguments and evidence presented in previous chapters suggest that the likely route to successful management of nationalism may be through democratically negotiated federal, even non-territorial organization of national communities within a framework of nation-states or possibly larger-than-national political entities. Nationalism in a benign form of non-territorial patriotism with political structures similar to cantons could be one way forward. Jürgen Habermas considers the world of nation-states obsolete and argued in favor of non-national allegiance to the *local and global* political structures based on the legitimacy of constitutional patriotism.

Supporters of liberal nationalism agree that in some cases only federal arrangements can limit the negative aspects of nationalist principles. So, for instance, Gregory Jusdanis argues that only non-territorial federalism can meet the challenges of poly-ethnic societies because, by eliminating the need for an all-encompassing culture, it removes from politics this seed of discord (Jusdanis 2001). He argues that people emphasize their own traditions, language and native land, not out of a commitment to liberalism, but out of a belief that they will lose their personal and social bearings without them. Precisely because the individual's own private identity is so tied to the identity of her or his group, cultural identities may become the foundation to launch a political movement. "Personal respect in this way is related to the dignity of the ethnic group" (Jusdanis 2001, 213). In order to protect the dignity of one group and not antagonize others, a nation-state could be reformed into federal arrangements, whereas government would be on the level of cultural communities, on the one hand, and on the level of federal authorities, on the other. However, as David Held points out, the problem of supra-national global governance cannot be solved through the extension of grass-

roots democracy alone; arguments for such a solution leave unanswered an important question:

> Which grass-roots and which democracy? There are many social move-
> ments—for instance, right-wing nationalist movements or the eugenics
> movement—which highlight how the very nature of grass-roots movements
> can be contested and fought over. Grass-roots movements are by no means
> merely noble or wise. (Held 1995, 286)

At the same time, according to Jusdanis, federal governments
should be framed into a system of transnational organizations con-
trolling federal bodies, so that they can restrain the abuse by individual states of their citizens. Collective functions such as education,
health care, cultural institutions, recreation and social services
would be funded and run on the level of such cultural communities.
Whether such an approach to fragmenting nation-states, dissolving
them down to territorial communities controlled by the UN like
global government, could be viable remains to be seen. In the present, any meaningful reform of the UN depends on the permanent
members of the UN Security Council, i.e., the most powerful nation-
states.

Similar views of non-territorial cultural autonomy arrangements for national minorities were popular at the end of the nineteenth and beginning of the twentieth centuries within the school
known as Austro-Marxism. Otto Bauer and Karl Renner attempted
to elaborate Marxism as a sociological theory of nationalities in order
to find a solution to the Habsburg dilemma of competing ethno-
cultural nationalisms. They believed that it was possible to separate
the principle of cultural nationality from territorial location and divorce nationalities, those "communities of character" as described by
Bauer (2000), from the right to territorial self-determination.

We know the fate of the Habsburg Empire, but are there better
times to come? Bill Bowring has investigated the attempt of scholars-
turned-politicians to revive the concept of non-territorial national
autonomy in the Russian federation in the late 1990s. The Russian
Federation inherited from the USSR an institutionalized ethno-
territorial division of the federal hierarchy of autonomous regions
and republics, and therefore inherently suffered from ethno-national

nationalisms. Chechnya was the most violent expression of the separatist movements which the federal Russian government had to deal
with, so it is not surprising that in 1996 (after the defeat of the Federal troops in the First Chechen war) Russia adopted a law on non-
territorial National Cultural Autonomy (NCA), aimed at liberalizing
policy toward national minorities, but at the same time taking away
the right to territorial self-determination. Bowring concludes that
whatever the result of Russia's experiment with NCA, it "will surely
generate a wealth of experience" (Bowring 2002, 229-250). The fact
that the Russian federal government decided in the end to break the
Chechen resistance by force illustrates that the NCA strategy should
have been applied before nationalism enters the stage of armed
struggle. In the end, the Russian government could find no better
solution than to criminalize any call for cultural autonomy that
could be perceived as an expression of "separatism" in the broadest
interpretation.

Yet, the NCA idea also reflects two competing schools of
thought in the Russian and the general post-Soviet space, concerning
views about the problem of nationalism. The "modernist," constructivist position on nationalism, similar to the one in the West, is still a
minority faith, although it is an elite minority in the Russian social
sciences. The most important representative of this school of
thought, and supporter of the NCA experiment, is the academician
Valeriy Tishkov, who energetically appeals to politicians to forget
the nation as a concept and adopt a "post-nationalist view of nationalism" (Tishkov 1998, 3-26). However, the majority of Russian scholars, as Tishkov himself admits, do not accept the constructivist interpretation of nationalism. The proliferation of neo-Eurasian ideology, with references to Lev Gumilev and Aleksandr Dugin, suggests
that the bio-spherical approach is much more popular in Russia than
its socio-biological counterpart, represented by Pierre van den
Berghe (1978) in the West. The failure to abandon the territorially
defined concept of nationality in Russia, despite the relative success
of re-institutionalized asymmetric federalism among Russian ethno-
national republics, illustrates the strength of the idea of the nation-
state, even within federal arrangements.

Indeed, the new assertive policy of President Putin, who managed to overpower separatist tendencies in the republics, led to a precedent that compelled the Republic of Buryatia to abolish its Declaration of Sovereignty (1990), as not corresponding to the new Russian Federal Constitution. James Hughes and Gwendolyn Sasse, therefore, argue that a democratic outcome is possible in the case of the FSU republics if state authorities manage to renegotiate the re-institutionalization of multi-ethnic autonomies. Reiterating Gellner's prediction about the possible deconstruction of territorial nationalism into non-territorial patriotism in Eastern Europe, the authors argue that the new federal institutional architecture provides a potential democratic solution in multi-ethnic states. Hughes and Sasse suggest that there are two variants of this:

> ...either the establishment of a new 'control' regime, or the reassembly and re-institutionalisation of provisions for multi-ethnicity in ways which may or may not draw on the autonomy arrangements of the discarded old regime. Both variants may be effective at managing multi-ethnicity, but only the latter comes with an international seal of approval. (Hughes and Sasse 2002, 239)

As would appear from the example of Kosovo, an "international seal of approval" comes in different forms at different times. However, the authors' point remains valid that ethnicity is manageable within a democratic framework if both sides are willing to negotiate. Hughes and Sasse also admit that the adoption of nationalizing and homogenizing policies in divided societies is likely to intensify minority discontent and conflict, hence the Russian Federation is the last one to hold on among the disintegrated post-communist federations.

So, why is the Russian Federation an exception? The authors' overall argument is that Russia was more successful in democratizing and negotiating federal arrangements on legislative and regional levels throughout the 1990s. This, however, contradicts Jack Snyder's elite-persuasion theory: i.e., that the early democratization of states with weak democratic institutions leads to the escalation of ethnic conflict. In fact, Snyder argues that "it is dangerous to unleash democratization before effective antidotes to nationalist conflict are in place" (Snyder 2000, 85), and it was precisely *weak* democratic institutions which gave Aleksandr Dugin and other proponents of neo-imperial Eurasianism such influence.

According to James Hughes, one of the key aspects of the "successful" re-institutionalization of ethnicity in Russia was a lack of transparency, leading to an information deficit of the bilateral power-sharing treaty process (Hughes 2002, 63). In other words, leaders of the ethno-territorial republics had to negotiate autonomy with the President of the Russian Federation in secret, not only from other federal republics, but to a large extent from their own publics. Therefore, successful nationalism management in the Russian Federation was not so much a result of democratic institution-building as neo-colonial elite manipulation. This, however, does not contradict the conclusion that a federation with asymmetric power sharing between the center and the republics, as in Russia, has an important stabilizing effect. In the long run, however, the logic of the elite's inclination to use nationalism to advance their goals could work as long as they can hold onto their territory. The re-instutionalization of an ethno-territorial structure of federation does not necessarily satisfy the general aspiration of ethno-nationalisms toward self-determination, but can only delay it. Specifically, the case of the FSU dilemma of the Habsburg type of nationalism will not be solved until the ruling elite in the center is confronted by the local intelligentsia in the regions, on the basis of ethnic markers. Therefore, the homogenization of society still provides a more effective solution, and federalization only buys time to accomplish it. Liberal democracy envisages either homogenization based on a dominant culture, effectively through the assimilation of local ethno-national cultures, or self-determination of political units based on local cultures. The case of Czechoslovakia is a good example of the latter, where relative homogenization of the nation-state culture was achieved via negotiations and, effectively, a "velvet divorce." Unfortunately, the Russian Federation under President Putin chosen homogenization of the "Russian civilization" based on Russian culture pursued via covert and overt coercion, first of its own federal subjects, and then other FSU countries. Valery Tishkov's comments on Russian society not being ready for a civic definition of Russians as one nation, in

2017, summed up what could have been a promising attempt at non-territorial National Cultural Autonomy. Instead, Putin's Eurasianism led Russia to ethno-geopolitical territorial disputes and armed conquests in Georgia and Ukraine, with continuing subversion of both nation-states. For Ukraine, Russian-induced "federalization" would mean acceptance of Russian culture as the basis for the homogenization of society where the majority is constituted of ethnic Ukrainians. Even were the ruling elites to accept such a proposition, in order to achieve peace and secure the Ukrainian sovereign state that they benefit from, the national identity of Ukrainians would be existentially threatened. At the same time, the modest attempts to homogenize Ukrainian society on the basis of the "titular" Ukrainian culture led to the illegal annexation of Crimea and armed conflict over territories that Putin proclaimed as the "New Russia." In other words, the Kremlin is forcing Kyiv to negotiate federal arrangements between the Ukrainian majority and the Russian minority at gunpoint, demanding at the same time the homogenization of Ukrainian society based on Russian culture. Facing the choice between the Russian civilization based on the super-ethnos concept and the EU supranational civilization, Ukrainians enshrined their "euro-atlantic" choice in the constitution and supported it in armed struggle. This, however, does not ease the confrontation between the neo-imperial Russian nationalism manifested by Putin's Eurasianism and the Ukrainian irredentist civic nationalism proclaimed by the Euro-Maidan "Revolution of Dignity." So, what does the development of two supra-national integration projects in Eurasia (the EU and the EAEU) tell us about the likely future of nationalism in Europe and the likely solution of the Russian-Ukrainian standoff?

Although the decline or, rather, potential self-withdrawal of the nation-state in Europe remains disputed, it is nevertheless substantial. When our world has been compressed by powerful technologies into a "global village," it looks as though there should be no room for the old-fashioned "blood-and-soil" national identities. If nationalism was invented as a result of uneven capitalist development, it can be un-invented by the development of a global economy and an all-encompassing information space.

This is the core argument of neoliberals, represented, for instance, by Percy Mistry (1999) in his account of the New Regionalism as an intermediate future between the age of the nation-state and global governance:

> In 1990, history made a choice in favour of markets offering the dominant economic paradigm for the world economy for the foreseeable future. There is no going back. For the next few decades, regionalism offers a better approach than either nationalism or multilateralism in the interregnum between the era of the nation-state, which is about to end, and the era of global governance which is still some distance from materializing in effective form. (Mistry, 1999, 152).

Globalization, however, evokes the resistance of regional European identities, be it Brexit in Western Europe or the *Russki Mir* (Russian world) in Eastern Europe. The world economy experiences not only globalizing tendencies, but also regionalizing ones. And the reason for both of these is the same capitalist development (Hazel 1991). Or, as Buzan put it: "The national idea is obviously not dying out ... but what is modified is the organisation of political space" (Buzan 1998).

Ideally, any new modifications of political space should reflect the interests of a regionalized world economy that would automatically reinforce local (national) identities. This could be achieved if uneven globalization would match regional social movements. Gellner and Habermas agree that political power should shift from the level of nation-states to sub-national and supra-national, or, in other words, regional and global levels. On the other hand, one can argue no less convincingly that the "regionalism and nationalism of the periphery are not atavistic throwbacks but rational responses to the growth of the modern state and can only be understood as such. Territorial relationships are a constant factor in politics, though changing in form and their means of expression over time" (Keating 1988, vii). Buzan made another important observation:

> Though economic improvements are crucial, the traditional liberal argument about overcoming nationalism through modernisation has to be modified in at least three ways. First, it is not the economic factors directly that creates nationalism but the psychological factors that have to be understood. Secondly, despite the arguments about the irrational nature of nationalism it is still pos-

sible that the mechanism will get started again at some level of economic development. This is not least because of the unsettling effects of modernisation and the relative nature of status, and thereby the constant possibility of humiliation. Thirdly, there is a difference between trying to prevent the eruption of nationalist logic by economic pre-emption and handling a conflict that is already started and run according to nationalist logic. (Buzan 1998, 75)

After all, "as an ideology or state of political feeling, nationalism can be conceived of [...] as attaching utility or value to having certain jobs held or certain property owned by members of the national group rather than by non-members of the national group" (Johnson 1965, 176). This point is reflected in the "America First" principle proclaimed by US President Trump, who has clearly rejected globalization in favor of isolationism and protectionism: "We reject globalism and embrace the doctrine of patriotism" (Quote from *Time*, 28 September 2018 https://time.com/5406130/we-reject-globalism-president-trump-took-america-first-to-the-united-nations/). It was a declaration of the supremacy of the nation-state sovereignty, and an invitation to other national leaders present at the UN General Assembly to embrace their own versions of Trump's "America First" foreign policy approach. In the case of the global economy and geopolitics, nationalism can be re-considered as a one of the unintended consequences of regionalization. The implications of worldwide globalization and its impact on regions as socio-economic units as well as regional identities are still highly debatable. However, federalism, in its various forms, might allow time for the political accommodation of ethno-territorial separatist aspirations, until the question of supra-nation building in Europe and the rest of the world is resolved one way or the other.

Another stabilizing factor, for the time being, could be the growth of civil society in both developing as well as mature democracies. In fact, it is the link between democracy and nationalism as a legitimizing factor that makes Civil Society-based polities superior in theory to democracy, which is simply based on the nation-state's majority. Gellner believes that:

The emergence of Civil Society has in effect meant the breaking of the circle between faith, power and society. ... The criteria of truth, the criteria of social efficiency, the social hierarchy and distribution of advantages in society—all

> these are not mutually linked, and the citizen can live with the clear awareness that indeed they are not linked, that the social order is not sacred, and the sacred is not to be approached through the social. Inquiry into truth and commitment to the maintenance of social order are separated. The social can become both instrumental and optional (Gellner 1994, 147).

In other words, civil society sought in theory to break with the modern tradition that links social legitimization with faith, in this case national myths and stereotypes, and therefore to break with the irrationality of nationalism. However, in reality, civil society has so far not produced a sufficiently effective substitute for democracy based on faith while maintaining national boundaries as well. International civil society, so far, is weaker and less effective than international organized crime, for instance. As can be seen in the above empirical findings, emerging civil society is not a guarantee against the revival of old blood-and-soil identities such as the Cossack one.

The above fieldwork findings suggest that the Cossack movement is a social phenomenon emerging "from below," i.e., it can be seen as part of civil society development. What induces people to join the "patriots" as opposed to the "cosmopolitans," and not only adopt a certain worldview, but also risk sacrificing their lives in the name of an "imagined community"? The question was succinctly formulated by James Kellas:

> The fact that so many people make the 'supreme sacrifice' of dying for their nation is testimony to a special force shaping human behaviour. Explaining that force must be the principal task of any theory of nationalism. (Kellas 1991, 170)

The research findings suggest that Cossack identity served the function of a positive national identity, something these people lacked as a result of the dissolution of their former national identification as Soviets. The very core of the idea of civil society is that its institutions will emerge naturally when the economy achieves a high degree of autonomy from the state. This condition did not exist in post-communist Eastern Europe, so effectively the national governments proclaimed civil society as their goal.

In this situation, it was easy for both the Ukrainian and Russian governments to influence the Cossack revival and shape it respectively as the renaissance of diversity and plurality or as a tool for ethno-national paramilitary mobilization. As Andre Reszler has noticed, nationalism never appears in isolation. It is often a facade for other policies and aggressions that never bear their own names:

> We live in a world where a more or less fixed set of values makes up the foundations of 'civil society'. Some of the values upon which our institutions are founded are well established and openly vindicated. Other values however are undeclared. They are at the basis of fundamental policy making, yet they never appear in the open. The will of power of organised groups, political movements and power-thirsty individuals, as well as the desire to dominate, are never mentioned among our openly declared values. We know nevertheless that we must never forget about their existence, if we want to understand the society in which we live. (Hieronimi 1980, 217)

However, the weakness of civil society at present does not mean a lack of strength in the future. Post-industrial social organization may need civil society as much as early modernity needed nationalism as a political principle and legitimizing ideology.

Summary und Conclusions of the Book

This monograph has mapped out a synthetic analytical framework for the study of nations, national identities and nationalism, and has provided new empirical evidence for the nationalist revival in Eastern Europe, using the example of the Cossack movements in Russia and Ukraine. It has also tested the theoretical notion of Societal Security in terms of identifying the explosive potential of nationalist movements. The summary of the research conducted can therefore be divided into theoretical and empirical findings.

Analysis of "modernist" vs. "primordialist" schools in the Western, and socio-spherical vs. bio-spherical schools in the Russian and Ukrainian, scholarly traditions illustrates that there is little agreement as to the time, causes, and genesis of the national phenomenon, even though there is a more coherent description of the contemporary state of nations and national identity. It is the historical evolution of nations and nationalism that is most disputed, including the definition of these terms. This can be explained by the fact that the nation-building process has not been universally completed and therefore the legitimization of "new" vs. "old" nations depends also on scholarly interpretation of "natural law and justice," especially when it comes to the right to self-determination.

Legitimizing national and ethno-national boundaries by means of scholarly justification was certainly evident in the case of the USSR, where Soviet Ethnography provided a "scientific" basis for ethno-social engineering and its political outcomes. Soviet Ethnography was dominated by a socio-spherical approach that combined aspects from both the "modernist" and "primordialist" Western traditions. Methodologically, it was based on historical materialism, resembling the approach of Western "modernists"; but, empirically, it emphasized the ethnic origin of nations as well, making it consistent with the views of Western "primordialists."

Debates in contemporary Western and Eastern European traditions have focused on components of national identity as a means of shedding light on the origins of nationalism. Nations could be "imagined communities," but their existence is no less real because of this fact. The projection of national identity onto social relations keeps nations alive and nations exist as long as they are reflected in national identities.

There are different and conflicting scholarly predictions as to the future of national identities, and nationalism as a political principle and as a legitimation of nation-states. So far, nationalism has proved resilient and adaptable, proliferating in various forms in most parts of the world. Nations and nationalism successfully transitioned from industrialization to post-industrial society, retaining as many irrational beliefs as they had during the transition from agrarian to industrial society.

This study defines national identity as a complex belief system that includes a set of beliefs of a rational and irrational-emotive nature, concerning the origin, history, common culture, political nature, and shared language(s) of a given people. These beliefs provide real or invented connections with previous historical identities and collectivities for both legitimization and a sense of community bonding. It is the irrational-emotional components of national identity, such as self- and hetero-stereotypes, as well as myths, which provide nations with a sense of communal sentiment that not only keeps the nations together but also makes national sentiment so emotive if it is rationally, rightly or wrongly, challenged.

Studies of the irrational-emotional components of national identity often do not receive sufficient attention from scholars studying national phenomena because of interdisciplinary difficulties. Sociologists avoid studying the emotive components of national identity, focusing instead on the rational actions of human beings, while social psychologists are preoccupied with the psychological mechanisms of stereotypes and consider social identity a part of the individual identity process, i.e., they leave the social aspects of national stereotypes to the sociologists. Comparative historical analysis of the stereotypes and myths and their role in the life of nations, therefore, remains largely unexplored. While there are numerous discussions in the scholarly literature of the "mythical" nature of nations and national identity, they fail to provide a methodologically sound basis for this analysis.

The suggested definition of national identity as a complex belief system helps to overcome such difficulties in defining rational and irrational components, by borrowing from cognitive psychology. From this point of view all human knowledge, irrespective of a rational or irrational origin, is technically managed in human minds as a set of single beliefs. This is because belief precludes the possibility of acquiring any knowledge, irrespective of its origin, rational or irrational. Such an approach provides a methodological framework allowing us to grasp the complexity of both the rational and irrational components of national identity and their role in initiating social action and change. This approach also brings different disciplines such as history, sociology, social anthropology, and social psychology, into the study of nationalism. The suggested framework provides an opportunity to develop an interdisciplinary perspective using different tools of research.

The proposed analytical approach was applied to historical "groups of patriots," activists of national movements, among the "new" nations that took the shape of a Cossack revival in Ukraine since the 1990s. The present study of the individual and collective identity construct of a "group of patriots" helped to shed light on the historical process of nation-building that took place in Eastern Europe relatively late in comparison with the "old" nations of Western Europe.

So-called national revivals among "new" nations are in fact belated nationalist projects of social and economic modernization that aim to catch up with the earlier developed nation-states of the continent. "Revivalist" and modernizing movements that started in Eastern Europe at the beginning of the nineteenth and sometimes twentieth century were not completed in Ukraine as a result of the Bolshevik conquest and then Soviet nationality policy. They re-started with the collapse of the USSR and so provided a good chance to study the processes of nation-building that had taken place in other regions two centuries earlier. In other words, the study of Ukrainian Cossacks, using contemporary methods of social research within the suggested theoretical framework, provided the opportunity to research the construction of national identity in its formation and therefore to expose the genesis of nation-building typical of most national revivals in Europe. This in turn provided empirical data important to issues central to debates in the study of nations and nationalism generally and in the case of Ukrainian and Russian nationalism in particular.

As discussed in Chapter 2, the key issue of discontent among the "modernist" and "primordialist" as well as socio-spherical and bio-spherical traditions concerned the role of ethnic heritage in national genesis and the components that might link national communities to previously existing ones. The fieldwork findings on the formation of a national identity construct leads to the conclusion that ethnic identity is an optional part of national identity, the importance of which is conditioned by historical and cultural traditions and can vary over time. It is also important to stress that the most important components of ethnic identity, self-stereotypes and myths, are formed differently during the transformation to the industrial era of mass society and might have no strict correspondence to pre-modern social reality.

In other words, the case study of the Ukrainian Cossacks suggests that their "revivalist" project of the ideal Cossack Nation in Ukraine involves as much invention as it does ideas taken from a historical social reality; therefore, what contemporary Cossacks believe the Cossack Nation to have been in the past has no strict correspondence to what the Cossack community actually was, as we can reconstruct it from history.

Employed more generally and applied to other nation-building projects, this approach would not contradict either "modernists," who believe that ethnicity does not play a substantial role in modern societies, or "primordialists," who believe in the ethnic origin of nations. "Primordialists," however, need to acknowledge that ethnic aspects of historical national memories in the modern world might have little, if anything, in common with the ethnic memories [realities?] of the pre-modern age.

The fieldwork findings and the case study of Russian and Ukrainian policies of nation-state building presented in Chapter 4 also suggests that there is no pre-determined path of ethnic vs. civic nation-building models, as the concept of ethno-national identity is optional and depends on the choices available to ruling elites in the newly-established nation-states.

The empirical findings suggest that the ruling elites in Russia opted for the path of institutionalized ethno-territorial national autonomies due both to the dominant scholarly tradition and to the real consequences of Soviet institutionalized ethnicity. A synthesis of dominant socio-spherical approaches, diluted with the bio-spherical concept of ethnos, led to the revival of ethno-geopolitics in the Russian Federation, demonstrated by the creation of the new ethnic community of Russian Cossacks, recognized as a separate people or a Cossack sub-ethnos. In contrast, the Ukrainian ruling elites, despite sharing a similar theoretical discourse, did not pursue the option of ethnic nation-building, as they had to acknowledge that the Ukrainian national project would compete with the Russian Supra-state national idea, and so could not afford to antagonize minorities in Ukraine by being exclusivist in nature. All successive Ukrainian governments have consistently supported a civic nation-building project that includes all minorities. This resulted in the orientation of the Ukrainian Cossack revivalists toward a civic organization propagating the creation of the Cossack nation as an ideal all-inclusive model of the Ukrainian people.

Supporting the theoretical conclusions of Chapter 2 and 3, the empirical findings presented in Chapter 3.3 and Appendices 1 and 2 indicate that characterizing ethnic nationalism as more potentially violent than civic nationalism is misleading. War-causing nationalism is characterized not so much by the criteria of national membership as by threats to national identity perceived through national interests. Nationalism provides a sense of cohesion in all democracies, irrespective of their possessing either a civic or ethnic model of nation. Violence, however, is likely to erupt, not necessarily because some minorities feel excluded from the particular national project, but because they prefer not to include themselves in the national project, i.e., they choose to pursue their own national project or the project of an already established neighboring nation-state.

A minority might choose to opt for another national project, not necessarily because it believes it is discriminated against, although this is often the case, but because members of the minority might legitimately believe in their right to self-determination, a right that is universally enshrined and cannot be rationally denied. At the same time, the more "ethnically" mixed the territory of this particular minority, the harder it is for the majority to agree to the division or redistribution of territory and therefore the national identity of the majority becomes threatened. A threat to the identity of the majority causes the whole community to change from a security community, where violence among its members is unimaginable, into a "no war community," where war preparations are made as a precaution.

The political ideology shared by the majority's ruling elite determines in such circumstances whether or not force is to be used against members of a minority favoring a different national project. If "legitimate" force were used indiscriminately, to the degree that minority members feel their lives or the existence of their community threatened, war preparations on their side might be inevitable, unless the oppression is total. In the case of the Ukrainian Cossacks, war preparation was inevitable, as they believed that Cossacks favoring a Russian supra-state project were preparing to provoke violence in order to involve the Russian state. Russian state policies aimed at dominating the former Soviet Republics and protecting Russian minorities on the territories of what had become sovereign states only worsened the anxiety of the Ukrainian national movement since the 1990s and turned out to be well justified. Some of the Ukrainian "groups of patriots" opted for the Cossack nation model precisely because they felt threatened by the possibility of violence on behalf of the Russian minority favoring the expansionist national project of a neighboring state.

This balance between identity threats and war preparations found in the empirical research demonstrates the utility of the notion of societal security for studying the relationship between national(ist) revival and the eruption of violence. Traditional state-as-actor security theories proved unable to predict the inter-ethnic violence that intensifies with the collapse of such powerful states as the Soviet Union and Yugoslavia, precisely because these theories do not treat societies within those states as independent objects of security. As soon as the USSR and the Federal Republic of Yugoslavia liberalized to the extent that they released previously repressed national projects, demands for what appeared as the "natural" right to self-determination began turning their "security communities," where violence in unimaginable, into "no war communities," where war preparations are underway. The institutionalized ethno-national identities of some minorities were threatened to the extent that they opted for violent secession.

Both the Russian Federation and the Yugoslavia successor states still suffer from processes of violent disintegration despite the fact that both Russian and Serbian supra-state national projects were inclusive of other national minorities and presupposed supra-state identities of *Rosiian* and Yugoslavs respectively. It is the threatened identity of the targeted minorities, the perceived possibility of their not being able to survive as national communities, which made confrontation between national projects inevitable.

Although in Ukraine inter-ethnic violence did not erupt into mass clashes between the Ukrainian majority and national minorities up until 2014, the threat to societal security was continually present. It manifested itself in the competition between the two Cossack projects reflecting paramilitary forms of two mutually exclusive nation-building projects. Cossacks supporting the "Russian World," the Russian Supra-Ethnos, Russian civilization projects were confronted by their Ukrainian counterparts, who favored the Ukrainian national project. Both the Russian Supra-Ethnos-state national project and the Ukrainian civic nation-building projects are therefore inclusive of their respective minorities, but mutually exclusive to each other and therefore both led to war preparations between Russian and Ukrainian Cossacks as paramilitary formations of their respective national projects.

Introducing the concept of societal security into security analysis allows us to see, therefore, what analysis based on state-as-actor security theory tends to obscure: that on a societal level preparation for war between Russia and Ukraine has been in process since the collapse of the USSR. Both Ukrainian national identity, with respect to the "upgrading" of Russia's nation-building project, and Russian identity, with respect to the Ukrainian national "irredentist" project, were and still are mutually exclusive and therefore threatened.

Such an analysis is not pessimistic in that it does not predict that war is inevitable every time a new national project gains momentum, as such possibilities are plentiful. Rather, it provides us with a better insight into the factors that can cause national self-determination projects to produce violent conflict.

The state of a No War/No Peace community, when undeclared war is waged by Russia on Ukraine by proxy, is better understood through a societal security lens. A prosperous and successful Ukrainian nation-state with its capital in Kyiv ("the mother of Russian cities," in Russian mythology) threatens the Russian (Eurasian) identity rather than Russian state-centered security. The Crimean Cossack narrative in 2019 was not about defending "Fortress Russia" from the advancing Ukrainian Nazi junta but "liberating" Ukrainians from EU/NATO domination and "reuniting" them with Russian civilization. The fact that Ukraine had enough volunteers (Cossacks or not) to sustain five years of defensive trench warfare against all Russian "liberation" attempts shows the overwhelming societal determination to defend both the Ukrainian nation-state and Ukrainian national identity. The Ukrainian Cossacks might have failed to protect the territorial integrity of their country but they certainly preserved their national idea (the Cossack Ukraine) in opposition to the "Russian World." Should Ukraine eventually succeed in joining the EU and NATO security community (as enshrined in the Ukrainian Constitution) it will become part of a postmodern attempt to create a community of European nations without nation-state borders. A successful, EU-bound Ukraine might also liberate Russian identity from the missionary delusion that requires charging Cossacks to force neighbors into the "Russian World." In this sense, the dilemma of the "Cossack nations" in Eastern Europe is universal. The cosmopolitan ideal of a post-nation-state global world might be realized one day, but until then the era of nationalism must be survived.

Appendix 1:
The Case Study of the Black Sea Cossack Revival

Introduction

The initial fieldwork research was conducted by the author in 1995-96. Some contacts with Cossacks were maintained via occasional face-to-face meetings and social media in the following two decades. The key Cossack leaders became public personalities in the Odesa region over this period of time and their activities, interviews and beliefs became available in the Ukrainian press and social media.

1.1. Fieldwork Methods

The nature of the topic required a combination of different field-research methods to obtain the most objective reconstruction of the primary subject, i.e., the Cossacks' group identity. "Groups of patriots," the main object of the research, are not representative of a whole society, as their historical task is to introduce a new national affiliation. Therefore *quantitative* methods of research, such as surveys based on statistical representation, are not suitable. It is possible, however, to introduce multi-step methodological procedures, in which different *qualitative* research methods are used, such as participant observation, qualitative interviews, group discussions, and so on.

The main method upon which qualitative analysis rests is analytic induction. In this, the researcher finds [proposes?] a hypothesis to explain the research problem, and then gradually adjusts this hypothesis to fit the data received from the fieldwork. Ideally, field data is gathered until it does not contradict the hypothesis and fits the description of the research problem, so the explanatory model corresponds with the formulated research objective.

The first two parallel steps combine (with the purpose of triangulation) a comprehensive analysis of the written sources (Cossack program documents, proclamations, etc.) with in-depth interviewing in the groups. The analysis of the written sources serves two main goals. First, it helps to define the concepts of Cossack nationalist identity and non-Cossack identity and measure them against the main indicative variables (i.e., national self-stereotypes, myths, and memories). Second, it helps, during the initial stages of research, to formulate both a rough definition and a hypothetical explanation of the research hypothesis, in order to start the collection of data by means of group discussions as well as participant observation.

This step was also followed by work on the "technical literature": relevant media reports, theoretical or philosophical papers, etc. Technical literature is used as a secondary source of data, in order to stimulate questions and, to some extent, for supplementary validation (Strauss and Corbin 1990, 48-52). There are a sufficient number of journalist publications on the Cossack movement for this purpose. Unfortunately, much less research had been done by academics. Almost all authors refer to the Cossack revival in rather an illustrative way, though without downplaying its importance for security issues (e.g., Twining 1993; Dawisha and Parrot 1994; Tishkov 1997). There were very few inquiries devoted exclusively to the subject (Plokhiy 1993; Hryb 1999). This, again, shows that the main material for analysis must come from fieldwork in the spirit of reconstructive theory. Reconstructive theory, as Alan Bryman explains,

> allows theory to emerge from data, so it does not lose touch with its empirical referent; it provides a framework for the qualitative researcher to cope with the unstructured complexity of social reality and so render it manageable; and it allows the development of theories and categories which are meaningful to the subjects of research, an important virtue if an investigation is meant to have a practical pay-off. (Bryman 1988, 84)

After determining the necessary field settings and some data collection, "categories" are developed which illuminate and support the data. In general, the "reconstructive" principle requires that the statements selected by the analyst and pursued subsequently by subjects be drawn from those actually made by the individuals involved with the discourse, and not contrived by the analyst. Procedures for sampling these statements, which ensure as much independence as possible from the particular interests (and potential biases) of the analyst, are necessary. Complete independence is of course impossible; however, qualitative methods such as grounded theory and interviewing provide an effective system of control by means of "saturation." This means that further instances of the developed categories are gathered until the researcher is confident about the relevance and range of categories for the research setting (Bryman 1988, 83). Connections between the categories are then considered. The researcher then develops hypotheses about the links among them, and the conditions in which these connections pertain.

At this point, the implications of the emerging theoretical framework are drawn for existing theoretical schemes relevant to the substantive area. The validity of the established connections is constantly reviewed and related to a variety of conditions. In our case, this re-considering was aided by the triangulation with the analysis of written sources carried out at the primary stage. Together, these procedures led to the reconstruction of the individual and collective Cossack self-identity constructs for the focus group of Ukrainian Cossacks.

The generalized, ideal model of Cossack self-identity was compared with the identity constructs of alternative Cossack groups, to show the actual, typical stage-by-stage involvement of an individual with a paramilitary organization and gradual self-identification as a Cossack. In this way, the suggested methodology for the empirical part of the research has to make possible the realization of our initial intention: to explore the conditions for the revival of paramilitary Cossack organizations on the Ukrainian Black Sea coast and discover possible explanations for individual self-involvement. The final stage of analytical synthesis is aimed at testing both existing and developing concepts of nationalism in the context of societal security. This is discussed in the summary of the procedures and development of the fieldwork in the sections that follow.

1.2. Phases of Fieldwork and of Fieldwork Methods Application

Formulation of the research problem/objective: The Odesa region is the focus of our examination of the Cossack Revival because this is where the last historical Cossack Troops in Ukraine were found, and it was the Cossack presence here that provided justification for the revival of both Russian and Ukrainian Cossacks. The historical Black Sea Cossacks (*Chornomors'ke Kozats'ke Viys'ko*, 1788-1792) or the Danube Cossacks (*Ust'-Dunays'ke Budzshats'ke Viysko*, 1806-1807; *Novorosiys'ke Kozats'ke Viys'ko*, 1828-1868) are a point of reference for legitimizing the historical claims of the Ukrainian Cossacks to this territory (ethnic Ukrainians represented the majority of the Cossack troops) and provides similar validation for the Russian Cossacks (troops were established by the Russian Tsars and commanded by tsarist generals). Odesa is a multicultural city and the administrative center of territories conquered by the Russian Empire at the end of the eighteenth century from the Ottomans. This region was inhabited by the native Tatars, Turkish-speaking Gagauz, Ukrainians and Moldavians when colonists from Russia (*starovery-nekrasovcy*), Greece, Albania, Serbia, Bulgaria, Germany, Poland, etc., were invited by the imperial Russian administration. Being so multicultural and, to an extent, cosmopolitan, the Odesa region adopted Russian as the common language of communication between the groups, but Ukrainian and Idish were widely spoken among other languages as well. Russian became the dominant language during the Soviet period as an official language.

Considering these historical facts, the first and most basic research question which came up regarding the existence or reappearance of Cossacks in the Odesa region was: who are the Cossacks in the Odesa region? This proved to be controversial, as was evident by the first contacts with ordinary residents as well as with members of the intelligentsia in Odesa in the summer of 1995. Answers to enquiries about Cossacks in Odesa were usually either negative (they had heard nothing about Odessian Cossacks) or, especially in the case of intellectuals, mostly skeptical-ironic (that there are certainly no Cossacks in Odesa but maybe some people just pretend to be such). Ordinary inhabitants of the city, like drivers, fellow passengers, hosts in rented apartments, journalists, etc., usually spoke of Cossacks in ways designed to distance themselves from Cossacks: we "Odessians," and "they" — "Cossacks." Most of the Russian-speaking contacts appeared to have a hostile attitude to the fact that some people were calling themselves Cossacks, assuming them to be Ukrainian nationalists. Nobody knew exactly who the Cossacks were, but inhabitants of Odesa seemed not to like them.

So, the next logical step in the initial phase of research was to find people who knew something more substantial about Cossacks or even members of a Cossack organization. To our surprise, we succeeded in this rather quickly. On our first day of field research we contacted, via a museum worker, people identifying themselves as Cossacks who were even organized in a specific group. By then the most important research question was: who are the Cossacks in contemporary Odesa? This question was particularly interesting because, historically, Cossacks as a social institution had always been clearly related to military service. So, questions about the national orientations and identifications of Cossacks in the multicultural Odessian region were especially important.

Fieldwork methods: At the initial stage (1995) the research team included a pair of researchers under the supervision of, and in collaboration with, the Marc Bloch Centre for Social-anthropological Research (Dr. Birgit Müller, Berlin). The methods of field research, as well as the strategies, changed in accordance with the situations and problems we encountered. One of the most difficult problems with which we had to deal was the lack of trust on the part of some of the Cossacks and, at times, a substantial part of the Cossack leadership. Therefore, the suspicions of Cossack circles had to be overcome with new strategies, which are best described in conjunction with a description of the fieldwork process.

In this context, the first phase of fieldwork, entering the field, was different from the following stages. As we managed to gain closer contact with at least one Cossack organization, the main emphasis of our field research focused on the question: who are these Cossacks? The results will be presented in Section 1.4, where we will describe how our image of Cossacks developed, based both on how they presented themselves as well as on how others perceived them. To complete this picture, we will try to reconstruct the shift toward Cossack identity using some personal life-stories (presented in Section 1.3). What we wanted to understand was whether what we were observing should be considered a revival or a creation, and to discover individual motives for joining the Cossack ranks. Another question, raised later on, turned out to be one of the most interesting: why did this Cossack movement start?

Entering the field: Our first image of Cossacks was generated from how they were perceived by others. It happened that the first people in Odesa with whom we spoke about Cossacks were intellectuals from one of the Odessian museums. Responses to our question — what do you know about the Cossacks in Odesa? — ranged from an ironic smile to extreme amazement that such existed. In general, the common opinion held that Cossacks in Odesa are not an ordinary phenomenon and opinions on the very existence of Cossack were divided.

There were two general comments about Cossacks we heard during our first few days of research. The first was that Cossacks were involved/concerned with reviving Ukrainian culture, history and old (actually Cossack) traditions. The second was that Cossacks were engaged in certain nationalist actions, such as opposing the city administration's plans to restore certain monuments in Odesa and replacing others (for example, Cossacks campaigned against restoring the monument to Catherine the Great where the monument to the battleship *Potemkin* now stands). Both opinions coexisted without necessarily being connected with one another.

However, we managed to find a historian (Anatoliy was his name), a lecturer at the University of Odesa, who was close to a Cossack group and described the situation with the Cossack movement as a "natural" revival of local Ukrainian traditions. As a historian he saw the Cossacks as having contributed a great deal to the creation of the city during the first decades of its existence in the late eighteenth century, and pointed out different stages of Cossack history in this region.

Anatoliy reported that Odessian Cossacks, as heirs of old Cossack families, were currently concentrating on two kinds of activity. First, they were reviving old Ukrainian traditions that had been neglected during the forced dominance of Russian culture. This concerned first of all military and craft traditions. Second, Cossacks were serving in private enterprises as security guards.

We met our first Cossack at a shop in the center of town. We were "lucky," in fact, to meet not only a simple Cossack but the head (Otaman) of the Cossack organization in the Odessian region. The Otaman was a tall, well-built man around thirty-five, and was dressed in the standard uniform of a security guard: black jeans and a dark blue shirt. He left his workplace near the entrance and agreed to talk for five minutes. He behaved with dignity and with a bit of suspicion about the aim of our visit and interests. Still, he invited us to a meeting of the Cossack council. That evening, the Otaman's adjutant, Sergiy, met us near the entrance to the Military Museum of Odesa. Sergiy was 24 years old at the time of this meeting, married, working as a guard in the same shop as the Otaman, and studying history part-time at the University of Odesa. In a friendly, casual manner, we were informed about the history of Cossacks in general and about the Odessian Cossack organization. During this and other meetings and interviews with Sergiy, we gained a picture of his perception of Cossackhood.

In this initial stage of our fieldwork, we did not feel particularly welcome by the Cossack leadership (with the exception of the adjutant), and therefore our strategy was to observe everything presented to us and record, in this way, what appeared to be the most important elements of Cossack self-representation. Participant observation was used along with in-depth interviews, which were frequently recorded. Sometimes Cossacks would allow us to take photographs of their insignia and uniforms, which altogether provided us with a variety of interesting and useful data.

Developing the field research and choosing new strategies: With the intensification of our contacts, it became clear that to maintain close and regular contact with the whole Cossack organization was impossible. Apart from meetings of the Cossack Council there was not much "useful" activity going on in the Cossack Headquarters. Also, the presence of researchers at these meetings was treated by the Cossacks as a distraction, and so was not productive for the research. We, therefore, adopted the strategy of establishing more personal contacts with members of the Cossack organization, and in this way maintained contact with the organization as a whole. As the leadership of the organization changed over the years (most Ukrainian Cossack organizations elected their leadership annually), so did the degree of trust in the researcher. Staying in contact with individual Cossacks and local Cossack communities also allowed us not only to learn about the daily life of Cossacks, but secured the acceptance of our presence among Cossacks from one elected leadership to another. Regular meetings with key contacts as well as group discussions followed every visit to Odesa and nearby towns. Sometimes participant observation seemed to suffice, other times interviews were arranged. This enabled us to develop an understanding of the self-representation of Cossacks as well as to learn about how Cossacks were perceived by others. As higher levels of personal trust were established, it became possible to observe contradictions, misunderstandings and conflicts within the Cossack communities. In addition, our trips to the countryside enabled us to interview local residents who did not share the Cossack worldview and in most cases were rather hostile to it. The additional information this provided was used to correct our research hypotheses and categories.

The main focus of research was on the Cossack organization in Odesa, which was part of a Ukrainian National Cossack organization and was run mostly by Ukrainian speakers. In addition, we had meetings and interviews with representatives of other regional Cossack organizations, which were independent and run by Russian speakers. The leaders of these organizations emphasized their legal or formal loyalty to the Ukrainian state, and that they did not share what, in their opinion, was the "savage" nationalism of the Ukrainian National Cossack organization. In the late 1990s Russian-speaking Cossacks in Odesa were seen by the rest of the Cossacks as a Russian fifth column. Although Cossack organizations of Russian speakers were not the central focus of our fieldwork, they were used as contrast groups to highlight the actual social boundaries among them, as well as boundaries in self-perceptions.

Selection procedure: Interviewees, as well as groups of Cossacks for participant observation, were initially selected, to a large extent, through "snowballing." However, during the process of accumulating data in various forms, it became possible to register saturation of some forms of research material, in the form of interviews and observations. At this point, the selection of interviewees was conducted according to patterns of behavior or appearance in the community. Altogether, our key contacts were around 25 Cossack leaders, ordinary Cossacks and non-Cossack members of the Cossack community in the Odesa region. Interviews, usually unrecorded, were also conducted with around 50 other Cossacks and local residents in various towns and villages of the Odesa region. As research inevitably took us into Cossack families, it was especially useful for comparative purposes to gather the opinions of Cossack wives and sometimes their older children. In addition, interviews were conducted in Cossack headquarters in Kyiv with leaders of the All-Ukrainian Cossack organization *Ukrains'ke Kozatstvo*. Study of the Cossack archives in Kyiv also provided important information and insights into the history and principles of the organization in general. A chronology of the fieldwork is presented in Table 1 below.

TABLE 1: Fieldwork chronology, contacts, places and methods

Time of fieldwork	Place and Contacts	Fieldwork methods
July -August 1995	Cossack communities in Odesa, Ananyevo, Nerubayske, Bilhorod-Dnistrovskyi	Interviews, participant-observation, group-discussions
January – March 1997	Cossack communities in Odesa, Korsuntsi, Ananyev, Bilhorod-Dnistrovs'kyi, Kotovs'k, Velyke Dolyns'ke	Interviews, participant-observations, group-discussions
January 1998; October 2000	Cossack Leaders in Kyiv Headquarters of *Ukrains'ke Kozatstvo* and General Assembly	Archive studies, interviews, observations
November 2001	Cossack Leaders in Kyiv Headquarters of *Ukrains'ke Kozatstvo*	Interviews

It is necessary to mention that a limitation of the research methods employed: it was nearly impossible to achieve full participant observation in Cossack life, as the status of a researcher inevitably drove a wedge between the parties. Sometimes it was possible to temporarily overcome this limitation by engaging in activities useful for Cossacks, such as facilitating dialogue among antagonistic organizations, or even dissident groups within one organization. In this case the neutral status of the researcher, and the relatively high degree of mutual trust that engendered, proved useful for engaging sides in dialogue. This in itself, however, ran up against the limitation imposed by the episodic presence of researchers in Odesa. At the same time, one can say that the shortcomings of the research were conditioned also by the degree of development of Cossack organizations at that time. Cossack movements historically and at present are traditionally divided and conflicting, and in this respect there is a clear continuity between past and present.

It makes sense therefore to start the description of the fieldwork by describing individual Cossack personalities. Overall, recorded interviews were transcribed as two sets of texts, according to the two major time periods of (1) 1995, and (2) 1997-98 and 2000, creating in this way two language corpora of research. Around 40 in-depth interviews that, transcribed averaged about 35 pages each, produced altogether over 1,400 pages of text. A separate collection of images was gathered, mostly photographs and drawings from the fieldwork, and analyzed separately. The text of field-notes from participant observation and group discussions were used by researchers as a reference throughout, to enhance their self-awareness and facilitate a further triangulation of the findings.

1.3. Evolution of Personal Identities — Shift Towards Cossack Identification

Our initial findings at the early stages of research allowed us to develop some theoretical assumptions and concepts concerning why the Cossack movement started; and whether the movement represented the revival or creation of Cossackhood.

Although aware that personal biographies may be misinterpreted by others with limited access to information about the individual's life history, we believe these were nonetheless important for identifying patterns in the evolution of personal identities which might have played a role in motivating individuals to join Cossack movements. Analysis of life histories was not among our field methods; instead, we attempted to reconstruct the evolution of Cossacks' identities in ways that were fragmentary and depended largely on the Cossacks' self-representation (i.e., their *current and past self-images*, or, in other words, how Cossacks perceive themselves "as they are now" and "as they used to be").[62] In this sense, our use of in-depth interviews, participant observation and so on, were practical tools to reduce the researchers' subjectivity in collecting and analyzing data on Cossack self-representation. Obviously, the focus of attention was the transition from pre-Cossack to Cossack identities.

---

[62]   Here, one's identity is understood as "the totality of one's self-construal, in which how one construes oneself in the present expresses the continuity between how one construes oneself in the past and how one construes oneself as one aspires to be in the future" (Liebkind 1989, 72).

In the process of research we found common features in the self-images and worldviews of Cossacks in the Odesa region. We also found common stages in their biographies, such as participation in a certain type of social organization before the turn to Cossackhood. In this, we can clearly distinguish two age groups: (1) one whose members were around 20-30 years old, and (2) the other whose members were aged 40-60 years. Both age groups included persons who opposed Soviet ideology and participated in civic organizations that formed an alternative to the Soviet ones. The ideology of these organizations varied, but was always different from the communist ideology of the USSR.

The Younger Generation: At least three Cossacks among the younger cohort had followed a similar pattern. They were about 25 years old, married, and students who also worked while pursuing their studies. These characteristics do not differentiate them much from non-Cossacks of this age and similar background. What makes them different is that, despite growing up in the city of Odesa, which is mostly a Russian-speaking urban center, all three were also Ukrainian speakers. Two of them married Ukrainian-speaking women from the Western, traditionally more Ukraino-phone, part of Ukraine. All three were members of Komsomol (the Youth Communist Organization in the Soviet Union), but were not very interested in making a career there. Their interests and social activities, especially their membership in independent movements, coincided with opportunities provided by *Perestroika*, when all of them joined "alternative to communist" organizations, including a Cossack one.

The most constant, intensive, but maybe not the easiest, contact we maintained was with a Cossack, Sergiy, whose friendly talks were one of the main sources of our information about Ukrainian Cossacks in Odesa. We found it interesting to investigate how this young man, educated in the Soviet state, came to the Cossack organisation—an organization that offered an alternative to the Soviet belief system.

At first glance, Sergiy had a more or less usual background for a man of his age in Ukraine. He graduated from secondary school, worked in the harbor as a guard, got married, and entered the University of Odesa as a part-time student of history. During the time of the Soviet state he was a member of Komsomol. However, he had never been overly interested in this, partly obligatory, organization; so he was not, in fact, motivated to be an active participant. Sergiy started to look for possibilities of joining the Cossacks after he first heard about them (around 1992). As he explained it, he just felt that this was the organization he needed. His reflections and memories concerning Cossacks, when we asked about this, focused on his early childhood. He remembered his summer vacations in the countryside (he lives in a village near Odesa), and his grandfather, who liked to talk about Cossacks, usually stressing very positive connotations: e.g., "A real man should be as brave as a Cossack." At that time, the image of Cossacks was associated first of all with history, folklore (especially songs) and even cartoons, but not with personal life histories. So, such childhood memories and, later, obligatory knowledge of Ukrainian history obtained in school and maybe in literature, contributed to the construction of Sergiy's perception of Cossackhood. Still, soon after joining the Cossack organization, he was so involved in and fascinated by different kinds of Cossack activities, such as their special way of riding horses (*dzshyhitovka*), traditional Cossack fighting *(hopack),* and some rituals, that now these activities take up almost all his free time. Even his new job as a guard in a private enterprise is connected with his membership in the Cossack organization.

When we first met in 1995 Sergiy had just been promoted within the Cossack hierarchy; five years later he was decorated. What is uncharacteristic, in his case, is that Sergiy sees no contradiction between his current self-image ("me as I am now") and past self-image ("me as I used to be") on the ideological level. Here, we can suggest two main, explanatory assumptions, based on Sergiy's self-image. First, his past identification with ideologically defined groups such as the Komsomol had never reached a substantially high level of personal involvement; in other words, his identification with groups based on non-Cossack belief systems was rather superficial. So, when Soviet ideology appeared to be "bankrupt," Sergiy did not experience much change in his worldview. Second, his smooth initi-ation into Cossackhood, later with empathetic [emphatic?] identifica-tion and a high degree of self-involvement, was accomplished prob-ably thanks to his familiarity with the Ukrainian folklore tradition (especially songs) from his early childhood. As mentioned above, it is folklore that preserved the emotionally positive image of Cossacks on a popular level during the development of "real socialism" in Soviet art and culture.

The evolution of Cossack identity in this way was similarly de-scribed by another young Cossack, Sashko. However, in Sashko's case the situation was a bit different: despite his living also in one of the villages near Odesa, he did not have folklore memories about Cossacks as Sergiy did (or at least none emerged from his self-reflections). Sashko's family was quite indifferent about their ethnic, national, or ideological allegiances. Like Sergiy, Sashko was also a member of Komsomol. However, unlike Sergiy, Sashko happened to meet, while studying in a technical college, a professor from the Odesa University's circles, who introduced him to an alternative (to the communist) system of values.

Here it is important to remember the general situation in the country at that time. *Perestroika* had caused the emergence of what were sometimes very critical attitudes on the part of the intelligent-sia to the existing Communist Party-dominated system. Facts about the repression of millions of people during Stalin's time and other terrifying facts of the previously hidden Soviet reality, such as the Great Famine in 1932-33, were a kind of shock for a society which had for some generations considered itself to be among the most humanistic and advanced in the world. It is rather unsurprising that it was first of all intellectuals who started to look for alternatives to what seemed to be a "bankrupt" Communist ideology. One of the most obvious avenues for them to pursue was to look to the old roots of their society, i.e., into history and traditions.

As Sashko came from a family of mixed ethnic origin (quite typical of multicultural southern Ukraine), he became deeply inter-ested in the history of national minorities (Moldavians, Bulgarians, Hahauzy) in the Odessian region, and, of course, in the history of the

Ukrainians, with whom he identified himself. At the same time he actively participated in *Rukh* and even created a local unit in his technical school (initially a People's Movement in support of *Perestroika*, and later simply a movement for an independent Ukraine). For a period of time, as he described it, he was under constant observation by KGB agents, especially before and after some of *Rukh's* public activities. Yet he was never prosecuted for his activities, though there were some informal "complications" with the teachers in his school. Sashko's decision to join the Cossacks was a rational choice just after he returned from his army service. As he explained in one of our interviews, he came back from the army when the independence of Ukraine was proclaimed and *Rukh,* as an alternative movement to the old regime, had lost its appeal. Formally, Sashko joined the "Congress of Ukrainian Nationalists" but, in fact, his ideal self-image ("me as I would like to be") was connected with a positive identification with Cossacks. Sashko even made an attempt to found a local Cossack unit in his neighborhood. However, this turned out not to be easy.

Being a Cossack for Sashko is not only the idealistic identification with a group of people whom he likes, but also a motivation for broadening his knowledge. He continued to search archives for knowledge about the history of minorities and learned the languages of these minorities. Consequently, he entered the Department of History at the University of Odesa and later studied the Turkish language at the University of Istanbul (Turkey). In addition, he taught history in his village school and worked as a part-time correspondent for a local Bulgarian newspaper. His main hobby was an activity connected with traditional Ukrainian art, wood fretwork, and he became a member of the Ukrainian Union of Artists. He learned a special traditional technique from one of the original craftsman at the Carpathian region and tried to develop it on his own.

As we see, Sashko enjoys a multiplicity of social roles and identifications; however, his value system and positive role model is bound up with his identification with Cossackhood. Our explanatory assumption here is that, by being a Cossack, Sashko can incorporate a maximum of his interests, giving them all a common meaning and value.

The Older Generation: Another age group of Cossacks is comprised of Cossacks aged 40-60 years old. Here, similarities are less demographic: most of these Cossacks are married, sometimes with grown-up children and with various professional careers. Also, in contrast to the younger generation, their worldviews were not in conflict with the dominant Soviet ideology until well into *Perestroika*. So, for instance, one of the founders of the Cossack organization in Ananyevo — the Poet — had strong communist convictions that dissolved only in the late 1980s. Other Cossacks simply kept their distance from any state-sponsored social activities during the Soviet time. A common feature of almost all Cossacks of the older age group is that, with *Perestroika*, they managed to find a mode of expression and took a socially active position. Both the Ataman in Odesa and the Poet in Ananyevo took part in *Rukh* activities. After Ukraine achieved its independence in 1991 *Rukh* lost its significance and both the Ataman and the Poet have found their way into other organizations. As neither accepted political forms of Ukrainian radical nationalist political movements, they soon founded the Cossack organizations in their respective city and town. Many of the former *Rukh* members were among the newly-qualified Cossacks in both organizations, so in a way this transition was typical, requiring a closer look.

The Poet was one of the founders of the Cossack unit in Ananyevo. He belongs to the post-World War II generation, so his biography is much longer and richer than in the two previous cases. The Poet remembered as a child the famine of 1947 in Eastern Ukraine, the first and very laborious and exhausting decade after the war. We had in this case an additional source of information about the Cossack's biography, namely, a book of his poetry published in 1992 (the year when he actually became a Cossack). The poetry is written in Ukrainian and Russian and reflects on the Poet's life from the early 1960s until 1992.

As we can conclude from the autobiographic poetry and our long discussions, the Poet did not at first have any identification conflict with Soviet ideology, despite having a critical and independent view of the world. His poetry up to the mid 1980s is devoted predominantly to personal and moral reflections. Though the latter might be construed as having to do with his personal position in society, they also express patriotism toward the Motherland, i.e., the USSR. Still, his past self-image never lacked an ethnic/national identification as a Ukrainian. One of his poems from 1962, devoted to a charismatic Ukrainian poet from the nineteenth century, Taras Shevchenko, could be considered highly patriotic (Ukrainian) or even nationalist. However, as a member of the Communist party and a state official (he worked for a long time as a policeman and later as a lawyer), he generally identified himself with the existing system of values.

With the emergence of *Perestroika*, the Poet became more and more critical about the existing political system and his previous past identification with Soviet ideology. By 1987, he had revised his values—in one of his poems he expressed extreme disappointment with his previous "deception." And in 1990 he wrote the poem, "Repentance of a Communist." Here, it is noteworthy that his extreme disappointment with Soviet ideology did not undermine his highly patriotic attitude toward the Motherland. However, with time, and especially after 1991, his perception of the Motherland narrowed, step by step, so that ultimately it included only Ukraine, which had formerly existed for him as the Ukrainian SSR. Starting from 1991, his poetry became openly anti-Soviet and, simultaneously, his patriotism was directed exclusively toward the independent Ukraine. The final shift to a new national ideology was symbolically completed in 1992, when the Poet proclaimed in another poem that the Testament of Taras Shevchenko about a liberated Ukraine had finally come true.

Similar to many other Cossacks, the Poet was one of the founders of *Rukh* in Ananyevo. With time, the goals of the movement appeared to be unrealistic, since it was not possible to improve a system which was "fundamentally wrong," as the Poet reflected in his poem "On *Perestroika.*" The same activists and founders of *Rukh* in Ananyevo also organized a Cossack unit on *Rukh*'s basis the year after the establishment of a sovereign Ukraine. At first it comprised only three persons; its membership doubled to six the following year. When we first met in 1995 there were around 15 members of this Cossack unit. As the Cossack leaders recognized at that time, the local population of the small town had generally ignored them as deviants, or even expressed open hostility. The latter, though, did not affect the Cossacks' optimistic view of the future, and, by 1997, around 50 members attended Cossack celebrations in Ananyevo.

Among other key contacts within the older generation was the Painter—a prominent intellectual figure in Odesa and an artist. The Painter was, perhaps the most experienced political activist among our interviewees. He claimed to have been a dissident since the 1970s and to have been under surveillance by the Soviet KGB. Although he did not formally join the Cossack organization, his intellectual authority was of great importance for the Cossacks. He also had much more developed convictions about Ukrainian nationalism compared with the rest of the Ukrainian Cossacks. His nationalist outlook became especially evident when we witnessed a debate between the Painter and one of his friends who dropped by his studio. As the Painter himself confessed, he supported the Cossack movement exclusively because the Cossacks were developing Ukrainian national consciousness among the local population. The Painter believed not only in the primordial origin of the Ukrainian Cossack nation, but also in the transcendental presence of his Ukrainian roots in his rather abstract paintings (see Appendix 2: A1).

The description sketched above is sufficient to illuminate our main explanatory assumptions and concepts concerning the evolution of the Cossacks' personal identities. We can identify the following characteristics and patterns in this evolution:

1. On the one hand, a substantial part of the Cossacks were not satisfied (and/or did not succeed) with their engagement in the previously existing social organizations of Soviet society such as the CPSU, Komsomol, etc. On the other hand, one can conclude that the identity constructs of these people included a need for group belong-

ing; in other words, social identity for these people was the most prominent or salient aspect of their identity process, unlike others for whom personal identity is more important. We could observe the need for artistic creativity among the Cossacks we interviewed. With Soviet reality collapsing all around, these people started to look for alternative forms of social activity. *Rukh* and similar organizations of the early 1990s became an alternative, until their function as an anti-Communist movement was fulfilled. Joining a Cossack organization was a new way forward for many. This explanatory assumption suggests a dialectical tension between personal and group-based distinctiveness; e.g., people try to balance a positive self-identity through group belonging on the one hand, and individual distinctiveness on the other. (Similar observations in other groups were described in Lemaine et al. 1978; Lange and Westin 1985; and in the sources cited in Liebkind 1989, 36.)

2. A need for positive self-esteem, together with the previously mentioned emphasis on *social* identity within the individual identity construct, would be another explanatory assumption about the shift to Cossack identity.

National identity appeared to be one of the most persistent forms of social identity in the ruins of Soviet society. Historically, national identities in Eastern Europe had strong ethnic markers. Invisible under Soviet rule, past positive ethno-national identification as Ukrainian, Russian, etc., simply took over national identification as "Soviet." However, being Ukrainian for many Russian-speaking ex-Soviet citizens was often devoid of much content besides ethnic identification in their "internal" Soviet passports (IDs). Hence, the "groups of patriots" discovered that the historical identity of Cossacks could fill the gap in constructing a positive self-identity.

All the Ukrainian Cossacks we met represented themselves as patriots and responsible men who wanted to do something positive for their ("new") nation. They all had a strong identification with the Ukrainian state and with the representation of themselves as Ukrainians. But it is not at all obvious what that meant in mostly Russian-speaking Odesa. Ukraine has, throughout its history, almost never been an independent state. The territory of contemporary Ukraine was rarely even under unified rule; more often it was divided among the Polish-Lithuanian Commonwealth, the Russian, Ottoman and Austro-Hungarian empires. An attempt at independence after World War I lasted for just a few months in Western Ukraine (1918), and a few short years in Eastern Ukraine (1917-1919). Thus, the "glorious history" of Ukraine, extolled by contemporary "groups of patriots," was in reality rather modest. Moreover, it was almost exclusively represented, at least in folklore, by the Cossacks: "free men," refusing to be dominated, famous for their military strategy and "know-how"; powerful, smart, shrewd and moral, respectable and responsible, all at the same time. This is almost the exact opposite to the way that the Cossacks we observed in our field-research judged the situation to be in the Ukrainian state. Corruption, organized crime; and a lack of power responsibility, morality, and national consciousness appeared to them to be the most important characteristics of post-Soviet Ukrainian society. Newly-independent Ukraine would not appear to offer a basis for a positive national identity. Some patriotic Ukrainians chose to identify themselves with the tradition and culture of historical Cossacks, a people who lived hundreds of years before them. Therefore it was clear that the attempt to build a positive self-image through the creation of an ideal model of Cossacks — real and respectful Ukrainians — was an attempt to build and/or re-establish positive self-esteem.

One of the most important consequences of such an explanatory concept is the assumption that Cossack identity is a sub-form of national identity. In support of this argument we can refer to our empirical data, in which Cossacks tend to claim that all Ukrainians are Cossacks at least potentially, and to actually hold as a goal making *all nationals* into Cossacks, i.e. "ideal fellows of the Ukrainian community." However, a counter-argument might be, in this case, the openness of the Cossack organization to other ethnicities: for instance, the Odessian Cossack organization accepted some Moldavian and Russian members loyal to the Ukrainian state. Indeed, historically the Cossack organization of Zaporizhska Sich was based on openness to all Christian membership (similar to medieval military orders), where non-Ukrainians constituted, according to different estimates, around one third.

At first glance, there is no contradiction between the argument and the counter-argument if we do not take into account the fact that, for the so-called Eastern model of nation, the ethnic principle has always been essential and functions in a rather exclusive way. Ukrainian nationalism is traditionally described as consistent with this Eastern model. Modern Cossackhood, however, was an attempt to establish a new positive civic national identification, as well as an attempt to "Westernize" the Ukrainian model of nationhood by eliminating ethnic exclusiveness from national identification.

Time and logistical constraints precluded our fieldwork from analyzing many other possibly relevant aspects to the evolution of personal identities: e.g., different degrees of vulnerability of individual identities to social change, the role of symbols associated with certain types of group identities, early childhood memories from grandparents' folklore and other possible reasons for the sudden affirmation of allegiance to Cossack identities, and so on. All of these could have also contributed substantially to our analysis of Cossack identity formation in Ukrainian society. However, the data we collected has allowed us, nonetheless, to capture a general trend.

1.4. Black Sea Cossacks — Self-Image and Perception of Others

Odesa is a vibrant, multicultural city, where the Russian language provides a common means of communication. Thus, "new" Ukrainian-speaking Cossacks were perceived by many city inhabitants as the "Ukrainian nationalists." Their appearance and activities were considered to be deviant and suspicious. The average Odessian would speak with irony and skepticism about Cossacks. This is important to highlight, because it shows how difficult and "unfriendly" the environment in which Ukrainian speakers have organized themselves was. The very first public Cossack action was staged in opposition to the city administration's plans to dismantle a monument to the sailors of the battleship *Potemkin*, and to erect in its place a monument to the Russian Empress Catherine the Great. Though Catherine ruled during pre-Soviet times, she was the ruler who destroyed the Cossack Sich in 1775 and also forced Ukrainian free farmers into Russian serfdom.

Yet, the stereotype of Cossacks as warriors did not necessarily fit with Odesa's contemporary reality. Although some of the Cossacks, especially the elected leaders, behaved toward the researchers in the distant manner of power-holders, most of the Cossacks, including the leaders when they found themselves in private situations, were reasonably friendly and polite. The "unconquered" Cossack spirit was more part of their self-perception than their code of behavior. Cossacks would pose in a warrior-like manner, for example, to allow the researcher to take pictures, but would then return to a more "casual" appearance. A similar pattern of behavior occurred when the Cossack unit marched through the town, and was watched by the amazed residents. It seemed that without an audience there was no need for Cossacks to appear warrior-like.

Representation of the past: Almost all Cossacks began their story with some reference to Ukrainian history. Surprisingly, they would stress not only past military glory, but also their great civic and economic achievements. The latter did not fit the perception of Cossacks as principally fighters. Interviewees would stress that the Cossack Sich was, until the eighteenth century, a type of male, Christian Republic of free warriors, in contrast to the despotic serfdom of the Russian empire.

According to Sergiy (the Otaman's adjutant), for instance, Cossackhood has been a form of self-organization of the Ukrainian people during their entire history. He never tried to find out the exact time when this type of movement started, but he assumed that it had been in existence as long as the Ukrainian people, i.e., at least since the period of *Trypill'a* culture, around 2,000 B.C. Sergiy said that during different historical periods Cossacks had had different names and slightly different functions. For instance, during the period of Kyivan Rus', Cossacks existed in the form of a *druzshyna* (private army) serving some *kniaz'* (prince). In the twentieth century, Cossacks reappeared as, for example, anarchists (*mahnovci*) in the 1920s and as the Ukrainian Insurgent Army (UPA) during World War II.

The representation of the past, unsurprisingly, was often idealized. Cossacks would emphasize the positive aspects of their history and would even cite events that are not a matter of historical record and therefore speculative. The Poet, for instance, insisted that Cossack roots could be traced from Antiquity and even earlier, which would make Cossack Ukrainian culture the original source of culture in Ancient Greece. Some Cossacks in his town insisted that the first wheel was invented on the territory of Ukraine and probably by Cossacks, and it goes without saying that the first horse was domesticated by them, as well.

Although other Cossacks did not usually go deeper into history during our discussions, all of them seemed to agree that Cossackhood is simply a natural way of living, since time immemorial. The Poet, from Ananyevo, who was at the time also *Pysar* (a Cossack rank), starts his proclamation—"Welcome to Cossackhood"—with the following words: "Cossackhood as a social-political phenomenon as well as a way of life originated in Ancient times. The name itself—the 'Ancient world' [*Antychnyi svit* in Ukrainian] is consequently the first, original name of the Cossacks—*Anty* [great, strong]."

The Cossack fascination with history would also sometimes translate into their activities. In both Odesa and other towns we visited, cemeteries had Cossack (Maltese-like) style crosses and sometimes plaques (see Appendix 2: A2). In fact, the Cossacks in Odesa regularly gather, or plan at least, to commemorate their predecessors, and for them, the graves of unknown people who died two centuries ago represent important markers of the Cossack presence in the region, which was, in their opinion, still disputed by others. Cossack crosses in Odesa became a symbol of the Cossack foundation of the city. In a town nearby, where crosses of this shape are sometimes not present, Cossacks refer to the dominant hills in the otherwise steppe-like landscape as *Kurhany*. Some indeed could have been used from the time of the Scythians as graves for the nobility; some of them are just natural hills. For Cossacks they are symbols of old, may be even ancient Cossack graves that stand there as a reminder of Cossack glory. In fact, these hills are used also for Cossack rituals and initiations (see Appendix 2: A3).

The moral code and esoteric knowledge: During our field-trips to various towns and in meetings with Cossacks in the city of Odesa, we found that Cossacks often refer not only to historical evidence of the continuity of Cossack existence, but to traditional moral codes too. Specifically, most claimed that it is Cossacks who have always preserved the purity of moral norms among Ukrainians. In their opinion the image of a Cossack is always associated with the highest dignity. Therefore the revival of Cossackhood in contemporary Ukraine facilitates also the revival of morality in a country that suffered from an inhumane totalitarian ideology for such a long time. It is not surprising, therefore, that among the items in the invitation to Cossackhood is the claim that the "fight against alcoholism, drug use, lawbreaking by children, teenagers and adults — citizens of Ukraine" is one of the principal domains of Cossack activity (another item is the "promotion of a healthy lifestyle").

Cossack public actions are preoccupied with promoting a revival of moral values and healthy lifestyles. One example is the investigation of Odessian Cossacks into the history of an old Cossack cemetery, neglected and partly destroyed during the Soviet time. They influenced public opinion in Odesa to force the City Hall to recognize this cemetery as a historical site and even to change their plan to use the territory of the cemetery for a motorway. In this way, Cossacks not only saved an architectural relic, but also drew public attention to the moral value of preserving the historical past. Another example is the action of Ananyevo's Cossacks in helping the Youth Scout organization in a nearby village. Their intention was to promote the scout movement and to frame it simultaneously as consistent with the "Cossack way of life"; to promote patriotism, the preservation of tradition, solidarity, and mutual help. The Scout organization of "little Cossacks' (*Kozachata*) performed songs and dances enthusiastically, and showed us their costumes, which were in the Ukrainian folk style. It was also interesting that among 11- and 12-year-old scouts, girls were in the majority.

On a personal level the Cossacks we met allowed themselves "small" exceptions from exclusive [exacting?] moral principles (illustrated in numerous life-situations). Despite the Cossack rule never to raise a hand against another Cossack, quite a few of them received serious injuries or even knife wounds as a result of personal conflicts or in fights. Preserving moral codes was in fact a matter of aspiration more than actual practice.

It was also surprising to us that religious affiliation, which was so important in Cossack culture historically, was now hardly discussed by the Odessian Cossack organization. Their general attitude toward the Orthodox Christian Church had both favorable and critical aspects. A lot of Cossacks were practicing believers; some were atheists, others were adherents of pre-Christian, or New Age, religions. In fact, contemporary Cossacks could *choose* either to read a prayer while taking an oath during their Cossack initiation, or just to read a formal text of allegiance.

Still, even with such internal religious tolerance, the Cossacks in most of the local organizations preferred to accompany their public events with a service by the local Orthodox priest. This probably was a matter of deferring to public opinion in their towns. In Ananyevo, for instance, Cossacks preferred to nominate an Orthodox priest as their "spiritual father," to a large extent in order to gain a more legitimate status in a town where social attitudes were rather unfavorable towards them. Cossack moral values were generally built not on religious morality as such, but on closely following it.

In this context, it is necessary to mention the independent character of the Cossacks' world-perception, based also to a large extent on the conviction that Cossackhood always possessed some non-traditional, "esoteric," knowledge and skills. This conviction originated not only in the fictional literature they read but was also based on certain memories and oral histories. One way or another, we can make the comment from our observation, interaction and communication that Cossacks believed in the existence of such knowledge. The possibility of practicing esoteric skills was an important influence in shaping their worldview and behavior. The belief that Cossacks could avoid bullets or survive terrible pain or wounds was typically offered as evidence of such skills (see Appendix 2: A4).

Symbols, stylization, attributes: A belief in special knowledge partly explains the special attention Cossacks give to their symbols, attributes and rituals. As an illustration we could use the example of a scene with a *kolodach* (a Cossack knife of a special shape, used in close-combat fights), performed for us by Sergiy, the Otaman's adjutant.

When Sergiy brought out his *kolodach* to show us what it looked like, he performed the ritual kissing of the *kolodach* before and after showing it to us. He told us that the *kolodach* is an item of special Cossack memorabilia to be passed down from generation to generation, a kind of sacral subject [sacred object?]. "It is not supposed to be unsheathed without a special reason and should be respected as a sacral symbol dealing with death and life — two things which do not really depend on human will." What was interesting to observe was that for Sergiy it was not important at all that his *kolodach* was produced in modern times using contemporary technology and is a stylization of those real blades that Cossacks had two hundred years ago. It was also clear in the case of the Ananyevo Cossacks that they felt comfortable to be effectively the new generation adherents of an interrupted Cossack tradition. They were fully aware of the fact that they have re-invented traditions of Cossackhood and yet deeply convinced in the natural continuity between the new and old (see Appendix 2: A5).

In other words, we can observe a kind of self-reconstructive belief system recruiting followers and simultaneously self-inventing, adapting to a new reality. For instance, one of the leaders of the Ananyevo Cossacks, spontaneously and in front of the researcher, postulated the need and validity of new Cossack symbols that diverge from traditional ones. This was in a situation where a resident of Ananyevo (a young man who had served in the Soviet special forces) objected to Cossacks wearing a black military beret, which for him was a symbol of the Soviet elite troops. The Cossack's comment was sincere and pragmatic: "Yes, what you say is the truth, but we can't fight in our traditional *papaha* (a kind of tall woollen hat) in contemporary times because it is too easy to be killed by snipers, so we need a kind of up-to-date combat uniform. A beret is simply convenient and we chose it." It did not look likely that residents of Ananyevo would find themselves on the battlefield at the time, but the answer offered was consistent with the thinking of people who consciously decided to be the defenders of their country, i.e., to be Ukrainian Cossacks.

Both examples clearly illustrate that to a large extent we are dealing not so much with the preservation of symbols and rituals as such, but with the creation of new Cossack "traditions" and the development of a new Cossack mythology.

Aims, tasks, boundaries: All the components of the Cossack belief system described above (i.e., representations of the past, moral codes, symbols and rituals) defined the general orientation of the Cossacks' activity and their goal as the defenders of their homeland. However, as our observation of Cossack life indicated, there was a contradiction between the wish to act so as to serve a particular goal and the opportunity to act in such a way. With no immediate military threat to Ukrainian independence, the Cossacks had no opportunity to be the defenders of their Motherland. Moreover, their knowledge of historical fighting traditions was not really relevant to modern warfare. The Cossack organizations of the 1990s had little domestic opportunity to be war-oriented (even simple para-military training was forbidden by law in Ukraine), so the Cossacks realistically had to opt for other peaceful social activity — economic, cultural, educational, etc. — and were not really good at it, or perhaps not really motivated. This was one reason why the Cossacks were not well known in the Odessian region as successful role models.

What the Cossacks really managed to achieve on their own was mostly symbolic, such as, for instance, action against the installation of the monument for Catherine the Great, or taking care of old cemeteries around Odesa. The Ananyevo Cossacks successfully collaborated with the youth scout organization. The Bilhorod-Dnistrovskyi

Cossacks were into promotion of private Cossack enterprise, such as beekeeping. The Cossacks in the Odesa region were searching for a new meaningful social organization rather than the revival of old traditional Cossacks activities based on military fortune.

The ambiguity of the Cossack orientation (action in self-representation vs. promotion of certain patriotic values in reality) also explains some of the negative perceptions of them within the context of emerging civil society. It appears that non-Cossacks expect the Cossacks to act, as they have been known throughout history, primarily as warriors and fighters. The appearance of uniformed Cossacks at the cemetery in a small town on one occasion triggered exceptional irritation from the locals and even verbal arguments. Local inhabitants argued that the Cossacks can do better than to look after old cemeteries, like, for instance, punishing the corrupt head of a collective farm. However, the Cossacks in Ananyevo seemed not interested in "punitive" actions and emphasized instead the "revival of the Cossack spirit."

Generally, the reaction of the local population split into two main attitudes toward the Cossack organization in the Odesa region: first, that Cossacks are trying to do something very positive for Ukrainian society but that they are too weak to be effective (this predominates among people who share a patriotic worldview similar to the Cossack one); second, that the Cossacks are not Cossacks at all but simply a group of people preoccupied with the artificial idea of Cossackhood (this attitude predominates among people who have a different perception of patriotism from Cossacks). As we can see, an ambiguity in the perception of Cossack organization exists among the Cossacks themselves (in self-perception as action- or ideology-oriented) and among the public whose expectations are not fulfilled.

Despite the ambiguity of the perceptions and self-perceptions of the Cossacks, it is possible to define the boundaries of their existing self-image. The Ukrainian Cossacks considered themselves to be a moderate patriotic organization in contrast with other political right-wing organizations in Ukraine. Cossacks seemed to be more interested in history, arts and martial-art hobbies than in anything else.

The majority of the public in the region therefore have not developed a clear image of who the contemporary Cossacks were and what exactly they were doing. Generally, the public perceived the Cossacks as "revivalists" of old traditions but would treat them with suspicion, as they would any other "nationalist" organization. The third, rather peculiar Soviet stereotype, was a perception of historical Cossacks as funny, cartoon-like characters. This was partly inherited from late eighteenth- and early nineteenth-century burlesque poems (e.g., "Eneida" by Ivan Kotliarevsky) and partly from Soviet cartoons for children. It is this cartoon-like image of a Cossack, with a laid-back lifestyle, that seems to dominate the popular imagination and which is widely used in the advertisement of food products, alcohol and cigarettes (see Appendix 2: A6).

We can conclude that Ukraine was in the process of developing a new image of Cossacks, both in their self-perception and in the perception of the surrounding communities, contributing together to the creation of a new functional myth of Cossackhood.

Summary

1. Revival or Creation? That was the initial research question regarding the (re)appearance of the Ukrainian Cossacks in the Black Sea Region. A simple answer to this question would not do justice to the complexity of the contemporary appearance of the Ukrainian Cossacks, which consists of a number of different and sometimes inconsistent trends. There are several aspects which seem to prove that it is primarily a creation. Almost all of the "Cossacks" we found during our field research did not have direct (family) links with Cossacks in the past. Cossack "tradition," therefore, is not based on the direct transmission of family customs or oral histories, and tends to rely on the study of literature and history regarding the Cossack past. But more important is the fact that the actual Cossack organization has a substantially new character compared to the historical organization. The social organization of the Ukrainian Cossacks was always bound up with life in a fortified settlement — *Sich*. *Sich* as a social and political organization, comparable to a state, served as the

socio-economic basis of life for community members, providing a means of fishing/a craft-based economy, a legal framework and profitable military service. Cossack membership influenced one's whole lifestyle, as one could not just join the Cossacks, but had to *be* a Cossack. In contrast to this historical picture, the contemporary Cossack organization is only a civil organization in a complex post-industrial society where it serves a quite limited function among many other public organizations. "Sich" today does not provide a socio-economic basis for its members or include extensive duties and obligations as before. Membership in contemporary Cossack organizations is a matter of choice that is not at all obligatory.

On the other hand, several field findings pointed in the direction of a revival. First of all, there is the great attention that contemporary Cossacks pay to the historical roots and origins of the Ukrainian Cossack tradition. Even though they often have a very "subjective" view of Cossack history, which does not always correspond to the scholarly version, this view is nevertheless based on some historical study and not just on the stereotypes inherited from tradition. Searching for information and facts regarding Cossack history, the new Ukrainian Cossacks pay special attention to the civil role of Cossackhood, despite the general association of Cossacks with their past military abilities and power. Even regarding the legitimization of their present Cossack organization, they refer more to the glorious past of Cossacks and their special importance for Ukrainian history than to the social and political situation in contemporary Ukraine.

Consequently, the past and historical tradition play a special role in the specific "styling" and (re-)creation of the "new" Cossacks. The hierarchical paramilitary order of the organization, the use of traditional symbols, signs and attributes, as well as the moral codes, are some aspects which refer directly to the reconstructed past. Additionally, contemporary Cossacks are trying to revive traditional activities, crafts and even the "folk-esoteric" knowledge of the historical Ukrainian Cossacks.

Altogether, our empirical findings allow us to conclude that the (re)appearance of Cossacks is both a creation and a revival. It is a creation since direct links, especially on the individual level, are almost completely missing and the traditional form of Cossackhood as a whole cannot be recreated in the present. It is at the same time a revival since indirect links on a collective level are established via the study of history, when contemporary Cossacks make an effort to relate their "Cossackhood" to traditions of the reconstructed past. It would be fair to say that, in fact, the Cossack revival is a national modernization project typical of nationalist discourse, incorporating Phases B and C of Hroch's definition of national revivals.

2. As our fieldwork developed over the years, there was one more very interesting question that was raised again and again during the research project: why had this new Cossack movement started at precisely this moment of history? Our empirical findings suggested two inter-linked theoretical explanations: *Lack of civil society and/or lack of a positive national identity.*

To understand its significance, we have to consider the actual situation in Ukraine in the historical context. During the Soviet period, almost all civil organizations were one way or another under the control of the state, some even directly run by the state authorities. Independent civil organizations were precluded by the absence of civil society. But this was not a significant problem for most Soviet citizens, until *Perestroika* and the breakdown of totalitarian Soviet social structures. During *Perestroika*, for the first time, a kind of independent civil "movement," *Rukh*, appeared in (still Soviet) Ukraine. This movement had a very clear aim: to open, reform or even replace the existing political system in order to achieve real independence for the formally sovereign Ukrainian Soviet Socialist Republic. When in 1991 this finally became a reality, *Rukh*, as a movement for independence, started to lose its purpose and legitimization. This happened simultaneously with the disintegration of many other civil organizations from the Soviet past. By then, the lack of institutions associated with civil society was quite evident, at least for those individuals who retained their internalized need for social participation. A lot of these people had been previously engaged in movements or organizations, so they found themselves in the vacuum of a crumbling social space. Some of them started to build new civil organizations with different aims and purposes, including the Ukrainian Cossack Organization. Many of the Cossacks we met during our field research had participated in at least one of the newly created organizations, before joining, sometimes in groups, the Cossack ranks just after independence.

This, however, only explains why Ukrainians started to build civil organizations and not why some of them came up with the idea that there should be a Cossack organization. As the analysis of individual and group interviews suggested, an explanation could be found if we consider Ukrainian Cossack identity as a form or manifestation of the newly-emerging Ukrainian national identity. On the one hand, the reality of the crisis-stricken Ukrainian state did not provide many opportunities for personal positive identification with the newly-established social group (nation), for various reasons, such as a failing economy and social services, corruption among the ruling elite, diminishing international prestige, etc. On the other hand, certain people with strongly developed or dominant social identities needed this positive identification with a group for (re-) establishing positive self-esteem. When existing reality did not provide a basis for such positive identification, these people chose to create a group with an ideal image for them to identify with. Ukrainian folklore and history suggested framing this ideal image in the form of Cossackhood. Such an explanatory hypothesis, in the context of newly-emerging civil society in 1990s Ukraine, offers a satisfactory answer to the question of why this Cossack movement started at this moment in history.

The daily life in Odesa offered plenty of other signs why the Cossack image was indeed popular. At the market, one could find Russian dolls painted as Cossacks, cigarettes are called "Otaman" or "Cossack," and TV shows played with the Cossack image—a humorous character of urban folklore in Odesa. There seemed to be a place everywhere for "Cossacks," or even some need for them.

Conclusions: There are a number of empirical findings suggesting that the Cossack movement in Ukraine is an activity by "groups of patriots" in the context of the Ukrainian national revival. The first decade of nation-building in Ukraine showed that post-Soviet society badly needed a unifying ideology for all members of society, irrespective of their ethnic, cultural or linguistic background. In conditions where civil society is weak or absent, and under an increasingly authoritarian state, the "Cossack myth" became one of the potential candidates for such a unifying ideology. Such a theoretical assumption, first put forward by historians (Armstrong 1993; Plokhiy 1995; Plokhiy 2001), finds justification in the sociological research conducted for the present study. The fieldwork reveals evidence of a current Cossack mythology attempting to create a new, "better" and "happier" Cossack Nation out of the population of ex-Soviet Ukraine. The Ukrainian Cossacks aim at the revival of their traditions, not for the sake of their own narrow group interests, but for the sake of a better "Cossack Ukraine," which for them is part of the nation-building processes from time immemorial. The fieldwork findings also support the hypothesis that Cossack groups are in fact comprised of revivalist "groups of patriots" and, as was the case historically, the Cossacks must still convince the majority of the surrounding population in South and Southeastern Ukraine of the attractiveness of their national project. In other words, contemporary Ukrainian Cossacks, just like their counterparts from other nations in the nineteenth century and elsewhere, are trying to "awaken" their fellow members in an "imagined" Cossack nation and encourage them to take an active part in competing with other national projects. Both the Cossack revivalist rhetoric, and their propaganda-oriented actions, illustrate that the theoretical parallel between the contemporary Ukrainian Cossack movement and the activity of historical "groups of patriots" is justified and reasonably accurate.

It also brings important insights to the scholarly discussion between "modernists," who claim that nationalist movements are based on totally "invented traditions" leading to the creation of "imagined communities," and "primordialists," who claim that there is an important ethnic source for the creation of modern nations.

On the one hand, the contemporary Cossack movement in Ukraine is to a large extent based on invented and reinterpreted traditions. Cossack activists mostly were neither Cossacks at birth nor particularly associated with Cossackhood before the early 1990s. On the other hand, the revivalist activity of the Cossacks, its aim of nation-building and the methods used to achieve that aim, do in fact represent the Ukrainian tradition of nation-building, which was interrupted for various reasons, but is at least two centuries old, since Kotliarevsky wrote his "Eneida." The Ukrainian Cossack movement therefore is a part of the same process of nation-building that began, but was not fully completed, in previous centuries. What the Ukrainian Cossacks really want is, in fact, the introduction of *a homogeneous high culture within a single nation-state.*

Yet what would be the role of the pre-modern and maybe ethnic content of the revivalist efforts of the contemporary "groups of patriots"? The answer is in the name of the movement; for the adjective, "Cossack," reflects the concept of the common origin suggested for the new Ukrainian state and its nationals. The whole concept of a Cossack Nation suggests a whole range of positive self-stereotypes, historical memories and myths, amounting to a complex system of beliefs about what is actually the Ukrainian (Cossack) Nation. Yet, the Ukrainian Cossack concept of the origin of the "new" Ukrainian nation leaves one with no definite answer as to the "ethnic" or civic nature of the community. Historically, it allows citizens of the nation-state to interpret membership of the Cossack nation in either an ethnic (Ukrainian Cossacks) or a civic way (Cossacks of Ukraine). In reality, as the fieldwork illustrates, this dilemma is not theoretical at all, since the two competing Cossack ideologies had different high cultures (Ukrainian and Russian) in mind when promoting their political ideals. With a resurgent Russia, Ukrainian society was faced with the existential choice of accepting one of the proposed high cultures: building a Ukrainian nation-state, or accepting a supranational culture of the "Russian World." The latter was actively promoted by the Russian Cossacks in Ukraine, who took their cue from the neo-imperial Cossack tradition in Russia. The Ukrainian state authorities managed (between 1991 and 2014) to keep the two movements apart, in relatively peaceful coexistence, with their mutually exclusive identities. The ideological differences of the two distinct Cossack movements were ignored, and in this way, the societal security of Ukraine was ignored as well.

Appendix 2:
Reflections of the Societal Security Concerns in the Conflict Situation Between the Two Cossack Organizations in the Black Sea Region.

2.1. Description of the Two Cossack Movements

The Ukrainian Cossack Organization in the Odesa region is part of the All-Ukrainian organization *Ukrains'ke Kozatstvo,* which has been known under its regional, registered name of *Chornomors'ke Podunayguliaypilske Kozatstvo* (the Black Sea Cossacks from Danube to Huliaypole) since 1990. The name is long and difficult to pronounce even in Ukrainian, but not without reason. The Black Sea Cossacks chose this name to indicate "their" territory from the Ukrainian-Romanian border on the Danube to the historically significant region in south-central Ukraine of Huliaypole, on the left bank of the river Dnipro (Dniepr). In this way, the Ukrainian Black Sea Cossacks claimed their monopoly on the hundreds of square kilometres from the Danube to Crimea because, as they recognized, they would have rivals.

The Ukrainian Cossack Organization has been electing its Otamans (leaders) in Odesa annually to ensure that their Cossack tradition of democratic leadership is preserved. The first Otaman and effectively, the founder of the Cossack movement in the region was a Cossack (by origin) who preferred to call himself by his patronymic, "Petrovych." Petrovych had extensive knowledge of Cossack history in Ukraine and Russia and had a family history in the region. He remembered his grandparents' stories of the Great Famine in Ukraine during 1932-1933, when some of his family starved to death. Petrovych believed that Cossacks should do their best to ensure that no aggressors take over Ukraine again. The Russian Cossacks in Ukraine are to be watched closely as they are often disguised Russian security service officers who already control Transdniestria and look forward to exercising influence in Odesa and Crimea. The

Ukrainian Cossacks believed that an armed conflict in Sevastopol would not be impossible if the Russians use security forces, like special unit "Alfa," to stir up confrontation and provoke Russian and Ukrainian Navy personnel. Petrovych believed that the Ukrainian Cossacks (not the demoralized Ukrainian Army or police) that would ensure that provocations are dealt with swiftly, minimizing if not eliminating Russian covert influence. To ensure that their fighting capabilities are at their best, some Ukrainian Cossacks are believed to have participated in the Bosnian war, on the Croatian side. It is in the Croatian and Chechen mountains that Ukrainian and Russian Cossacks clashed for the first time, and the time could come when they clashed in Ukraine itself. Or so the Ukrainian Cossacks believed, because none would confess to being a mercenary abroad. Petrovych, however, was certain that neither Russia nor the West was really interested in attacking Ukraine openly. Such a military venture would not benefit either of them and warfare would only strengthen Ukrainians. However, Russia and the West also understand that Ukraine is attractive in its weakness, as a country that could be persuaded to take sides. Whoever includes Ukraine in its sphere of influence would gain geopolitically. It is in Ukrainian interests not to take sides, but establish a self-sufficient economy based on traditional Cossack values. These are, however, distinctly socially-oriented and do not recognize the exploitation of a Cossack by another Cossack. Cooperatives could be one choice and shared ownership of companies another. The Cossacks do not believe in political struggle and prefer to advance their cause by their own affirmative actions; however, in reality their achievements in the Odesa region are very modest.

In the early 1990s a Russian Cossack organization was formed in the region, and immediately alarmed all Ukrainian public organizations in Odesa *oblast'*, which borders the breakaway Transdniestrian Republic, in which the Russian Cossacks took sides in armed confrontation and formed their own Black Sea Cossack Organization. The first Russian Cossack organization in the Odesa region was disbanded under pressure from Ukrainian law enforcement bodies after they discovered that it included in its ranks ethnic Russian officers serving in the newly-established Ukrainian Armed Forces. However, victory for the Ukrainian Black Sea Cossacks did not last long.

A new Russian Cossack organization was founded in the town of Bilhorod-Dnistrovskyi (bordering Romania, Moldova and the unrecognized Transdniestrian Republic) in January 1995 that acquired the name of *Budzhacka Sich* (from the geographical name of the Budzhak steppe), claiming in this way a chunk of territory from the Ukrainian Black Sea Cossacks. The organization was established by an ex-musician from the Odesa symphonic orchestra, who claimed to be Kniaz Vladimir Dolgorukiy Arsakid and the only legitimate descendant of the medieval Royal House of Riurikovichi, which ruled Kyivan Rus' and Grand Duchy of Moscow until the seventeenth century. Kniaz Vladimir claimed to be a patron of all the Cossack forces aiming to reunite ex-Soviet republics under a joint monarchy blessed by the Russian Orthodox Church. He admits to being an imperialist, as his ultimate goal is to recreate a state with Russian imperial borders that existed before the 1917 Bolshevik revolution. However, being a Ukrainian citizen and resident of Odesa, Kniaz Vladimir admits that his imperial goal is not achievable in the near future, therefore he recognizes the Ukrainian independent state for the time being. Kniaz Vladimir believes that the Cossacks should become the backbone of a new state in Eastern Europe that opposes the American-Israeli domination in the world. In Europe he hopes for collaboration with Germany, which historically has close ties with Russia.

Kniaz Vladimir dismissed any possibility of collaboration with the Ukrainian Black Sea Cossacks unless they accept his suzerainty, which he admits is impossible. The Ukrainian Black Sea Cossacks considered Kniaz Vladimir to be a fake royal and the leader of a Russian fifth column in Ukraine, while Kniaz Vladimir dismissed the Ukrainian Black Sea Cossacks as a "bunch of underachievers and vulgar Ukrainian nationalists." Considering that his first Russian Cossack organization in Odesa, of which he was a member, was disbanded, Kniaz Vladimir met with the then All-Ukrainian Cossack Hetman, General Muliava, to discuss the possibility of joining with the Ukrainian Cossack Organization *Ukrains'ke Kozatstvo* directly, without linking up with the Black Sea Cossacks in Odesa. Neither side expressed any particular enthusiasm in this respect, although Kniaz Vladimir said in the interview that his organization was given some time to learn the Ukrainian language. Formally, the Cossacks of *Budzhak Sich* adopted contemporary military uniforms and the insignia of *Ukrains'ke Kozatstvo* (See Appendix 2: A7). This was despite the fact that some of them admitted participation in war hostilities in Transdniestria on the side of Russian Cossack units. Having more interest in business activity than in negotiations, Kniaz Vladimir discontinued talks with *Ukrains'ke Kozatstvo*; satisfying Kyiv with the formal acceptance of Ukrainian symbols on the uniform, yet not bothering with the Ukrainian language. In 1999 Kniaz Vladimir moved to an unspecified location in Slovakia for reasons of security and "better working conditions." The remains of his Cossack organization either later agreed to join the Ukrainian Black Sea Cossacks or the Russian Black Sea Cossacks organization established across the border in breakaway Transdniestria.

Another alternative to the Ukrainian Cossack organization was registered in 1997 in Odesa *oblast'*. It was founded by Ataman Driamov, a Don Cossack by birth, who at the time of the interview in 1997 was also a retired officer of the Soviet Armed Forces and head of the Odesa Association of Soldiers-Internationalists and Veterans.[63] This new organization also took the name "The Black Sea Cossacks," but in Russian, i.e., *Chernomorskoye Kazachestvo,* after the historical eighteenth-century Cossack formation, which was part of the Russian Imperial troops and located in what is now the Odesa *oblast'*. Ataman Driamov did not recognize the existence of the Ukrainian "Black Sea Cossacks of Danube and Huliay Pole," after he once tried unsuccessfully to contact this "unknown" organization. He was aware, though, of Kniaz Vladimir and his Cossacks and said that, with all due respect, he did not see any particular need to get in touch with them either. After all, Cossack organizations are regis-

---

[63]   "Soldiers-Internationalists" is from the Russian *–voiny-internatsionalisty* — veterans of the Soviet war in Afghanistan or other local wars in which the Soviet Union was involved in the countries of the Third World.

tered as perfectly legitimate independent public organizations with similar objectives: to "educate youth to be defenders of their Motherland." Accordingly, all claim to organize sports events and festivals and attract young people to join their ranks before going into the Armed Forces as conscripts. The understanding of the Motherland, however, differed somewhat from one organization to another. Ataman Driamov stated that as a patriot and "internationalist" he wished that the Soviet Union had not disintegrated and that "we" had a big strong state. Although he "does not mess with politics" and recognizes the independent Ukrainian state, he believes that the collapse of the Soviet Union was staged by the West and was not in the interests of the three Slavic peoples (Ukrainians, Belorussians and Russians); after all, they "lived happily together for hundreds of years before.". He believes that American Foreign Policy is outrageous and that so-called Ukrainian independence is in fact full of dependence and humiliation. Ataman Driamov was always against the Party *nomenklatura* in Soviet times, so he is not in favor of Communist restoration of the USSR. He wants to see a recreated strong state in place of the Soviet Union, but believes that it should be some sort of confederation, with much stronger ties than that of the Commonwealth of Independent States.

The new Russian Black Sea Cossack organization made an impression on the personal project of Ataman Driamov, who is a Cossack in spirit and for whom his Cossack uniform might be an expression of nostalgia for his military past (See Appendix 2: A8). He has few Cossack followers, but more importantly he leads a strong organization of Afghanistan War Veterans, which serves as a private security agency for private businesses in Odesa. Effectively, Ataman Driamov, having just started a new Cossack movement, already had the most efficient and professional "Cossack" force in the region, one with enough income to maintain themselves and their sports schools for local youth. Training young people for combat is not only good for the education of patriots ready to defend their country, but also a source of new members. With symbolic support from the Russian Cossacks in the Russian Federation and little interest in politics, Driamov's Cossack organization in the end had little choice but to formally join *Ukrains'ke Kozatstvo*, although they clearly had an antagonistic ethos. Talking about the history of Cossacks in an interview, Driamov refused to discuss the Ukrainian Cossack tradition, as he does not recognize the division of Cossacks into "Russian" and "Ukrainian." Having lived in Odesa for more than a decade, this true "internationalist" did not read or speak Ukrainian and had no interest in Ukrainian or other cultures. The only language he spoke at the time of the interview was Russian, although he believed that the Cossacks are a separate people from the Russians. He was convinced that Kyivan Rus' still exists and must be reintegrated, so there would be no divisions among the Eastern Slavs.

The Ukrainian regional organization of *Ukrains'ke Kozatstvo*, the "Black Sea Cossacks of Danube and Huliaypole," might have gained a certain satisfaction from the fact that after a decade of existence it had managed to unite under its jurisdiction the rest of the Cossack movements; however, the ideological differences remained. No Cossack organization dominated Odesa in public life either, be it in educational or commercial activity. Until hidden economic and ideological contradictions between Cossack organizations are solved, alternative and competing Cossack organizations will likely appear in the future. Therefore it makes sense to outline the main differences in the conflict of interests among existing Cossack parties. For convenience it is sufficient to divide parties in two categories:

1. "The Ukrainian Cossacks" category, representing the "older" Ukrainian organization of Black Sea Cossacks and its dissident groups, who share the objectives of the All-Ukrainian organization *Ukrains'ke Kozatstvo*, i.e., Ukrainian national(ist) revival, according to the principle "one culture, one state";

2. "The Russian Cossacks" category, which represents other Russian-speaking organizations that, despite formal recognition of Ukrainian state independence as well as the organization of "Ukrainian Cossacks," are in favor of the re-creation of a Slavic state larger than Ukraine, i.e., a Russian Supra-state or "Russian civilization."

2.2. The Origin of Conflicting Interests

The conflict originates in the idealistic conviction that each new or old organization exclusively represents "the real" Cossack movement, whereas the others are fake and pretentious. The ideological conflict between the Cossacks in Odesa had lasted for 6 or 7 years when the field research began. Since a new Russian Cossack organization was founded in January 1995, ideological conflict with the older Ukrainian organization had developed. The Ukrainian Cossacks denied the legitimacy of Russian organizations, as they claimed exclusive representation of the Cossacks in the region. They accused the Russian Cossack organizations of being a "fifth column" of a foreign state in Ukraine and claimed moreover that there was no historical evidence of such Cossack organizations in the past. The focus of their criticism was first of all on the national affiliation and orientation of the Russian Cossack organizations in which the majority of members are not Ukrainian-speaking individuals of different nationalities, but mostly ethnic Russians.

The Russian Cossack organizations claimed that nationality (ethnicity) is not substantially important, referring to the history of the Cossack phenomenon, which always absorbed representatives from various religious, ethnic and national backgrounds. Therefore Russian Cossacks considered national criteria to be "primitive and nationalist" in relation to Cossack organizations. However, they also held true to both the old Soviet political cliché that "true internationalism" is possible only on the basis of the Russian language and culture, and the old Tsarist political cliché that "real" spirituality is possible only with the Russian Orthodox Church. In other words, the Russian Cossacks were truly tolerant of all nationalities as long as they speak and pray in Russian.

Assuming that conflict is a perceived divergence of interest, then, in the Cossack situation, the divergence would concern the interpretation of interests rather than their formal content. On the formal level, both organizations call for the revival of Cossack culture and old Cossack traditions, as well as the preparation of youth for army service. Yet each organization has its own vision of how to do it. Moreover, since it is clearly impossible for both organizations to resurrect historical worldviews and lifestyles as they existed hundreds of years ago, the root of the matter concerns to what extent, and on the basis of which criteria, such reinvention should be carried out. In other words, the revival of old traditions in contemporary society implies a high degree of innovation and creativity. The character, degree and orientation of these innovations create ideological disagreement and conflict.

2.3. Self-Perception of Parties

The strong emphasis on "us" vs. "the other" by both parties in this conflict well explains both the psychological and physical segregation of the Cossacks in Odesa. With both parties often located in different towns in the Odessian region, the possibility of interaction is rather limited. This physical segregation was followed by a psychological rejection of the other after a number of failed attempts to resolve the confrontation. Despite formal unification under the umbrella of the Kyiv-based *Ukrains'ke Kozatstvo*, the perceived potential to integrate was very low and determined by conflicting aspirations.

As already mentioned, both parties possessed the idealistic belief that only one of them is "the real [true?] one." As both organizations were relatively new and did not have substantial accomplishments, their aspirations were directed rather to gaining future benefits from their position, i.e., developing their own potential rather than being involved in current confrontation. This is partly due to the parties' moderate perception of their past achievement.

This absence of interaction also led to misperception of each other's capabilities. Both sides tended to underestimate the capability of the other as "fake." Underestimating the strength of a competing paramilitary movement could also lead to escalation of conflict, but this was not the case in Odesa. An important factor here was the lack of group legitimacy in the eyes of the broader community. Both Cossack groups were in a similar situation, with neither of them having significant support among the public. To be a Cossack in

Odesa was clearly considered by the majority to be maverick behavior, no matter what language one spoke.

The lack of interaction explained the few or absent changes in perception of each other. The representatives of the national Cossack organization from Kyiv attempted to play the role of mediator.

2.4. An Attempt to Solve the Problem

The national Cossack organization had a regional structure, including the 25 administrative regions (*oblast'*) in Ukraine. On the one hand, regional organizations are included in the national organization with formally strict subordination. On the other hand, each regional Cossack organization was registered with a regional administration as an independent public organization. This caused a certain ambiguity in the vertical structure of the All-Ukrainian Cossack organization, where some regional structures refused to recognize Kyiv's authority. The first group of Ukrainian Cossacks was registered as a regional body of the national Cossack organization in Odesa *oblast'*. This was also one of the reasons why they perceived themselves as the exclusive representatives of Cossacks there.

For the Russian Cossacks, there was no practical sense in joining the Ukrainian organization. Firstly, they differed in their objectives, and secondly, the Russian Cossack leaders believed in their own superiority. Most importantly, there was no real need either to cooperate or mutually recognize the All-Ukrainian organization.

The Ukrainian Cossacks, as a "revivalist" group, were culturally oriented in Odesa, and did not have the financial means to begin any action leading to confrontation with the other party. Their access to mass media was negligible and they lacked an efficient leadership capable of effective mobilization. The Ukrainian Cossacks also had the formal recognition of, if not support from, the national Cossack organization and this provided them both legitimacy and a positive self-identity without the need to improve the status quo.

The national Cossack organization maintained a delicate balancing act, supporting the loyal regional organizations and keeping the peace as a moral higher authority. By then, however, no public organization had any say over another public organization even if one was national and the other regional. It was up to the good will of the Russian Cossacks in Odesa to join or not to join the National organization of Ukrainian Cossacks. After the experience of being disbanded for wearing Russian insignia, they opted to use national Cossack Ukrainian symbols to ensure their legitimacy and keep within Ukrainian law. In a way the status quo of formal mutual recognition was sufficient for each side at this stage. The Ukrainian Cossack groups in Odesa gained the moral satisfaction of enforcing the Ukrainian insignia. The Russian Cossacks had the opportunity to pursue their commercial interests: by tolerating the Ukrainian symbols of *Ukrains'ke Kozatstvo* as well as acceding to formal subordination, they were provided with additional legitimacy and freedom of action. The third party (the national All-Ukrainian Cossack organization) exercised its moral authority and avoided an open confrontation or conflict escalation.

2.5. The Social Context

The social context antagonistic to both Cossack parties played a stabilizing role in this conflict situation. Neither side seemed to be particularly legitimate in the eyes of Odessians. The Ukrainian Cossacks were considered grotesque because of their historical costumes and attributes. The Russian Cossack organizations were even less well-known to the public and their image was marred by the ambiguous [suspicious?] background of their leaders.

The lack of public support made the mobilization of mass support from outside of the Cossack organizations impossible, so both organizations were in an equally unfavorable situation. The minimal possibility of competitive interaction between both movements minimized the chances of conflict escalation. However, potentially, the conflict could have easily escalated under the following circumstances:

- First, if the organization of the Ukrainian Cossacks switched to competitive activity, such as offering private security services, and therefore invaded the "turf" of the other party.

Such intentions were declared but the Ukrainian Cossacks seemed to be more at ease with "revivalist" cultural agenda.

- Second, if the organization of the Russian Cossacks became so commercially successful as to undermine the image of the Ukrainian Cossacks as the "real" ["true"?] and exclusive Cossack organization. This would have been of special concern if the commercial activities of both organizations in private security business were to cross.

- Third, if there had been a local armed conflict in Odesa or nearby, similar to that in the Transdniestria region or particularly in Crimea, and if public opinion rapidly changed in favor of any organization, provoking an escalation of confrontation into open armed conflict. (This did not happen until 2014.)

- Fourth, if the state were to lose control over public law and order to the extent that the economic interests of Ukrainian oligarchs linked with the Cossack movements led to a violent confrontation escaping state control.

Summary

The Cossacks might be an increasing daily reality in Southwestern Ukraine, but the hidden ideological conflict between the two main Cossack movements remain as acute as ever. The mainstream Ukrainian Cossacks perceive their identity to be threatened as the newly-established Ukrainian nation-state struggles to maintain its independence. Being essentially revivalists, the Ukrainian Cossacks tended to have a defensive attitude with respect to Ukrainian language and culture, which were undermined during the Soviet period for the sake of Soviet "internationalism" based on Russian language and culture. For the same reason, Russian-speaking Cossacks in the region were hostile to any attempts to change the status quo of the still-dominant Russian language and mass culture in Odesa. In fact, their own identity would be threatened by the development of a single unified culture shared by the whole population of the developing Ukrainian nation-state and not based on the Russian tradition. In other words, one of the objectives and certainly the main motivation for the Russian Cossacks was to resist the creation of the new Ukrainian homogenous high culture that would be shared by the whole nation-state, if that culture and state were not Russian. The conflict of interests is obvious, but not unusual if we accept the definition of nationalism as being of the "one state, one culture" principle, where, historically, there has been more than one competing national(-ist) project at any time during the nation-building process. What is unusual in the case of the Odessian Cossack organization is that both trends of the Cossack movement ended up under the same umbrella organization, *Ukrains'ke Kozatstvo*. Under pressure from the Ukrainian authorities trying to ensure state security, the ideological conflict of interests was "frozen" until open Russian state aggression and the takeover of Crimea took place in 2014. Until then, both conflicting Cossack movements had been "united" under the umbrella of the centralized organization of *Ukrains'ke Kozatstvo*, whose new leadership was increasingly associated with the ruling elite in Kyiv by the end of the 1990s. Facing a similar choice to that of Russia in the early 1990s, the Ukrainian state authorities refused to consider Cossack communities in Ukraine to be ethnic entities that would provide the Russian-speaking Cossack community with ethnic minority status and the related constitutional guarantees. This choice could probably be partly explained by the fact that the Russian-speaking Cossacks did not aim at regional separatism. Quite the contrary, their ideology was expansionist and aimed at the creation of a supra-national entity, in which Russian language and culture would be the common currency of social communication; in other words, a Russian Supra-state/civilization.

P.S. Twenty years later, Odesa remained formally bilingual and practically a Russian speaking city, so the Odessian Cossacks have to live with this status quo. The Russian Cossacks under Ataman Driamov were accused of supporting the Russian Cossacks in Crimea, but no prosecution by the Ukrainian authorities followed (https://rgb-ua.com/zvity/14824/). Otaman Sergiy, who started as a young adjutant with the first Ukrainian Cossack organization, established his own Cossack organization, "The Black Sea Haidamaky Force," in 2005. He was a prominent figure in the 2013-14 Revolution of Dignity and volunteered to serve in the Ukrainian Armed Forces to fight against the Russian separatists in Donbas (2016-17). When asked about his dreams while on the Donbas frontline Sergiy replied: "My first dream is Odesa developing as a European city. The second is to achieve victory over the enemy. Peace without our victory is a capitulation we do not need' (https://odesa.depo.ua/ukr/odesa/na-viyni-yak-v-shkoli-treba-pravilno-sebe-postaviti-odeskiy-atovec-sergiy-gucalyuk-20181012852244).

The conflict situation between divergent Cossack ideologies is still frozen in Odesa and other government-controlled parts of Ukraine. However, as Soviet and post-Soviet Ukrainian history has illustrated, ignoring contradictory nationalisms without attempting to address their conflict potential is shortsighted. Sooner or later the interests of the conflicting Cossack movements will merge with the economic interests of relevant political elites, and this could lead to open confrontation as it happened in 2014, when dozens of people died in mass street clashes. In other words, while enforcing the state security of Ukraine, the Ukrainian authorities still struggle to address the conflict of threatened identities at the ground level, i.e., they ignore the societal security of Ukraine.

Appendix 3: Photo-Pictures

A1   Cossack motifs in art from the Painter's studio. Odesa. 1995.
       Oil. Source: author.

A2   This is the cemetery on the outskirts of Odesa near the village of Nerubayske where Cossacks installed a plaque commemorating historical graves. Source: author.

A3   The Cossack unit *'palanka'* pictured after the ritual initiation of new members on a hill thought to be an ancient grave (Ananyevo, January 1997). Source: author.

A4   One of the founders of the Cossack movement in Odesa, known as "Petrovych," is posing next to the spot in a wall used to keep Cossack memorabilia with special "force," occupied at the moment by a pistol. Source: author.

A5   Otaman of the Bilgorod-Dnistrovskiy Cossack unit (*kish*) is
         pictured thanking Cossacks for his re-election. The *pernach* in
         his hand is a Cossack symbol of power (1997). Source: author.

A6   A Cossack family in Odesa (1997). Source: author.

A7   Russian speaking Cossacks of Budzhak Sich also use Ukrain-
        ian Cossacks' chevrons, in this case on a Soviet Army uni-
        form (Bilgorod Dnistrovskyi, 1995). Source: author.

A8   The uniform of a Russian Don Cossack does not seem to be
        used too often as not even all members of Afghan War Vet-
        eran organisation were aware of the Cossack background of
        their 'Ataman' (Odesa, 1997). Source: author.

BIBLIOGRAPHY

Abrams, D. and Hogg, M. A. (eds.) *Social Identity Theory* (New York: Springer Verlag, 1991).

Ackroyd, S. and Hughes, J. (eds.) *Date Collection in Context* (London and New York: Longman, 1981).

Adorno, Theodor W., *The Authoritarian Personality* (New York, 1950).

Agenstvo Voyennykh Novostey, *Surplus of Cossack Volunteers for Russian Armed Forces*. AVN web site. Moscow, in English 0628 gmt 4 July 2000 (BBC Mon FS2 FsuEcon kg).

Allport, G., *The Nature of Prejudice* (Garden City: Anchor Books, 1954).

Anderson, B., *Imagined Communities: Reflections on the Origin and Spread of Nationalism* (London and New York: Verso, 1991).

Apanovyc, O., "L'activité historique constructive de la Cosaqueri Ukrainienne," in Cadot, Michel and Emile, Kruba (Eds.), *Les Cosaques de l'Ukraine. Role historique, represéntations littéraires et artistiques* (Paris: Presses de la Sorbonne Nouvelle, 1995), 67-74.

Arbenina, V.L., "Metodologicheskiye problemy etnosociologicheskih issledovaniy," in *Kharkivski sociolohichni chytannia* (Kharkiv: Sotsiologichna assotsiatsiya Ukraiiny, 1995), 45-50

Armstrong, J.A., *Nations before Nationalism* (Chapel Hill: The University of North Carolina Press, 1982).

Armstrong, L.A., "Ukraiinskyi Natsionalism," in *Zustrichi.*—1991.—No. 2., 111-122.

Artanovskiy, S.N., "Etnotsentrism I 'vozvrat k etnichnosti': kontseptsii I deystvitelnost," in *Etnograficheskoye obozreniye.* -1992.- No. 3, 15-23.

Artyuh, L.F. and Kosmina T.V., "Istoricheskoye soznaniye I etnicheskiye stereotypy v sovremennoy materialnoy kulture ukraincev," in *Traditsii v sovremennom obschestve: issledovaniya etnokulturnyh procesov* (Moskva: AN SSSR, I-t. etnografii im. Mikluho-Maklaya. 1990), 208-215.

Arutyunyan, Yu.V., Drobizsheva, L.M., Kondratyev, V.S., Susokolov A.A., *Etnosotsiologiya: tseli, metody I nekotoryye rezultaty issledovaniya* (Moskva: Nauka. 1984).

Aslund, A. and Olcott, M.B. *Russia after Communism* (Washington D.C.: Carnegie Endowment for International Peace, 1999).

Aves, J., "The Caucasu States: The Regional Security Complex," in: Roy Allison and Christopher Bluth (eds.), *Security Dilemmas in Russia and Eurasia* (London: The Royal Institute of International Affairs, 1998), 175-188.

Bachynskyi, A.D. and Bachynska, O.A., *Kozatstvo na pivdni Ukrainy* (1775-1869) (Odesa: 1995).

Baev, P., "Ukraine's Army under Civilian Rule," *Jane's Intelligence Review*, January 1996.

Baev, P., "Will Russia Go for a Military Victory in Chechnya?" *Occasional Brief* 74, Conflict Studies research Centre, January 2000.

Balakrishnan, G. (Ed.), *Mapping the Nation* (London: Verso, 1996).

Baldwin, D., "The Concept of Security," in *Review of International Studies*, No. 5, 1997, .5-26.

Bar-Tal, D., *Stereotyping and Prejudice: Changing Conceptions* (New York: Springer, 1989).

Bassin, M. (Ed.), *The Politics of Eurasianism: Identity, Popular Culture and Russia's Foreign Policy* (Rowman & Littlefield International, 2017).

Bauer, O., *The Question of Nationalities and Social Democracy*, trans. Joseph O'Donnell (University of Minnesota Press, 2000).

Bayev, P. and Bukkvoll, T., "Ukraine's Army under Civilian Rule," *Jane's Intelligence Review*, January 1996.

Bayev, P., "Will Russia Go for a Military Victory in Chechnya?" January 2000. Available online: https://www.globalsecurity.org/military/li brary/report/2000/ob74.htm

Benner, E., *Really Existing Nationalisms: A Post-Communist View from Marx and Engels* (Oxford: Clarendon Press, 1995).

Bezsoznatelnoye, Priroda, Funktsii, Metody Issledovaniya. (Tbilissi: AN Gruzinskaya SSR, I-t psikhologii im. D. Uznadze, Metsniereba, Vol.3, 1978, Vol. 4, 1985).

Billig, M., *Banal Nationalsim* (London: SAGE Publications, 1995).

Billig, M., *Ideology and Opinions: Studies in Rhetorical Psychology* (Newbury Park, CA: SAGE, 1991).

Bloom, W., *Personal Identity, National Identity and International Relations* (Cambridge: Cambridge University Press, 1990).

Blumer, H., "Society as Symbolic Interaction," *Sociological Review*, vol. 21/no. 6 (1962), 683-690.

Boldetska, O.A., *Etnichna samosvidomist' v ukrayino-rosiyskomu prykordonni.* Tekst. Dys. K.s.n. (Kharkiv: KhDU, 1996).

Boldetskaya, O.A., "Simvol v structure etnicheskogo samosoznaniya," in *Kharkivski Sotsiologichni Chytannia* (Kharkiv: Sotsiologichna Asotsiatsia Ukrayiny, 1995), 54-57.

Bondar, V., "Suchasna istoriografija natsiyetvorennia v Ukrajini 1990-2000s," in *Ukrainskyi istorychnyi zbirnyk*. Issue 15. 2012.

Bowring, B., "Austro-Marxism's Last Laugh?: The Struggle for Recognition of National-Cultural Autonomy for Rossians and Russians," *Europe-Asia Studies*, Vol. 54/No. 2 (2002), 229-250.

Breakwell, G., *Coping with Threatened Identities* (London and New York: Methuen, 1986).

Breuilly, J., *Nationalism and the State* (Manchester University, 1993).

Brilmayer, L., "The Moral Significance of Nationalism," *Notre Dame Law Review*, vol. 71/no. 1 (1995).

Bromley, Yu.V. *Ocherki Teorii Etnosa* (Moskva: AN SSSR, I-t. etnografii im. Mikluho-Maklaya. Nauka. 1983).

Bromley, Yu.V. and Kozlov, V.I., *Etnischeskiye protsesy v sovremennom mire* (Moskva: AN SSSR, I-t. etnografii im. Mikluho-Maklaya. Mysl'. 1987).

Bromley, Yu.V. and Podolnyi, R.G., *Chelovechestvo – eto narody* (Moskva: Mysl. 1990).

Bromley, Yu.V., *Etnosotsialnye protsesy: teoriya, istoriya, sovremennost'* (Moskva: AN SSSR, I-t. etnografii im. Mikluho-Maklaya. Nauka. 1987).

Bromley, Yu.V. and Kozlov, V.I., *Sovremennye etnicheskiye protsesy v SSSR* (Moskva: Nauka, 1975).

Bromley, Yu.V., *Sovremennye problemy etnografii: otcherki teorii etnosa I istorii.* (Moskva: AN SSSR, I-t. etnografii im. Mikluho-Maklaya. Nauka. 1981).

Brown, R., *Group Processes: Dynamics Within and Between Groups* (Oxford, UK and Cambridge, USA: Blackwell, 1988).

Brubaker, R., "Myths and Misconceptions in the Study of Nationalism," in Hall, J.A. (ed.), *The State of the Nation: Ernest Gellner and the Theory of Nationalism* (Cambridge University Press, 1998), 272-306.

Brubaker, R., *Nationalism Reframed: Nationhood and the National Question in the New Europe* (Cambridge: Cambridge University Press, 1996).

Bryman, A., *Quantity and Quality in Social Research* (London, 1988).

Budjeryn, M. and Sinovets, P. "Interpreting the Bomb: Ownership and Deterrence in Ukraine's Nuclear Discourse," in *NPIHP Working Paper #12*, December 2017.

Bukkvoll, T., *Ukraine and European Security* (London: The Royal Institute of International Affairs, 1997).

Burnell, P.J., *Economic Nationalism in the Third World* (Brighton: Wheatsheaf Books, 1986).

Buzan, B., "The Level of Analysis Problem in International Relations Reconsidered," in Booth, K. and Smith,S. (eds.), *International Relations Theory Today* (Cambridge: Polity, 1995), 198-215.

Buzan, B., *People, States and Fear: The National Security Problem in International Relations*, 2nd edn. (Hemel Hempstead: Harvester Wheatsheaf, 1983).

Buzan, B., Waever, and de Wilde, J., *Security: A New Framework for Analysis* (London: Boulder, Lynne Rienner Publishers, 1998).

Cadot, M. and Kruba, E. (eds.), *Les Cosaques de l'Ukraine. Role historique, représentations littéraires et artistiques* (Paris: Presses de la Sorbonne Nouvelle, 1995)

Carr, F. and Ifantis, K., *NATO in the New European Order* (London: Macmillan Press, 1996).

Chalasinski, J., *Antagonizm niemecko-polski w osadzie fabrycznej „Kopalnia" na Gornym Slasku* (Warszawa, 1935).

Cheh, M., "Vyity na zupynci 'samostiynist'," in *Zustrichi.*—1991.—No. 2, 2-21.

Chesnokov, Ya.V., *Etnicheskiy obraz / Etnoznakovyie funktsii kultury* (Moskva: AN SSSR, I-t. etnografii im. Mikluho-Maklaya. Nauka., 1991).

Chugrov, S.V., "Etnicheskiye stereotypy I ih vliyaniye na formirovaniye obschestvennogo mneniya," in *Mezhdunarodnaya ekonomika I mezhdunarodnye otnosheniya.*—1993—No. 1, 41-47.

Connor, W., *Ethnonationalism: The Quest for Understanding* (Princeton, NJ: Princeton University Press, 1994).

Dashdamirov, A.F., "K metodologii issledovaniya natsionalno-psikhologicheskih problem," in *Sovetskaya Etnografiya.*—1983—No. 2, 62-74.

Dashdamirov, A.F., *Natsiya I lichnost* (Baku: AN AzSSR, ELM, 1976).

Dashkevych, Ya., "Perehuk vikiv: try pogliady na mynule I suchasne Ukrainy," in *Ukraina: Nauka I kultura* (Kyiv: 1993—Issue 26-27), 44-78.

Dawisha, K. and Parrot, B., *Russia and the New States of Eurasia: The Politics of Upheaval* (Cambridge: Cambridge University Press, 1994).

Deutsch, K., *Political Community at the International Level: Problems of Definition and Measurement* (Hamden, CT: Archon Books USA, 1970).

"Deputaty Zaproponuvaly Denonsuvaty Dohovir pro Nerozpovsiudzhennia Iadernoii Zbroii [Deputies Propose Withdrawal from the Nuclear Nonproliferation Treaty]," in *Dzerkalo Tyzhnia*, 20 March 2014 (https://dt.ua/POLITICS/deputati-zaproponuvali-denonsuvati-dogovir-pro-nerozpovsyudzhennya-yadernoyi-zbroyi-140070_.html).

Dogan, M., "Sravnitelnyi analiz spada natsionalizma v Zapadnoy Yevrope: dinamika, vzgliadov pokoleniy," in *Mezhdunarodnyi zhurnal sotsialnykh nauk.* 1993—No. 3.

Donchenko, E.A., *Societalnaya psihika.* (Kyiv: Naukova Dumka, 1994).

Dontsov, D., *Nationalism.* (London and Toronto: Ukrainska Vydavnycha Spilka, 1966).

Drobizsheva, L., "Inteligentsiya I natsionalism. Opyt post-sovetskogo pros-transtva," in *Etnichnost I vlast' v polietnicheskih gosudarstvah* (Moskva: Nauka, 1994).

Drobizsheva, L.M., "Rol' inteligetsii v razvitii natsionalnogo samosoznaniya narodov SSSR v usloviyah perestroyki," in *Duhovnaya kultura I etnicheskoye samosoznaniye.* (Moskva: 1991, Issue 2).

Drobizsheva, L.M., "Izmenieniya etnokulturnyh oriyentaciy I samosoznaniya u narodov SSSR," in *Etnicheskiye protsesy v SSSR I SShA* (Moskva: Nauka, 1987).

Drobizsheva, L.M., "Natsionalnoye samosoznaniye: baza formirovaniya I sotsialno-kulturnye stimuly razvitiya," in *Sovetskaya Etnografiya* — 1985. — No. 5, 3-16.

Dubnov, V., "Tales from the Cossack Lands," in *New Times*, 14 November 1994, 18.

Dudnik, V., "To Discord or to Order," in *Moscow News*, no. 15, 9 April 1993, 11.

Dyson, S. and Parent, M., "In His Own Words: Vladimir Putin's Foreign Policy Analyzed," in *War on the Rocks*, 26 April 2017. (https://www.youtube.com/watch?v=MQ-uqmnwKF8)

Eiser, J.R., *Social Psychology* (Cambridge: Cambridge University Press, 1986).

Eley, G., "Nationalism and Social History," in *Social History*, vol. 6., no. 1 (1980), 83-107.

Etnonatsionalnyi rozvytok Ukrainy. Terminy, vyznachennia, personalii. (ed.) Rymarenko, Yu.I. and Kuras, I.F., (Kyiv: I-t derzhavy I prava AN Ukrainy. 1993).

Etnos I sotsium. (ed.) Popov, B.V., Piddubnyi V.A., Shkliar A.O. (Kyiv: Naukova Dumka, 1993).

Evera, S., "Hypotheses on Nationalism and War," in *International Security*, vol. 18/no. 4 (Spring 1994), 5-39.

Fearon, J.D., "Commitment Problems and the Spread of Ethnic Conflict," in Lake, D. and Rotchild, D. (eds.), *The International Spread of Ethnic Conflict. Fears, Diffusion, and Escalation,* (Princeton, NJ: Princeton University Press, 1998), 107-127.

Filosofskyi Slovnyk. (ed.), Shynkaruk, V.I (Kyiv: URE, 1986, 2nd edn.).

Fishman, J., *Language and Nationalism: Two Integrative Essays* (Rowley, MA: Newbury House Publishers, 1973).

Formuvannia ukrainskoyi natsii: istoriya ta inteprytatsii: Materialy kruhlogo stolu istorykiv Ukrainy (Lviv: NTSh, LDU, 1995).

Gadzshiev, K.S., *Vvedeniye v Geopolitiku* (Logos: Moskva, 1998).

Galeotti, M., "A Military Future for the Cossacks," in *Jane's Military Review*, (March 1993), 104-106.

Garfinkel, H., *Studies in Ethnomethodology* (Englewood Cliffs, NJ: Prentice Hall, 1967).

Geertz, C. (ed.), *Old Societies and New States* (New York: Free Press, 1962).

Gellner, E., *Nations and Nationalism* (Oxford: Basil Blackwell, 1983).

Gellner, E., "The Rest of History," *Prospect*, May 1996, 34-38.

Gellner, E., *Anthropology and Politics: Revolutions in the Sacred Grove* (Oxford, UK and Cambridge, USA: Basil Blackwell, 1995).

Gellner, E., *Conditions of Liberty: Civil Society and Its Rivals* (London: Hamish Hamilton, 1994).

Gellner, E., *Culture, Identity and Politics* (Cambridge: Cambridge University Press, 1987).

Gellner, E., *L`avvento del nazionalizmo, e la sua interpretazione. imiti della nazione e della classe* [The Coming of Nationalism and Its Interpretations. The Myths of Nation and Class], in Anderson, P. (ed.), *Storia d`Europea* (Einaudi: Torino, 1993).

Gellner, E., *Nationalism* (London: Phoenix, 1997).

Gellner, E., *The Psychoanalytic Movement* (London: Paladin, Granada Publishing, 1985).

Gellner, E., *Thought and Change* (London: Weidenfeld & Nicolson, 1964).

Gerth, H.H. and Wright-Mills, C. (eds.), *From Max Weber: Essays in Sociology* (London: Routledge and Keagan, 1948).

Giddens, A., *The Construction of Society: An Outline of the Theory of Structuration* (Cambridge: Polity Press, 1984).

Giddens, A., *The Third Way: The Renewal of Social Democracy* (Cambridge: Polity Press, 1998).

Giedymin, J., "Antypositivism in Contemporary Philosophy of Social Science and Humanities," in *British Journal for the Philosophy of Science*, vol. 26., no. 4 (1975), 275-301.

Glaser, B.G. and Strauss, A.L., *The Discovery of Grounded Theory* (Chicago: Aldine, 1967).

Goble, P., "Moscow Tightens Control Over Its Cossacks," in *Eurasia Daily Monitor*, vol. 16, no. 103. https://jamestown.org/program/moscow-tightens-control-over-its-cossacks/

Gorodetskaya, N., "National Unity Fails to Withstand Criticism: Controversial Draft Law Renamed," *Kommersant* website, 5 March 2017

Grani http://graniru.org/

Graumann, C.F. and Moscovici, S. (eds), *Changing Conceptions of Conspiracy* (New York: Springer Verlag, 1987).

Gray, C.H., *Post-Modern War: The New Politics of Conflict* (London: Routledge, 1997).

Greenfeld, L., *Nationalism: Five Roads to Modernity* (Cambridge, MA: Harvard University Press, 1992).

Grudzinski, P. and van Ham, P., *A Critical Approach to European Security* (London and New York: Pinter, 1999).

Guba, E.G., and Lincoln, Y.S. "Epistemological and Methodological Bases of Naturalistic Inquiry," in *Educational Communication and Technology Journal*, vol. 30., no. 4 (1982), 233-252.

Gumilev, L.N., *Etnogenez I biosfera Zemli* (Leningrad: Gidrometeoizdat. 1989, 3d Issue).

Gumilev, L.N., *Ot Rusi k Rosii. Ocherki teorii etnosa* (Moskva: Ekopros. 1989).

Gumilev, L.N., *Ritmy Yevrasii: Epohi I cyvilizatsii* (Moskva: Ekopros. 1993).

Habermas, J., "The European Nation-state — Its Achievements and Its Limits: On the Past and Future of Sovereignty and Citizenship," in *Mapping the Nation*, 1996, 281-294.

Hammerslay, M. and Atkinson, P., *Ethnography: Principles in Practice* (London and New York: Tavistock Publications, 1983).

Hammersley, M., *The Dilemma of Qualitative Method* (London and New York: Routledge, 1989).

Hammond, P. and Herman, E. (eds.), *Degraded Capability: The Media and the Kosovo Crisis* (London: Pluto Press, 2000).

Harman, H., *Language in Ethnicity: A View of Basic Ecological Relations* (Berlin; New York; Amsterdam, Mouton de Gruyter. 1986).

Hazel, J., *Dispelling the Myth of Globalization: The Case for Regionalization* (New York and London: Praeger, 1991).

Heintz, S., *Ukraine at the Crossroads*, Report for European Studies Center of the Institute for East/West Studies (Prague, 1994).

Held, D., *Democracy and the Global Order: From the Modern State to Cosmopolitan Governance* (Cambridge: Polity Press, 1995).

Hieronimi, O. (ed.), *The New Economic Nationalism* (London: Macmillan Press, 1980).

Hill, F. and Gaddy, C., *Mr. Putin: Operative in the Kremlin* (Washington, DC: Brookings Institutions Press, 2012).

Hmelko, V., "Tretiy god nezavisimosti: chto pokazali vtorye presidentskiye vybory," in *Sovremennoye obschestvo.* — 1994. — No. 4. — 16-24.

Hnatenko, P.I., *Natsionalnyi kharakter* (Dnepropetrovsk: DGU, 1992).

Hobsbawm, E.J. and Ranger, T. (eds), *The Invention of Tradition* (Cambridge: Cambridge University Press, 1983).

Hobsbawm, E.J., *Nations and Nationalism since 1780* (Cambridge: Cambridge University Press, 1990).

Hogg, M.A. and Abrams, D., *Social Identifications* (London: Routledge, 1988).

Holobutskiy, V.A., *Zaporozshskoye kazachestvo* (Kyiv: Gospolitizdat USSR, 1957).

Hroch, M., "Real and Constructed: The Nature of the Nation," in *The State of the Nation: Ernest Gellner and the Theory of Nationalism* (Cambridge: Cambridge University Press, 1998), 91-107.

Hroch, M., *Social Preconditions of National Revival in Europe* (Cambridge: Cambridge University Press, 1985).

Hrushyn, B.A., *Massovoye soznaniye: opyt opredelieniya I problemy issledovaniya* (Moskva: Politizdat, 1987).

Hryb, O., "New Ukrainian Cossacks—Revival or Building New Armed Forces," in *Ukrainian Review*, vol. 46, no. 1 (Spring 1999), 44-54.

Hryb, O., *Natsionalna ta etnichna svidomist' yak sotsiokulturnyi fenomen.* Aftoreferat kandydatskoi dysertacii (Kharkiv: University of Kharkiv, 1998).

Hrytsak, Ya., "Ukrainske natsionalne vidrodzshennia: tiaglist I perervnist tradytsii," in *Zustrichi,*—1991.- No. 2.—21-29.

Hrytsak, Ya., *Narys istorii Ukrainy: formuvannia modernoi ukrainskoi natsii 19-20 stolittia* (Kyiv: Geneza, 1996).

Hrytsak, Ya., *Strasti za natsionalizmom: stara istoriya na novyi lad* (Kyiv: Krytyka, 2011).

Huboglo, M.N., "Tipologiya etnicheskih sred pri etnosotsiologicheskom issledovanii yazykovyh protsesov (na primere Moldavskoy SSR)," in *Problemy tipologii v etnografii* (Moskva: Nauka, 1979), 11-25.

Huboglo, M.N., "Integriruyaschaya funktsiya yazyka," in *Sotsiolingvisticheskiy problemy razvivayuschihsia stran* (Moskva: Nauka, I-t yazykoznaniya AN SSSR, 1979), 223-239.

Hughes, J. and Sasse, G., *Ethnicity and Territory in the Former Soviet Union: Regions in Conflict* (London: Frank Cass, 2002).

Hunt, R., *Guide to Advanced Industrial Society* (New York, 1984), 204.

Huntington, S., *The Clash of Civilizations and the Remaking of World Order* (London and New York: Touchstone Books, 1996).

Ignatieff, M., *Blood and Belonging: Journeys into the New Nationalisms* (London: Chatto and Windus, 1993).

Ionin, L.G., *Sotsiologiya kultury* (Moskva—'Logos', 1996).

Ipolitov, K.H., *Ideologiia natsionalnoy bezopasnosti* (Metodologiia problemy). Natsionalnaiya elekronnaya biblioteka (www.nns.ru/analytdoc/idnb .html) (1997).

Janovitz, M., *The Reconstruction of Patriotism: Education of Civic Consciousness* (Chicago and London: The University of Chicago Press, 1983).

Johnson, H.G., *Economic Nationalism in Old and New States* (London: George Allen and Unwin, 1967).

Johnson, H., "A Theoretical Model of Economic Nationalism in New and Developing States," in *Political Science Quarterly*, 80 (1965), 176-80.

Johnstone, D., "NATO and the New World Order: Ideals and Self-Interest," in Hammond, P. and Herman, E. (eds.), *Degraded Capability: The Media and the Kosovo Crisis* (London: Pluto Press, 2000).

Jusdanis, G., *The Necessary Nation* (Princeton and Oxford: Princeton University Press, 2001).

Kaldor, M. (ed.), *Global Insecurity: Restructuring the Global Military Sector* (London and New York: Pinter, 2000).

Kaldor, M., *New and Old Wars: Organized Violence in a Global Era* (Cambridge: Polity Press, 1999).

Kasyanov, G., *Teorii natsii ta natsionalismu* (Kyiv: Lybid, 1999).

Keating, M., *State and Regional Nationalism: Territorial Politics and the European State* (New York: Harvester, 1988).

Kellas, J.G., *The Politics of Nationalism and Ethnicity* (London: Macmillan, 1991).

Keohane, R. (ed.), *Realism, Neo-realism, and the Study of World Politics* (New York: Columbia University Press, 1995).

Kinnear, R., *Ethnicity and Nationalism*. Course Module (Prague: the CEU Press, 1992).

Kohn, H., *The Idea of Nationalism: A Study in Its Origins and Background* (New York: Transaction Publishers, 1967).

Kohut, Z., "Rozvytok malorosiyskoyi svidomosti I ukrayinske natsionalne budivnytstvo," in *Zustrichi* — 1991. — No. 2 — C.161-174.

Kohut, Z., "The Ukrainian Elite in the 18th Century and its integration into the Russian Nobility," in Ivo Banac and Paul Bushkovitch, (eds.), *The Nobility in Russia and Eastern Europe* (New Haven: Yale Concilium on International and Area Studies, 1983), 65-98.

Kohut, Z., "Problems in Studying the Post-Khmelnytsky Ukrainian Elite (1650s to 1830s)," in I. L. Rudnytsky (ed.), *Rethinking Ukrainian History* (Edmonton: Canadian Institute of Ukrainian Studies, 1981), 103-119.

Kołakowski, L., *Modernity on Endless Trial* (Chicago and London: The University of Chicago Press, 1990).

Kon, I.S., "Natsionalny kharakter—mif ili realnost?" in *Inostrannaya literature.*—1968—No. 9—215-229.

Kon, I.S., "Nesvoyevremennye razmyshleniya na aktualnye temy," in *Etnograficheskoye obozreniye.*—1993—No. 1—3-8.

Kondratyev, V.S., "Tipologiya I vyborka v etnosociologicheskom issledovanii," in *Problemy tipologii v etnografii* (Moskva: Nauka, I-t etnografii im. Miklukho-Maklaya AN SSSR, 1979), 115-122.

Krawchenko, B., *Social Changes and National Consciousness in Twentieth Century Ukraine* (Edmonton: Canadian Institute of Ukrainian Studies, 1980).

Ktsoyeva, G.U., "Metody izucheniya etnicheskih stereotipov," in *Sotsialnaya psikhologia I obschestvennaya praktika* (Moskva: Nauka, I-t psikhologii AN SSSR, 1985), 225-231.

Kuchma, L.D., "Suverenna Ukraina—zakonomirnyi vyiyav istoriii," in *Panorama*, no. 4 (1999), 3.

Kuchma, L.D., *Pro Naygolovnishe* (Kyiv: USPP, 1999).

Kuhn, T.S., *The Structure of Scientific Revolutions* [1962], 2nd edn. (Chicago: Chicago University Press, 1970).

Kuzio, T., "Paramilitary Groups in Ukraine," in *Jane's Intelligence Review* (March 1994).

Kuzio, T., "The Ukrainian Armed forces in Crisis," in *Jane's Intelligence Review*, vol. 7, no. 7 (August 1995).

Kuzio, T., *Viyna Putina proty Ukrainy* (Putin's War against Ukraine). (Kyiv: Dukh i Litera, 2018)

Kuznecov, A.I., "O sootnoshenii poniatiy 'obschestvo' I 'etnicheskaya obschnost'," in *Sovetskaya Etnografiya.*—1989—No. 4—19-31.

Kymlicka, W., "Misunderstanding Nationalism," in Beiner, R. (ed.), *Theorizing Nationalism* (Albany, NY: State University of New York Press, 1999).

Kymlicka, W., *Multicultural Citizenship: A Liberal Theory of Minority Rights* (Oxford: Clarendon Press, 1995).

Lacan, J., "The Four Fundamental Concepts of Psychoanalysis," in *Bezsoznatelnoye, Priroda, Funktsii, Metody Issledovaniya* (Tbilissi: AN Gruzinkaya SSR, I-t psikhologii im. D. Uznadze, Metsniereba, Vol. 3, 1978).

Lau, J., "Siedlungsraum' im Osten," in *Zeit Online* (2013) http://www.zeit.de/2013/12/Alexander-Rahr

Leontyev, A.N., *Deyatelnost, Soznaniye, Lichnost.* (Moskva: Politizdat, 1982).

Lévi-Strauss, C., *Structural Anthropology* (London: Penguin Books, 1963).

Lévi-Strauss, C., *The View from Afar* (London: Penguin Books, 1983).

Levkovich, V.P. and Pankova, N.G., "Sotsialno-psikhologicheskiy podhod k strukture etnicheskogo soznaniya," in *Psikhologicheskiy zhurnal* — 1983 — No. 4 — 64-74.

Levkovich, V.P. and Pankova, V.P. "Sotsialno-psikhologicheskiye aspekty problemy etnicheskogo soznaniya," in *Sotsialnaya psikhologiya I obschestvennaya praktika.* (Moskva: Nauka, I-t Psikhologii AN SSSR, 1985), 138-153.

Lichtenberg, J., "How Liberal Can Nationalism Be?" in Beiner, R. (ed.), *Theorizing Nationalism* (Albany, NY: State University of New York Press, 1999).

Liebkind, L. (ed.), *New Identities in Europe: Immigrant Ancestry and the Ethnic Identity of Youth* (London: Gower Publishers, 1989).

Lihachev, D.S., *Natsionalnoye samosoznaniye Drevney Rusi* (Moskva — Leningrad: AN SSSR, 1945).

Lippmann, W., *Public Opinion* (New Brunswick, NJ and London: Transaction Publishers, 1998).

Llobera, J.R., *The God of Modernity: The Development of Nationalism in Western Europe* (Oxford and Providence, RI: Berg, 1994).

Losev, A.F., *Filosofiya. Mifologiya. Kultura* (Moskva: Politizdat, 1991).

Lysiak-Rudnytsky, I., "Politychna dumka ukrainskih radianskyh dysydentiv," in *Zustrichi* — 1991 — No. 2 — 187-197.

MacMillan, J. and Linclater, A. (eds.), *Boundaries in Question: New Directions in International Relations* (London and New York: Pinter Publishers, 1995).

Mala entsyklopediya etno-derzhavoznavstva (Kyiv: Dovira, I-t derzhavy I prava im.Koretskogo, NAN Ukrainy, 1996).

Malewska-Peyre, H., "Identity Crisis in Migrant's Children and their Consequences," in *Polish Sociological Review* 2 (106), 1994.

Manzhola, V.A. and Galaka, S.P., "A Nuclear Weapons-Free Zone in Central and Eastern Europe: A Ukrainian Perspective," in Albright, D.E. and Appatov, S.J. (eds.), *Ukraine and European Security* (London: Macmillan Press, 1999).

Martin, M., *Why We Fight* (London: Hurst & Company, 2018).

Marx, K. and Engels, F., *Tvory*: Pereklad z 2-go rosiyskogo vydannia. (Kyiv: derzhpolitvydav URSR, 1958). 30 Volumes.

Marx, K. and Engels, F., *Collected Works*, 35 vols. (London: Lawrence and Wishart/ Moscow: Progress Publishers, 1975-).

Maxwell, A. (ed.), *The Comparative Aproach to National Movements: Miroslav Hroch and Nationalism Studies* (London and New York: Routledge, 2012).

McSweeney, B., *Security, Identity and Interests: A Sociology of International Relations* (Cambridge: Cambridge University Press, 1999).

Mearsheimer, J., "The Case for a Ukrainian Nuclear Deterrent," in *Foreign Affairs* 72, no. 3 (1993), 50–51.

Melnykov, A.N., "Natsionalnoye soznaniye: metodologicheskiye problemy genesisa," in *Soznaniye I lichnost* (Barnaul: Altayskiy universitet, 1986), 82-91.

"Mify massovoyi svidomosti v suchasniy Ukrayini," in *Universum* — 1997 — Nos. 3-4 — 11-18.

Mihayilov, F.T., *Obschestvennoye znaniye I samosoznaniye individa* (Moskva: Nauka, I-t Filosofii, AN SSSR, 1990).

Mishan, E., *Economic Myth and the Mythology of Economics* (Worcester: Wheatsheaf Books, 1986).

Mistry, P.S., "The New Regionalism: Impediment or Spur," in Bjorne Hettne (ed.) *Globalism and the New Regionalism* (London: Macmillan Press, 1999), 116-155.

Mitterrand, F., "Programme of the French Presidency," in *Debates of the European Parliament*, 17 January 1995, No. 4-456, Luxembourg, Office 4, Official Publications of the European Community, 45-52.

Molchanov, M., "Ukraine Between Russia and NATO: Politics and Security," in *Ukrainian Review*, vol. 45, no. 3 (Autumn 1998).

Motyl, A., *Sovietology, Rationality, Nationality* (New York: Columbia University Press, 1990).

Muliava, V., "Ukrains'ke Kozatstvo," in *Ukrains'ke Slovo*, 5 September 1996, 3-4.

Nationalism (1966) *A Report by a Study Group of Members of the Royal Institute of International Affairs. Reprints of Economic Classics*. New York.

Natsionalni vidnosyny na Ukrayini: Zapytannia I vidpovidi. (ed.), Bezpalyi, V.A., and Brytchenko, S.P. (Kyiv: Ukraina, 1991).

Natsionalnyie interesy I problemy bezopasnosti Rossii. (1997) Natsionalnaya elekronnaya biblioteka. Internet version: http://www.nns.ru/analyt doc/dok97_4.html

Nel'ga, O.V., "Samosvidomist' osobystosti ta yiyi etnichnyi zmist," in *Filosofska i sotsiologichna dumka* — 1993 — Nos. 7-8 — 111-129.

Nikitina, S.E., "Yazykovoye znaniye I samosoznaniye lichnosti v narodnoy kulture," in *Yazyk I lichnost'* (Moskva: Nauka, I-t ruskogo yazyka, AN SSSR, 1989), 34-40.

Okamura, J.Y. (1965), "Situational Ethnicity," *Ethnic and Racial Studies*, 4: 4.

Olcott, M.B. and Tishkov, V., "From Ethnos to Demos: The Quest for Russia's Identity," in Anders Aslund and Martha Brill Olcott (eds.), *Russia After Communism* (Washington D.C.: Carnegie Endowment for International Peace, 1999), 61-91.

Orlov, O., "The Support, but of What Russia?' in *Moscow News*, no. 15, April 9, 1993.

Pantelyuk, M., "Kozak tse ukrayinets, a ukrayinets tse kozak," in *Misto*, 18 Jan 2017, http://misto.vn.ua/news/item/id/10028.

Pavliv, S., "Rosiiski otamany demonstruyut' loyalnist' do "kozac'koho" prezydenta," in *Shliah Peremohy*, 4 June 1994.

Pelenski, J., "The Cossack Insurections in Jewish-Ukrainian Relations," in Potichnyj, P.J. and Aster, H. (eds.), *Ukrainian-Jewish Relations in Historical Perspective* (Edmonton: Canadian Institute of Ukrainian Studies, 1988).

Perepelytsia, H., "Problems of Ukraine's Military Integration into European Security Structures," in Albright, D.E. and Appatov, S.J. (eds.), *Ukraine and European Security* (London: Macmillan Press, 1999).

Pifer, S., "What the Death of the INF Treaty Means for Kyiv," 14 Feb 2019 https://www.atlanticcouncil.org/blogs/ukrainealert/what-the-death -of-the-inf-treaty-means-for-kyiv/

Plamenatz, J., "Two types of Nationalism," in Kamenka, E. (ed.), *Nationalism: The Nature and Evolution of an Idea* (Canberra: Australian National University Press, 1973).

Plavich, V.P., *Ubezhdennost': filosofsko-sotsiologicheskiy anali.* (Kyiv: Lybid', 1991).

Plokhy, S.M., "Historical Debates and Territorial Claims: Cossack Mythology in the Russian-Ukrainian Border Dispute," in *Russian Littoral Working Paper*, No. 10, UMCP/SAIS (May 1993).

Plokhy, S.M., "The History of a 'Non-historical' Nation: Notes on the Nature and the Current Problems of Ukrainian Historiography," in *Slavic Review*, vol. 54, no. 3 (Fall 1995).

Pomerantsev, P., "Russia and the Menace of Unreality," in *The Atlantic*, 9 September 2014.

Popova, I.M., "Ruskoyazychiye na Odeschinie—kak k niemu otnositsia?" in *Sovremennoye obschestvo*—1994—No. 1—58-66.

Popova, M.V., "Metody izucheniya protsesov identifikatsii," in *Voprosy psikhologii*—1988—No. 1—C.143-168.

Popovych, M. (ed.), *Natsionalna ideya I sotsialni transformatsii v Ukrajini.* (Kyiv: Ukrainsky Tsentr Dukhovnoi Kultury, 2015)

Posen, B.R., "The Security Dilemma and Ethnic Conflict," in *Survival*, vol. 35, no. 1, 1993, 27-47.

Prager, J. (1993), 'Politics and Illusion: A Psychoanalytic Exploration of Nationalism," 303-322, in *Psychoanalytic Sociology*, Vol. 2. An Elgar Reference Collection. Hunts.

Prizel, I., *National Identity and Foreign Policy: Nationalism and Leadership in Poland, Russia and Ukraine* (Cambridge: Cambridge University Press, 1998).

Psikhologiya. Slovar'. (ed.), Karpenko, A.D., (Moskva: Politizdat, 2nd edn., 1990).

Ramet, S.P., "Eastern Europe and the Natural Law Tradition," in *The Donald W. Treadgold Papers*, No. 27, August 2000. The Henry M. Jackson School of International Studies. The University of Washington.

Ratner, P., "The Dangerous Philosopher Behind Putin's Strategy to Grow Russian Power at America's Expense," in *Big Think*, 18 December 2016.

Reiter, D. and Stam, A., *Democracies at War* (Princeton and Oxford: Princeton University Press, 2002).

Reshetar, J.S., *The Ukrainian Revolution, 1917-20: A Study in Nationalism* (Princeton, NJ: Princeton University Press, 1952).

Richmond, A.H., "Ethnic Nationalism and Postindustrialism," in *Ethnic and Racial Studies*, vol. 7, no. 1 (1984), 5-16.

Riggs, W.F., *Politics and Ethnicity: A Conceptual Mapping Exercise* (Honolulu: University of Hawaii Press, 1990).

Roche, M., *Rethinking Citizenship* (Cambridge: Polity Press, 1992).

Rokeach, M., *Beliefs, Attitudes and Values* (San Francisco: Jossey-Bass Publishers, 1968).

Rokeach, M., *The Nature of Human Values* (New York: Free Press, 1969).

Rubchak, M., "Vid peryferii do tsentru: rozvytok ukrayinskoyi natsionalnoyi svidomosti u Lvovi XVI stolittia," in *Filosofska I sotsiologichna dumka* — 1993 — No. 1 — 96-112.

Russian government official website publication: http://government.ru/docs/17248 in Russian version or http://goverment.ru/eng/docs/17248/ in English

Ryabchuk, M., *Dylemy ukrainskoho Fausta: hromadianskie suspilstvo I rozbudova derzhavy* (Kyiv: Krytyka, 2000).

Rybachuk, M., *Vid Malorosii do Ukrainy: paradoksy zapiznilogo natsiyetvorennia.* (Kyiv. Krytyka, 2000).

Rymarenko, U. (ed.), *Short Encyclopedia of Ethno-State-Science.* NAN Ukrainy. — Kyiv. Dovira — Geneza. (1996).

Samus, M., "Termination of INF Treaty: Implications for Ukraine and Beyond," in *UNIAN*, 6 Aug 2019 https://www.unian.info/world/1064 2002-termination-of-inf-treaty-implications-for-ukraine-and-beyond. html

Sapozshnikov, I.V., Sliusar, Yu.A. and Shuvalov, R.O., "Typologiya kamyanyh namogylnyh hrestiv Pivdenno-Zakhidnoyi Ukrayiny," in *Starozhytnosti Prychornomorya* (Odesa: 1995, 2nd edn.), 16-47.

Schlesinger, P., "On National Identity: Some Conceptions and Misconceptions Criticized," in *Social Science Information* (London: Sage, 1987), vol. 26, no. 2, 219-264.

Seton-Watson, G., *Nations and States: An Enquiry into the Origins of Nations and the Politics of Nationalism* (London: Westview Press, 1977).

Sherr, J. and Main, S., *Russian and Ukrainian Perceptions of Events in Yugoslavia* (The Conflict Studies Research Centre, May 1999).

Shkliar, L.E., *Etnos. Kultura. Lichnost'* (Filosofsko-metodologicheskiye aspekty issledovaniya) (Kyiv: Naukova Dumka, 1992).

Shmilo, A., "The National Guard of Ukraine and Its Enemies," in *Ukraine*, September 1993.

Shotter, J., *The Cultural Politics of Everyday Life* (Milton Keynes: Open University Press, 1993).

Shporliuk, R., "Doslidzhuyuczy dramu istorii? Abo natsionalni shliahy do suchasnosti," in *Zustrichi* — 1991 — No. 2 — 79-86.

Shporliuk, R., "Ukrayinske natsionalne vidrodzhennia v konteksti yevropeyskoyi istorii kintsia XVIII — pochatku XIX stolittia," *Ukrayina. Nauka I Kultura* (Kyiv: AN Ukrayiny, Znannya, Issue 25, 1991), 159-167.

Silverman, D., *Qualitative Analysis for Social Scientists* (Hants: Gower, 1985).

Skalkovskyi, A.O., *Istoriya Novoyi sichi, abo ostannyiogo Kosha Zaporizkogo.* (Dnipropetrovsk: Sich, 1994).

Smirnov, S., "Kazachestvo I Geopolitika," in *Vozrozshdeniye Kazachestva: Nadezshdy i Opaseniya* (Mokva: Carnegie Endowment for International Peace, 1998).

Smith, A., "Ethnic Myths and Ethnic Revivals," in *European Journal of Sociology* vol. 25 (1984a), 283-305.

Smith, A., "National Identity and Myths of Ethnic Descent," *Research in Social Movements, Conflict and Change*, vol. 7 (1984b), 95-130.

Smith, A., "National Identity and the Idea of European Unity," in *International Affairs* 68: I (1991b), 55-76.

Smith, A., "Social and Cultural Conditions of Ethnic Survival," in *Journal of Ethnic Studies.* Ljubljana. Treaties and Documents (21 December 1988a), 15-26.

Smith, A., "The Myth of the 'Modern Nation' and the Myths of Nations," in *Ethnic and Racial Studies*, 11 (1), 1988b: 1-26.

Smith, A., "Towards a Global Culture?" in *Theory, Culture and Society*, Vol.7, Nos. 2-3 (1990).

Smith, A., *National Identity* (London: Penguin Books, 1991a).

Smith, A., *Nations and Nationalism in a Global Era* (Polity Press, 1995).

Smith, A., *The Ethnic Origins of Nations* (Oxford: Basil Blackwell, 1986).

Smith, A., *Theories of Nationalism* (New York: Holmes & Meir Publishers, 1983).

Smoliy, V.A. and Gurzhiy, O.I., *Yak I koly pochala formuvatysia ukrayinska natsiya* (Kyiv: Naukova Dumka, 1991).

Sniezshkova, I.A., "K probleme izucheniya etnicheskogo soznaniya u detey I yunoshestva (po materialam Kyivskoy I Zakarpatskoy oblastey)," in *Sovetskaya etnografiya* — 1982 — No. 1. — 80-88.

Snyder, J., *From Voting to Violence: Democratization and Nationalist Conflict* (New York: W. W. Norton & Company, 2000).

Snyder, T., "How a Russian Fascist Is Meddling in America's Election," in *The New York Times*, 20 September 2016.

Sociollogicheskiye teorii natsionalisma: nauchno-analiticheskiy obzor (Moskva: AN SSSR, I-t nauchnoy informatsii po obschestvennym naukam, 1991).

Stalin, J.V., "Report on the National Question," in *Sochineniia*, vol. 4 (Moscow: Gospolitizdat, 1947).

Strauss, A. and Corbin, J., *Basics of Qualitative Research: Grounded Theory Procedures and Techniques* (Newbury Park — London — New Delhi: SAGE Publications, 1990).

Strauss, A., *Qualitative Analysis for Social Scientists* (Cambridge — New York — Sydney: Cambridge University Press, 1987).

Svobodivtsi Zareestruvaly Zakonoproekt Shchodo Vidnovlennia Iadernoho Statusu Ukraiiny [Svoboda Deputies Registered a Bill on the Renewal of the Nuclear Status of Ukraine]," UNIAN, 23 July 2014 (https://www.unian.ua/politics/943019-svobodivtsi-zareestruvali-zakonopro ekt-schodo-vidnovlennya-yadernogostatusu-ukrajini.html).

Svod etnograficheskih poniatiy I terminov. Etnografiya I smezhnyie discipliny (Moskva: Nauka, AN SSSR, I-t etnografii im. Mikluho-Maklaya, 1988).

Sysyn, F., "The Problem of Nobilities in the Ukrainian Past: The Polish Period, 1569-1648," in Rudnytsky, I.L. (ed.), *Rethinking Ukrainian History* (Edmonton: Canadian Institute of Ukrainian Studies, 1981), 29-102.

Tajfel, H., *Human Groups and Social Categories* (Cambridge: Cambridge University Press, 1981).

Tajfel, H., "Aspects of Ethnic and National Loyalty," in *Social Science Information* 13 (1970), 65-93.

Tajfel, H., "The Formation of National Attitudes: A Social Psychological Perspective', in M. Sherif (ed), *Interdisciplinary Relationships in the Social Sciences* (Chicago: Aldline, 1969).

Tajfel, H., *Social Identity and Intergroup Relations* (Cambridge University Press, 1982).

Talmon, J., *Myth of the Nation and Vision of Revolution* (New Brunswick, NJ and London: Transaction Publishers, 1981).

Tamir, Y., *Liberal Nationalism* (Princeton, NJ: Princeton University Press, 1993).

Taylor, D.M. and Moghaddam, F.M., *Theories of Intergroup Relations* (Westport, CT: Praeger, 1994).

The Cossacks (1992) *Eastern Europe Newsletter*, 6, no.15 [20 July 1992], 5-7.

"The Cossacks: A Super-ethnos in Russia's Ribs," in *The Economist*, 21 December 1996,

"The Most Dangerous Philosopher in the World," in Big Think, 18 December 2016. https://bigthink.com/paul-ratner/the-dangerous-philosopher-behind-putins-strategy-to-grow-russian-power-at-americas-expense

"The Strugle for Ukraine" (Timothy Ash, Janet Gunn, John Lough, Orysia Lutsevych, James Nixey, James Sherr and Kataryna Wolczuk), *Russia and Eurasia Programme* | October 2017 | Chatham House

Thomas, W.I., *The Unadjusted Girl* (Boston, 1931).

Tishkov, V., "Zabyt' o natsii. Post-natsionalisticheskoye ponimaniye natsionalisma," in *Etnograficheskoye Obozreniye*, No. 5, 3-26 (1998).

Tishkov, V., *Ethnicity, Nationalism and Conflict in and after the Soviet Union:The Mind Aflame* (PRIO. UNRISD, 1997).

Tishkov, V.A., "Natsionalnosti I natsionalism v post-sovetskom prostranstve," in *Etnichnost I vlast' v polietnicheskih gosudarstvah* (Moskva: Russian Academy of Science 1994).

Turner, J.C. and Giddens, A. (eds.), *Social Theory Today* (Cambridge: Polity Press, 1987).

Turner, J.C., "Social Identification and Psychological Group Formation', in Tajfel, H. (ed.), *The Social Dimensions* (Cambridge: Cambridge University Press, 1984).

Trenin, D., "To Understand Ukraine," in *Russia in Global Affairs*, 27 December 2017.

Trenin, D., *Zagliadyvaya na 5 let vpered*. Moscow Carnegie Center website, 3 April 2018. https://carnegie.ru/commentary/75903.

Twining, D., *The New Eurasia: A Guide to the Republics of the Former Soviet Union* (London: Praeger, 1993).

"Ukraiintsi Ne Viriat' Vladi I Khochut' Povernennia Iadernoho Statusu — Opytuvannia [Ukrainians Do Not Trust Their Government and Want the Renewal of Nuclear Status — Survey]," *Ukraiinska Pravda*, 7 October 2014 (http://www.pravda.com.ua/news/2014/10/7/7040018/).

Van den Berghe, P., "Race and Ethnicity: A Sociobiological Perspective," in *Ethnic and Racial Studies*, vol. 1, no. 4 (1978), 402-411.

Vasilyeva, T.E., *Stereotipy v obschestvennom soznanii: sotsialno-filosofskiye aspekty*. Aftoreferat disertacii. D.f.n. (Moskva: AN SSSR, INION, 1988).

Vernadskiy, V.I., *Himicheskaya struktura Zemli I yeyo okruzheniya* (Moskva: AN SSSR, I-t geohimiyi I analiticheskoy himii im. Vernadskogo. 1965).

Volodina, L., "Kazaki za Yeltsina," in *Rossiyskiye Vesti* (22 March 1996), 1.

von Hagen, M., "Does Ukraine have a history?" in *Slavic Review*, vol. 54, no. 3 (Fall 1995), 658-673.

von Wright, G.H., *Explanation and Understanding* (London: Routledge and Kegan Paul, 1971).

Vyrost, I.S., "Natsionalna svidomist: problemy vyznachennia ta analizu," in *Filosofska I sotsiologichna dumka*. Kyiv: 1989 — No. 7 — 20-25.

Walker, R., "An Introduction to Applied Qualitative Research," in Walker, R. (ed.), *Applied Qualitative Research* (Aldershot: Gower, 1985), 3-26.

Wallensteen, P., *Understanding Conflict Resolution: War, Peace and the Global System*. London: SAGE Publications, 2002)

Waltz, K., "The Origins of War in Neorealist Theory," in Rotberg, R.I. and Rabb, T.K. (eds.), *The Origin and Prevention of Major Wars* (Cambridge: Cambridge University Press, 1989).

Waltz, K., *Man, the State, and War: A Theoretical Analysis* (New York: Columbia University Press, 1959).

Waver, O., Buzan B., Kelstrup, M. and Lemaitre, P., *Identity, Migration and the New Security Agenda in Europe* (London: Pinter, 1993).

Weber, E., *Peasants into Frenchmen. The Modernization of Rural France 1870-1914*. (Stanford, CA: Stanford University Press, 1976).

Weinreich, P., "Variations in Ethnic Identity: Identity Sructure Analysis," in Liebkind, L., *New Identities in Europe: Immigrant Ancestry and the Ethnic Identity of Youth* (London: Gower Publishers, 1989).

Wilson, A., "Myths of National History in Belarus and Ukraine," in Hosking, G. and Schopflin, G. (eds.), *Myths and Nationhood* (London: Hurst & Company, 1997), 182-198.

Wilson, A., *The Ukrainians: Unexpected Nation* (New Haven: Yale University Press, 2000).

Yack, B., "The Myth of the Civic Nation," in Beiner, R. (ed.), *Theorizing Nationalism* (Albany, NY: State University of New York, 1999), 103-19.

Yaniv, V., *Narysy do istorii ukrayinskoyi etnopsykhologii* (Miunhen: UVU, 1993).

Yavornyckyi, I., *Istoriya zaporizkyh kozakiv.* (Lviv: Svit, Vol. 1-3, 1991, 1992).

Yefremov, I., "Vazhnoye zveno v tsepi sviazey cheloveka s prirodoy," in *Priroda.*—1971—No. 2.—77-80.

Zabuzshko, O.S., *Filosofiya ukrayinskoyi ideyi ta yevropeyskyi kontext: frankivskyi period.* (Kyiv: Osnovy, 1993).

Zaporozke Kozatstvo v ukrainskiy istorii, kulturi ta natsionalniy samosvidomosti. (Kyiv: Zaporizhya, 1997).

Zshmyr, V.F., "Na shliahu do sebe," in *Filosofska ta sotsiologichna dumka*—1991—No. 2.—143-162.

Zubkov, I.F., *Kurs dialekticheskgo materialisma* (Moskva: Universitet Druzhby narodov, 1990).

SOVIET AND POST-SOVIET POLITICS AND SOCIETY

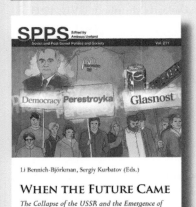

Editor: Andreas Umland

Founded in 2004 and refereed since 2007, SPPS makes available, to the academic community and general public, affordable English-, German- and Russian-language scholarly studies of various empirical aspects of the recent history and current affairs of the former Soviet bloc from the late Tsarist period to today. It publishes approximately 15–20 volumes per year, and focuses on issues in transitions to and from democracy such as economic crisis, identity formation, civil society development, and constitutional reform in CEE and the NIS. SPPS also aims to highlight so far understudied themes in East European studies such as right-wing radicalism, religious life, higher education, or human rights protection.

JOURNAL OF SOVIET AND POST-SOVIET POLITICS AND SOCIETY

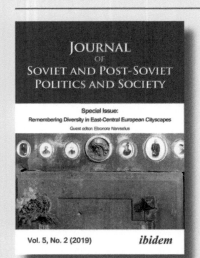

Editor: Julie Fedor

Review Editor: Gergana Dimova

The *Journal of Soviet and Post-Soviet Politics and Society* is a new bi-annual journal that was launched in April 2015 as a companion journal to the *Soviet and Post-Soviet Politics and Society* book series (founded 2004 and edited by Andreas Umland, Dr. phil., PhD). Like the book series, the journal will provide an interdisciplinary forum for new original research on the Soviet and post-Soviet world. The journal aims to become known for publishing creative, intelligent, and lively writing tackling and illuminating significant issues and capable of engaging wider educated audiences beyond the academy.

Ukrainian Voices

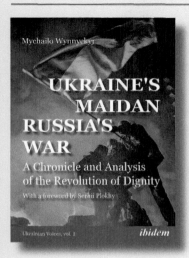

Collected by Andreas Umland

The book series *Ukrainian Voices* publishes English- and German-language monographs, edited volumes, document collections and anthologies of articles authored and composed by Ukrainian politicians, intellectuals, activists, officials, researchers, entrepreneurs, artists, and diplomats. The series' aim is to introduce Western and other audiences to Ukrainian explorations and interpretations of historic and current domestic as well as international affairs. The purpose of these books is to make non-Ukrainian readers familiar with how some prominent Ukrainians approach, research and assess their country's development and position in the world.

FORUM FÜR OSTEUROPÄISCHE IDEEN- UND ZEITGESCHICHTE

Editors: Leonid Luks, Gunter Dehnert, Nikolaus Lobkowicz, Alexei Rybakow, Andreas Umland

FORUM features interdisciplinary discussions by political scientists—literary, legal, and economic scholars—and philosophers on the history of ideas, and it reviews books on Central and Eastern European history. Through the translation and publication of documents and contributions from Russian, Polish, and Czech researchers, the journal offers Western readers critical insight into scientific discourses across Eastern Europe.

European Studies in the Caucasus

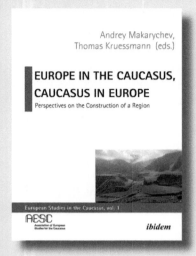

Editor: Thomas Krüssmann

The book series *European Studies in the Caucasus* offers innovative perspectives on regional studies of the Caucasus. By embracing the South Caucasus as well as Turkey and Russia as the major regional powers, it moves away from a traditional viewpoint of European Studies that considers the countries of the region as objects of Europeanization.

Journal of Romanian Studies

Editors: Lavinia Stan, Margaret Beissinger

Review Editor: Radu Cinpoes

The *Journal of Romanian Studies*, jointly developed by The Society for Romanian Studies and *ibidem* Press, is a biannual, peer-reviewed, and interdisciplinary journal. It examines critical issues in Romanian studies, linking work in that field to wider theoretical debates and issues of current relevance, and serving as a forum for junior and senior scholars. The journal also presents articles that connect Romania and Moldova comparatively with other states and their ethnic majorities and minorities, and with other groups by investigating the challenges of migration and globalization and the impact of the European Union.

BALKAN POLITICS AND SOCIETY

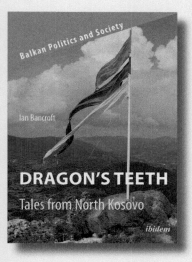

Editors: Jelena Džankić, Soeren Keil

The book series *Balkan Politics and Society* (BPS), launching in 2018, focuses on original empirical research on understudied aspects of the multifaceted historical, political, and cultural trajectories of the Balkan region.

IN STATU NASCENDI

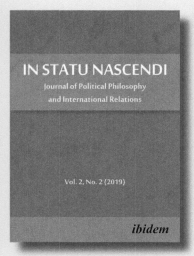

Editor: Piotr Pietrzak

In Statu Nascendi is a new peer-reviewed journal that aspires to be a world-class scholarly platform encompassing original academic research dedicated to the circle of Political Philosophy, Cultural Studies, Theory of International Relations, Foreign Policy, and the political Decision-making process. The journal investigates specific issues through a socio-cultural, philosophical, and anthropological approach to raise a new type of civic awareness about the complexity of contemporary crisis, instabilities, and warfare situations, where the "stage-of-becoming" plays a vital role.

ibidem
Press